D1327394

TRANSPORT MUSEUMS

TRANSPORT MUSEUMS
IN BRITAIN
AND WESTERN EUROPE

by

JACK SIMMONS

London

GEORGE ALLEN AND UNWIN LTD

RUSKIN HOUSE · MUSEUM STREET

PRINTED IN GREAT BRITAIN
in 11 *on* 12 *pt. Bell*
BY UNWIN BROTHERS LIMITED
THE GRESHAM PRESS
WOKING AND LONDON

PREFACE

The number of museums devoted to transport, wholly or in part, has grown rapidly in recent years. Of the thirty-four discussed in this book, nearly two-thirds have been opened since the end of the second World War. My main concern has been with the British Isles; but I hope that even those whose interests are confined to these islands will find it useful to get a comparative view of the good, and sometimes outstanding, work that has been accomplished in this field in some countries of Western Europe. Ideally this survey should have comprehended Eastern Europe too, and stretched across the Atlantic. But it is already long enough.

My study is concerned mainly with commercial transport, in the normal conditions of peace. I have therefore very little to say about battleships, tanks, or military aircraft. For reasons explained in the Introduction, I have dealt with railways a good deal more generously than with other forms of transport. Maritime museums, for example, are not accorded here the treatment they deserve. They cry out for a survey of their own.

The book is to be read as a statement of one man's interests and opinions. It is not a compendium put together from information supplied by the museums. I have visited them all myself, some of them several times over, since 1964. The choice of the objects discussed here is mine personally; so are the comments passed on them, and on the way in which they are presented to the public. I have sought no special facilities and seen nothing that the ordinary visitor cannot see for himself.

I have thus felt free to say what I like by way of praise or criticism. The criticism is infrequent, and I hope constructive. For my work in preparing this book has given me a mounting respect for the care and skill that have gone into the making of these museums. If I am able to contribute to enlarging the appreciation of their work and to persuading those who allocate funds to them to increase the measure of their support, I shall indeed be very glad.

The museums described here are arranged on a pattern of two continuous routes. Few readers, I imagine, will be tempted to follow out either of them in full. The second journey, on the Continent, is straightforward: just over 4,200 miles by train and ship. The first cannot be made very easily by public transport—the stretches from Beaulieu to Swindon, from Old Warden to Stoke Bruerne and on to Crich, make tedious going that way, though they are easy enough by car. The whole length of this journey is some 1,750 miles. The visitor who wants to see two or three of these museums at a time may be glad to have them grouped together, as they are here, topographically. Utrecht, Lucerne, and Milan, for example, all lie on the very comfortable main line from England to Italy by the Hook of Holland.

Certain changes have taken place in these museums while the book has been in the press. In any museum that is energetically directed, exhibits are likely to be moved, the display altered, from time to time. I have made a few changes in the text to bring it up to the present moment; but I have not attempted to do this throughout. The book is, after all, intended only to introduce the reader to the collections, to what the museums actually hold. Two cases of special difficulty have arisen. The Brighton Motor Museum was closed in 1968. I have decided nevertheless to retain my account of it, as it included some pieces of unusual interest, and its contents form part of the Montagu collections, described in the following chapter. The Swedish Railway Museum, described here in its temporary quarters at Tomteboda, is now being transferred to Gävle, to be opened there in 1970.

It would, I feel, be invidious for me to single out museum curators and members of their staff who have given me particular assistance. I hope that those who remember helping me will understand that I am not the less grateful to them. I especially obliged to those who have supplied me—as a rule very liberally and promptly—with the photographs I have asked for to illustrate the book. I should like to name two friends in Leicester who have been kind enough to comment on the text in draft and have helped me to understand, in many ways, both what museums are and what they ought to be: Mr T. A. Walden, Director of the City Museums and Art Gallery, and Mr H. R. Singleton, Director of Museum Studies in the University.

J. S.

The University
Leicester
January 1970

8

CONTENTS

II. WESTERN EUROPE

ILLUSTRATIONS

14

Illustrations

15

between pp. 264 and 265

54 Clapham: Midland compound No. 1000
Beaulieu: the Southern Railway's 'Bournemouth Belle', which ran from 1931 to 1967, with 'Schools' class locomotive *Stowe* attached to three Pullman cars

55 Lucerne: Lötschberg Railway electric locomotive (1913)
Belfast: Co. Donegal Railways locomotive *Phoenix*

56 Clapham: drawing-room in Queen Victoria's saloon
Nuremberg: saloon built for King Ludwig II of Bavaria

57 Clapham: electric kettle from Queen Victoria's saloon
Clapham: engraved glass from Queen Victoria's service

58 Stockholm: King Oscar's II's saloon, built in Berlin in 1874
Hamar: royal saloon for the Røros Railway (then metre-gauge) built in the USA in 1876

59 Science Museum: advertisement with cut of Robert Davidson's electric locomotive, tried out on the Edinburgh and Glasgow Railway in 1842

60 Science Museum: letter sent by balloon out of Paris during the siege of 1870
Royal Scottish Museum: Percy Pilcher's glider *Hawk* (1896)

between pp. 280 and 281

61 Shuttleworth Collection: Deperdussin monoplane (1910)
Science Museum: Avro triplane, 1909

62 Science Museum: Col. S. F. Cody standing by his biplane at Lark Hill in 1912
Science Museum: another historic photograph. Alcock and Brown take off from Newfoundland on their transatlantic flight, June 14, 1919.

63 Shuttleworth Collection: aeroplane starter devised by B. C. Hucks
Munich: the Aeronautical Gallery

64 Science Museum: the Aeronautical Gallery

The photographs have all been supplied by the museums concerned. The author and publishers are grateful for permission to reproduce them.

1   Science Museum: Land Transport Gallery, opened in 1967

2a Lucerne: general view of the Museum, showing (*centre*) the locomotive hall, with railway vehicles in the open air. The Gotthard main line runs across the foreground of the picture

b Stoke Bruerne: general view of the Museum

INTRODUCTION

A museum of transport! The idea is surely a contradiction in terms, an absurdity. For a museum seems to most of us to be something static—it freezes and preserves things—whereas transport moves, or it is not transport. How can this conflict be reconciled?

Very incompletely, if we are to be candid. Let us admit that at the outset. The purpose of a museum is to collect and display things for our study as perfectly as possible. It can only simulate motion—by showing working models; or a full-sized machine whose parts move, while it remains itself fixed to the spot; or at best, as in the Norwegian Museum at Hamar, a train that travels a few hundred yards under its own steam. The truest railway museum, it might be argued, is a railway that remains in service, fulfilling the social and economic purposes for which it was built, though perhaps by methods and with equipment that belong to an earlier day. The line from Havant to Hayling Island was a good example, until it was closed in 1963: for owing to the restriction on the weight that might be placed on the Langstone bridge it was worked till the end by the little 'Terrier' tank engines of the Brighton Company, some of them more than eighty years old by the time the service ceased. Or again, I might say that this very paragraph is being written in a similar museum, of a rather grander kind: one of the Pullman cars of the *Golden Arrow* running from Paris to Calais. For these Pullman cars are a reflection of a social and economic world that has passed away. When the train was first put on in 1926 it consisted solely of Pullman cars. There are now two cars only, attached to the ordinary express, but they continue to provide some of the most entirely comfortable accommodation ever offered to the railway traveller in Europe—a whole class better than that of the Trans-Europe Expresses put on in the 1950s. Moreover, at the time of writing, the train is still hauled from Amiens to Calais by steam engines: the noble Pacifics that gave splendid service for half a century from 1910 and have now been replaced by electric locomotives on nearly all the main lines of France. To travel in one of these Pullmans is to project oneself back into the world of thirty or forty years ago. It is an experience worth having, not to be available much longer.[1]

The museums described in this book are museums in the conventional sense of the word: depositories of objects gathered there for study. Most are indoors, though some have sections in the open air. Under the severe handicap that has been mentioned, all are designed to show changing means of transport, and most of them at least try to suggest something of the impact that these changes have had on the society in which they occurred. Between them they illustrate all forms of transport: by road, sea, inland waterway, rail, and air. They exemplify all the instruments that have been devised to promote it, from the tram to the jet aeroplane, the dug-out canoe to the motor-scooter. And some of these museums glance aside from the machine to consider the ends it has served, which leads them, for example, into postal services and tourism.

For 'transport' is a very wide-ranging subject. It comprehends the movement of men and women and their goods by all possible means from place to place; and, properly considered, it ought to take account of the changing demands that affected it and the consequences it produced. It is a mere device for serving human needs, and unless those needs are kept in mind the study of it loses all touch with reality. It may become a romantic pursuit of curious or beautiful machines. But they were not created as such. They were intended to meet needs that arose, in precise and specific forms, for conveyance that should be quicker or safer or cheaper or more commodious, or that should combine several of these advantages together. We shall not understand them or appreciate their true importance unless we understand the jobs they were designed to do.

Museums like those described in this book have a triple task to perform: to collect and preserve, to display their exhibits, and to explain them, telling us why each has been thought worthy of occupying the space allotted to it. In some of them, parts of this task are discharged well, other parts badly or not at all.

Something is said in this book of every kind of transport museum, from great national collections like the Science Museum, which treat transport as one of their departments, to those that are

---

[1] The change came while this book was passing through the press. The French Pacifics disappeared from the service in January 1969.

concerned exclusively with a single aspect of transport, like the Narrow-Gauge Railway Museum at Towyn or the Tramway Museum at Crich. A critical reader will notice some disproportion in the choice and treatment of the museums discussed here, and that calls for explanation.

This is not a guide-book, attempting to furnish a comprehensive list of all the museums in this field, with an inventory of their principal contents. Under 'Transport' and 'Shipping' the current edition of *Museums and Galleries in Great Britain and Ireland* lists over eighty institutions; only twenty-two of these are described here. The purpose of this study is not to catalogue but to discuss: to see what can be learnt about the evolution of transport from the study of collections of this kind. In a book of modest compass, which is designed to be read, not used as an encyclopaedia, only a comparatively small number of museums can be chosen for examination, by way of example. Some of those that are left out are important in their own right.[1]

The book will be found to give much fuller attention to railways than to any other branch of transport. There are several reasons for this. It seemed desirable to treat one branch of the subject fairly comprehensively, allowing at some points detailed discussion and comparison. And, at least up to the present time, it can fairly be said that the railway is more completely displayed in museums than any other branch of transport. No museum of the air can do much more than show 'stills' of flight, and machines perpetually grounded or hanging motionless in the air. Maritime museums, which are numerous and often distinguished both in Britain and on the Continent, suffer from the great disability that ships have to be represented by models and photographs. The preservation of ships complete and in their original form presents formidable problems, and with few, though notable, exceptions— the reconstructed Viking ships and *Vasa* in Scandinavia, *Peggy* at Castletown, *Cutty Sark* at Greenwich, the paddle-steamer *Rigi* at Lucerne, the German *Ewer* at Munich—it has not been attempted in Europe. Nor is a working model of a ship to be compared with that of a railway or a road. You can build a simulacrum of the Gotthard railway; you cannot convincingly mimic the Atlantic Ocean.

Museums of road transport suffer from different disadvantages.

---

[1] On this point, see further, p. 273.

One of them at least, though serious, could be removed without great difficulty. We urgently need a good text-book on the evolution of horse-drawn carriages and coaches, classifying them and defining the terms employed, with the help of photographs or line-drawings. What is the difference between a barouche and a landau, between a phaeton, a curricle, and a gig? A modest book of this kind, carefully prepared, would be invaluable. Even if it dealt only with vehicles used in Britain, the demand for it would be widespread. English carriages figure prominently in many Continental museums: at Lucerne, for example, and Milan.

The other handicaps to the display of road transport in museums are perhaps less easily remediable. From times before the development of the bicycle and the internal combustion engine the range of material that is available for exhibition is, apart from vehicles, rather limited, and much of it offers little visual interest. The evolution of the wheel has, it is true, been admirably managed at Milan. But the research that has gone into this display, and the workshop facilities it has required, would put it beyond the resources of most museums; and a mere series of pictures is too flat to convey very much. The gallery devoted at Munich to the building of roads and bridges is a demonstration of the way in which this challenge can be imaginatively met. Here again, however, this is an achievement far too costly and elaborate to be widely imitated.

When we come to the machines, we need to know a great deal more than we do about prices and running costs and reliability in service if their merits and defects are to be understood; if we are to be shown, as we ought to be, what were the genuinely important improvements made during their evolution, which changes proved to lead into blind alleys, and which were mere pieces of window-dressing. All this could be made clearer in a museum than anywhere else; but it presupposes knowledge that, at many points, we still lack.

With railways, on the other hand, all these difficulties are less formidable. A substantial proportion of the material that is worth showing can appear in its original state; there is no need to present so much in the form of models or mock-ups. Most of the exhibits have, or can be given, a visual interest of their own. Some of them can legitimately be called beautiful in their own right. (Anyone who doubts this should try walking unprepared into the Museum at Swindon; the effect made by the splendid machines in the entrance hall, displayed in an ample space, is overpowering.) Moreover, though there is much work that still needs to be done on the history of railways and their equipment, we already know more of what is significant in it than we do of the other branches of transport, except shipping. And finally, though the railway continues to play its part in the world's economy, and will go on doing so as far ahead as we can see, it is no longer a dominant part; whereas for Britain and all Western Europe there was, somewhere between 1830 and 1914, a 'Railway Age', when railways did regulate in a substantial measure the economic and social life of the communities they were built to serve. This gives a natural point of focus to a railway museum, a pattern and a sense of completeness, that can rarely appear in other forms of transport.

It is always a mistake, however, to look at transport in watertight divisions; the railway can be properly understood only if it is looked at side by side with the ship, the road vehicle, and the aeroplane. For these reasons it has seemed best to treat the railway more fully here, but always as one branch of a larger subject.

The greater part of this book is devoted to museums in the United Kingdom. But it would be a mistake to consider them in isolation, and twelve museums on the Continent have also been chosen for discussion. The number of these might well have been larger, and their range might have been widened to include some of the interesting museums of Eastern Europe, the rich collections of royal coaches in Spain and Portugal, the outstandingly fine displays in the United States, headed by that in the Smithsonian Institution in Washington. But again—this is a book, not a com-Institute in Washington. But again—this is a book, not a compendium of universal information, and it must be limited in size. It is intended primarily for British readers, to open up to them the chief collections of their own country and those that are within easy reach on the Continent. One theme that will be found to run throughout the book is the export of British skill and techniques, British capital and manufactures, abroad; balanced, in the case of the internal combustion engine, by a corresponding traffic in the opposite direction.

The Conclusion, which follows the account of individual museums, ranges over the whole field they cover and does not confine itself to the collections described in the book. It attempts to analyse the knowledge and understanding they afford us, to suggest improvements that might be made and gaps that remain to be filled.

A word should be said, in conclusion, about the history of the idea of the transport museum. It may be held to have originated with the collections of royal coaches that tended to accumulate in capital cities, from piety towards deceased sovereigns or from reluctance to destroy such costly monuments of departed fashion. Richard Ford gave a few lines to those in Madrid in his incomparable *Handbook for Travellers in Spain*. 'Now visit *La Real Cochera* and *Las Caballerizas*', he writes. 'These enormous coach-houses and stables lie to the N E [of the Royal Palace]: the latter were once filled with the mules and horses which conveyed the kings to their daily shootings. This antediluvian museum contains carriages of all forms and ages, from the cumbrous state-coach to the Cupid-bedizened car, from the oldest *coche de colleras* to the newest *épuipage de Paris* and the last hearse.'[1] The collection is still to be seen in Madrid today. There are others like it in Lisbon, Munich, and Vienna. Swedish royal coaches ornament superbly the entrance hall of the Northern Museum in Stockholm.

These objects were preserved as show-pieces; they formed part of the reverence traditionally paid to royalty. The systematic illustration of the history of transport has other and later origins. It can be seen emerging in the museums that formed an element in the new scientific education of the nineteenth century. In Britain the story begins with the Great Exhibition of 1851 and the establishment of the 'South Kensington Museum' of science and the pure and applied arts that sprang from it in 1857. Augustus Hare was much more intent on pictures and the romantic past than on the engineering wonders of his own century; but even he paused in his account of the Museum in 1878 to single out *Puffing Billy* and the *Rocket* for mention, and the original engine of the paddle-steamer *Comet*.[2] In the eighties it began to take on its present character, to become the national museum of applied science. It remained part of the Victoria and Albert Museum, however, until 1909, and the East Block of its separate premises

[1] *Handbook* (3rd ed., 1855), 720.
[2] A. J. C. Hare, *Walks in London* (1878), ii, 486.

in Exhibition Road was not completed until 1928. Even this, however, represented only one instalment of a three-stage plan.[1]

Thus the development of the Science Museum has been a gradual one, stretching over more than a century. Its transport collections have been important from an early stage, and they have benefited from some of the most recent extensions that have been made to the buildings: the new Land Transport Gallery, for example, was opened only in 1967.

The national museums of applied science on the Continent have a similar character to our own, though their histories are widely different. The oldest of them is the Musée des Arts et Métiers in Paris, which is one of a group of museums and galleries created by the Revolutionary Government in 1794. It has been established since 1798 in the incongruous premises it still occupies: the former priory of St Martin-des-Champs. The Deutsches Museum in Munich was opened to the public in 1906. The latest addition to the company in Western Europe is the Leonardo da Vinci Museum in Milan, installed like its French counterpart in a disused medieval monastery. It was opened in 1952.

In all these museums the section accorded to transport is only one of many, for they aim at illustrating the entire range of the applied sciences. The notion of devoting a whole museum to transport, or to one of its branches, is much more recent. Perhaps the earliest naval museum was the one established at Greenwich in the new Royal Naval College in 1873. But naval museums are necessarily concerned in the main with methods of warfare rather than with transport; and it seems as if the earliest true transport museum was the collection formed to illustrate the development of the Bavarian railways, which grew out of an Industrial Exhibition held at Nuremberg in 1882. It was not opened to the public, however, until 1899. By that time the Norwegians had opened their Railway Museum, at Hamar, in 1897. In the years immediately before the outbreak of the first World War the Danes and the Swedes became actively interested in maritime museums: those at Elsinore, Gothenburg, and Stockholm all date from 1913–14. The earliest museum to be devoted entirely to the road seems to be that now at Compiègne, which was opened there in 1927.

In this country the idea of a railway museum was canvassed in

---

[1] For the painfully slow expansion of the Science Museum in the twentieth century, see pp. 29–30 below.

the 1890s, when an Association was founded for promoting this object with a Council that included the venerable Archibald Sturrock of the Great Northern, W. M. Acworth, and A. R. Bennett, and was presided over by Charles Rous-Marten. The attitude of the railway companies proved to be discouraging, and the project dropped. It was revived by Bennett in 1908, but by that time Rous-Marten's enthusiasm had cooled. He considered that 'the really valuable and important and interesting locomotive relics have gone'. Taking a purely antiquarian view, he declined to admit that any later locomotives were 'epoch-making', like the 'Jenny Linds', the 'Problems', and the Sinclair singles of the Caledonian. '*What* still-existing engines', he asked, 'are worth "museumizing" at heavy cost? I really can't think of any that inspire me with a particle of zeal.' All he would say, rather grudgingly, was that he hoped that the 8-foot singles of the Great Northern Railway, then on their way out, would 'not be wholly allowed to disappear'.[1] When the former leader of the movement for a railway museum had come to regard the scheme with so little favour, it is not surprising that it failed. The project was not realized in Britain until 1928.

Transport museums in the full sense of the term, existing in their own right independently of the national museums of applied science and comprehending many or all branches of the subject, do not appear until after the second World War, at Clapham, Glasgow, Belfast, and Lucerne.

The premises occupied by these collections are a diverting assortment. The two monasteries that have been mentioned are not the only medieval buildings that have been turned over to this purpose: the Museum of Carriages is established in a range of fifteenth-century stables at Maidstone. For the rest, this book will take us to a royal palace; country houses; a barracks; a corn exchange; a building erected as a men's lodging-house, which then gave eighty years' service as a Wesleyan chapel; a quarry; an aquarium; bus garages; tram depots; a canal basin; and several railway stations. Only a small minority of European transport museums—those at South Kensington and Munich, at Nuremberg, Hamar, and Lucerne—are accommodated in buildings specifically designed for them. Almost everywhere the story is one of adapting and improvisation, of making one pound do the work of

[1] *Railway Magazine*, xxii (1908), 186–9.

two or five. But that has been a condition of life in most museums outside America; and like their colleagues in other institutions, the curators of these have faced up to their difficulties, as well as to the deeper challenges inherent in the very nature of museums, with a spirited determination and endless ingenuity.

I. BRITAIN

1

SCIENCE MUSEUM
SOUTH KENSINGTON

The origins of the Science Museum reach back to the Great
Exhibition of 1851. A number of the things that were shown there
were acquired by the Government after the Exhibition closed,
and with some additional material they formed the nucleus of a
Museum of Ornamental Art. The whole collection was accommodated in a corrugated-iron building, on a site purchased out of
the proceeds of the Exhibition, and the 'South Kensington Museum'
was opened to the public in 1857.

What that public saw was a motley assemblage, serving, as
we should now think, several quite distinct purposes. It was at
once a museum of science and of the decorative arts, and a picture
gallery as well. These functions did not become completely
separated for over fifty years, until in 1909 the Victoria and
Albert Museum, catering for the pure and applied arts, was
opened, leaving the scientific collections to form a Science Museum
on their own, on the other side of Exhibition Road.

Meanwhile those collections had changed their character
beyond recognition. They had been systematized, developed, and
very much enlarged. The Museum began to acquire ship models
on a large scale in the sixties. Then the extensive collection of
machinery in the hands of the Commissioners of Patents came to
be linked with it—a most important step, for the Commissioners
held not only models but such original machines as *Puffing Billy*;
the collection was formally transferred to the Museum in 1884.
Men of science pressed Governments continually to improve the
provision made for housing and displaying these things, but
change was very slow to come. The separation of the science and
art collections was recommended by a Parliamentary Committee

in 1897. In 1909, when that necessary first step had at length been taken, the Board of Education turned its attention to the Science Museum, accepting the advice of a strong committee headed by Sir Hugh Bell (Chairman of Dorman Long) that entirely new buildings were required; and in 1913 the first of these (the East Block) was begun. The arrival of the first World War postponed its completion, and it was not opened to the public until 1928. The second (Centre) Block was started in 1949; it took twelve years to complete, and it is coming into full use only now. The third (West) Block has not yet been begun (the third of three that were shown to be absolutely necessary more than half a century ago). In that half-century, as anyone can easily imagine, the collections have continued to grow apace, into fields that were not dreamt of even by the far-sighted Bell Committee.[1]

So much of the Museum's history must be understood if its achievement, and at some points its limitations, are to be properly appreciated.

The transport collections are all housed in the new Centre Block: land transport on the ground floor, shipping above it on the second floor, aeronautics on the third. The Aeronautics Gallery presents some original and interesting features of construction. But the building as a whole is extremely conservative in its architectural character, no more than a repetition of the East Block, which was designed fifty years ago. The task of presenting the exhibits is made much more difficult by the multiplicity of pillars; and instead of playing them down visually, rendering them as unobtrusive as possible, the architect has chosen to decorate them (if that is the right verb) with dreary panels of concrete aggregate.

If, in a strictly architectural sense, these new galleries are disappointing, the whole Museum has been transformed in recent years by the lavish use of colour. Here it is unquestionably superior to its counterparts in Europe. The Deutsches Museum is fatiguing to the eye, and therefore depressing to the spirit, of the visitor from the endless monotony of its grey walls. The decoration of the church that houses the main transport collection at the Arts et Métiers

---

[1] The history of the Museum is clearly summarized in C. R. Fay, *Palace of Industry* (Cambridge, 1951), Chap. vii, and *The Science Museum: the First Hundred Years* (1957). The Reports of the Bell Committee are Cd. 5625 (1911) and Cd. 6221 (1912–13).

in Paris is drab beyond the power of words to describe. Here, in South Kensington, everything is varied, stimulating, cheerful.

The Land Transport collections have benefited immensely from their rehousing.[1] In the past their very richness was a drawback. It was a glaring shame that it should be necessary to crowd up such important exhibits so closely together; and even when they had been crowded up the Museum was able to display to the public only a small part of its possessions. Now it has been possible to bring a number of things out of store and to give more ample room to most of the objects that are shown.

Take, for example, the bicycles: a collection of outstanding value, comparable in quality to that in Paris and much richer in quantity. They used to be shown packed closely side by side in a long row in the corridor leading up to the north entrance on the ground floor. There it was not possible to see any of them in isolation, still less to study them adequately, which was all the more provoking to the visitor who was interested in these machines because the collection had been so admirably described in one of the Museum's publications.[2]

The Science Museum can show examples of all the chief ancestors of the modern bicycle. The earliest is a hobby-horse of 1818, made in London by Denis Johnson on the pattern established by Baron von Drais in France in the same year. The hobby-horse was a bicycle in the literal sense of the word, making use of two wheels, placed one in front of the other; but its motive power was supplied solely by the action of the rider's feet on the ground. The first advance on this invention came from Kirkpatrick Macmillan, a Dumfriesshire blacksmith, who produced a machine in 1839 that was actuated by cranks and treadles. No bicycle made by Macmillan himself is known to exist today. But the design was copied by a number of other Scots. One very early imitation is that of Gavin Dalzell, now at Glasgow (see p. 174). The Science Museum has another, somewhat later—it dates from

---

[1] The rehousing was still incomplete when this book went to press. I am obliged to the Director of the Science Museum for permission to see the new Land Transport Gallery while it was still being arranged, and to the Museum's Publicity Officer, Mr Smart, for guiding me round it and answering my questions. Since it was opened, there has been a good deal of minor adjustment and re-arrangement. The Unic taxi, for example, referred to on pp. 35–6, is not now on exhibition.

[2] C. F. Caunter, *The History and Development of Cycles* (1955), and *Handbook of the Collection Illustrating Cycles* (1958). The old arrangement is shown in the frontispiece to the *Handbook*.

about 1860—made by Thomas McCall. It can also show several examples of the three and four-wheeled velocipedes of the 1850s, which were likewise actuated by treadles.

There is controversy still about the origin of the pedal-cycle. What is certain is that this type of machine, the 'boneshaker', was first manufactured by Pierre Michaux and his son Ernest in Paris in the early 1860s. The Museum has one of these, and also an English imitation, dating from about 1865, that once belonged to J. B. Dunlop, the creator of the pneumatic tyre as we know it. Michaux bicycles began to be made at Coventry in 1869, a development that 'not only rescued the city from commercial depression, but eventually made it the capital of the world's cycle production'.[1] The boneshaker gave place to the 'ordinary' or 'penny-farthing' in the seventies and to the 'safety' bicycle with the diamond frame, which established itself about 1890 and remained the standard pattern for nearly three-quarters of a century, until its supremacy was challenged by the Moulton design in the 1960s. A long series of examples, very carefully assembled and described, down to and including the Moulton, illustrate this evolution in the Science Museum.

The bicycles lead on naturally to the motor-cycles, and the collection is rich in them too. Von Drais's hobby-horse, which captured the fancy of the gay, mad Parisian world for a time, had its counterpart in a hobby-horse actuated by steam. It was christened, with an elegant terseness, the Velocipedraisiavaporianna and probably did not progress far beyond its inventor's head, though a contemporary print, shown here, bears a legend claiming that it was actually tried out in the Luxembourg Gardens.

Many other false starts occurred in the emergence of the power-driven bicycle, and it was not until very late in the century that any model went into commercial production. The first was that developed by the Hildebrand brothers of Munich, and it was powered by a steam engine—though Gottlieb Daimler had already built his first petrol-driven motor-cycle in 1885.[2] The Science Museum possesses what is probably the prototype of the Hildebrands' motor-cycle, and certainly one of their earliest productions. It was found abandoned in a corner of a railway depot at Newhaven.[3]

[1] Caunter, *History and Development of Cycles*, 10.
[2] A replica of this machine is in the Deutsches Museum: cf. p. 240.
[3] Cf. Caunter, *Handbook of the Collection Illustrating Motorcycles*, 3.

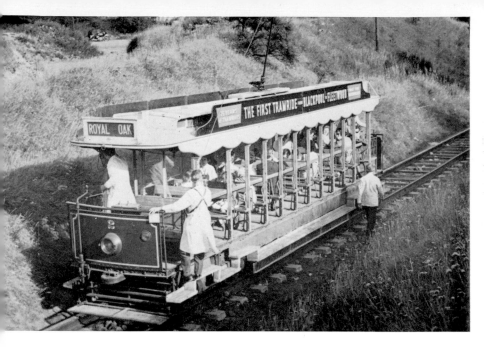

3a Crich: the tramway along the Cliff Side, with Blackpool–Fleetwood toast rack car

b Utrecht: the Railway Museum, formerly the Maliebaan station

4a Birmingham: bringing the locomotive *City of Birmingham* into the Museum

b Glasgow: moving the North British locomotive *Glen Douglas* into the Museum. The 'Jones Goods' of the Highland is behind

Again, however, this was a false start. In the Paris Exhibition of 1889 Félix Millet first showed his petrol-driven motor-cycle (now in the Arts et Métiers: cf. p. 196); and although his countrymen were for the moment more interested in the motor-tricycle, the brothers Werner developed the motor-bicycle in Paris in the late nineties. Two of their machines are here, dating from 1899 and 1902.

By this time Britain had entered the field of motor-cycle manufacture, in which she soon came to play an eminent part. There are Humber, Singer, and Triumph machines in the Museum, all dating from 1902–4. Many of the later variants of the motor-cycle are also represented here: the early scooters that appeared at the close of the first World War, the 'monocars' that were designed to improve the comfort of the rider. A very interesting example of these last is that designed by Sir Alliott Verdon-Roe, one of the chief pioneers of British aviation, in 1926. Its body is made of light alloy, enclosing much of the motion; the rider sits low, as in a motor-car, well protected by a windscreen. This machine was extensively used by its designer, on long journeys between Southampton and Manchester. He gave it to the Museum himself. Coming down to very recent times, the Ariel Square Four of 1959 is a notable machine: the last heavy touring motor-cycle to be produced in Britain. It is large and handsome, and capable of 100 m.p.h. But price killed machines of this kind: they cost as much as a small car.

The bicycles and motor-cycles occupy the south-west corner of the Land Transport Gallery. Next to them there is a series of models in cases illustrating the evolution of transport, with animals and men, from prehistoric times. Historically, this is the starting-point of the whole exhibition. Its placing, in the middle of the south wall, is rather odd, and it is a pity that visitors are not directed to it by a prominent notice. The display has been admirably thought out. Each figure stands in a little alcove, on a stepped frame. Here, and in all the new cases, as on the walls, the use of colour is effective and pleasing. Clear strong tones are used throughout—what a pleasure it is to move through a long sequence of colour-schemes free from the harsh, muddy greens and browns, the metallic purples that are so drearily characteristic of the taste of the 1960s! The selection of examples is admirably comprehensive, extending also to transport on ice. Beside the cases stand some fine original sledges. The Museum's collection includes some delightfully elegant examples of the eighteenth century, with French decoration.

The horse-drawn carriages include some splendid exhibits, and their new setting affords enough room to allow one to walk round and examine them closely. Even now, however, only a part of the collection can be displayed. The earliest English vehicle here dates from about 1770. It is a phaeton of great distinction, with a 'crane-neck' frame. The heavier vehicles include a mail-coach of 1827 and one superb example from the late nineteenth century, the Earl of Caledon's dress chariot, built for him by Hooper in 1891. (The Museum now has, in its large and important archives, the records of that leading firm of coachbuilders.) Among the lighter town carriages, one is of outstanding historical interest: the original brougham, built in 1838 by Robinson and Cook of Mount Street, London. It was made to the special order of the cantankerous politician after whom it came to be called, and it was the progenitor of a large family of small closed town carriages, used particularly by professional men such as doctors. This first example carried two passengers only and was drawn by one horse; but later there were two-horse broughams, for four passengers, as well. 'Electric broughams' appeared in the Edwardian age—one is in the Gallery here, on the north wall among the motor-cars. There were motor-broughams too: one made by Rolls Royce was presented to Dr Warre, the Headmaster of Eton, at Christmas 1904.

At the furthest end of the Gallery is a noble group of fire-engines. It begins with a little Newsham manual engine of 1734. It belonged to the borough of Dartmouth. One may suspect that it had gone out of use only very lately when the Town Council presented it to the Museum in 1875. There are two handsome horse-drawn steam fire-engines of the Victorian Age, one of 1863 by Merryweather, the other a Shand Mason engine of 1894. These are matched by two motor engines, one of 1904, the other a splendid machine of 1936, complete with a 100-foot ladder on a turntable. With their brilliant scarlet paint and bright burnished metalwork, they close the Gallery with a gorgeous display: a worthy tribute to one of the most heroic of our public services.

The motor-cars are of exceptional interest, and they are described in meticulous detail in the Museum's *Handbooks* devoted to them. The collection is especially rich in early vehicles: it includes eight cars built in the nineteenth century, besides two motor-cycles and a quadricycle. The earliest of them, one of Karl Benz's Model III, dates from 1888. It is the oldest petrol-engined car in this country and one of the oldest anywhere that is still capable of running—it went from London to Brighton in 1958 at an average speed of 9 m.p.h.

Moving forward ten years, we come to F. W. Lanchester's second car. This proved notably successful on its trials and won a gold medal for design and performance at the Royal Automobile Club's Show at Richmond in 1899.[1] It encouraged Lanchester in his progress towards the production of cars for the market, which began in 1901.

There are also two early English Daimlers: one (built by the Motor Manufacturing Company in 1897) with a wagonette body seating six passengers, the other a light 4 h.p. car built at Coventry in 1901. The French had already started to make small cars in substantial numbers—like the 5 h.p. Peugeot, dating from the following year, which is also in the Science Museum. They led in this field in Europe until the British and the Italians drew level with them in the 1920s. An interesting British competitor is the 5 h.p. Vauxhall, a very early example of which is here (it bears the works number 6): this was the model that first established the reputation of the firm, which was still operating at Vauxhall in London and did not move out to Luton until 1905.

These cars are mostly arranged in echelon against the north wall of the Gallery, except for two steam cars, by Stanley and by White, which are beyond, on the other side of the wall; a long series of engines and some demonstrations of the development of individual parts of the automobile—brakes, suspension, magnetos, lamps— are mounted opposite and dispersed among them. The Edwardian period is well displayed here, as in a number of other museums,[2] by cars that help, better than most things, to make us realize the leisured opulence of those years, when the old world was moving towards the verge of its own destruction.

From the new, very different world that emerged from the war we may single out first a Unic taxicab of 1922 and applaud the discernment that has placed it in this collection, where it properly belongs, in London. The motor-taxi conquered the capital only

[1] Cf. P. W. Kingsford, *F. W. Lanchester* (1960), 38–9.   [2] Cf. pp. 94–5.

gradually—even more slowly and hesitantly than the motor-bus. It had to conform to exacting police regulations—to be able to turn in a 25-foot circle, for instance; and, at first, it was undoubtedly less manœuvrable than the horse-cab. But the Unic established itself from 1907 onwards, both in Paris (the firm was French) and in London. Thousands of the type, modified only a little as the years went by, were produced; the last of them were still to be seen on the streets in the 1950s. The London taxi deserves more study than it has yet received, both of its technical development and of the social and economic functions it has discharged. Perhaps the sight of this vehicle will stimulate someone to undertake it. And perhaps the Science Museum will consider adding a corresponding taxi, of the years following the second World War. A good many are still about—a few in London, many more demoted to provincial towns.

Another outstanding car of the 1920s here is the Austin Seven of 1922. It was the precursor of a very long series: 350,000 of them were manufactured in Birmingham in the next sixteen years, not to mention large numbers more built under licence in France, Germany, and the United States. It was among the most famous of all British products, and deserved its fame: for it was a design of much ingenuity, executed in first-class materials, and it played a great part in making motoring a popular family pastime.

The last forty years of the motor-car's development are less fully illustrated. The outstanding original vehicle of recent times that is here is the Rover gas-turbine car of 1950: herald of a type of propulsion that has not yet come into its own. It is much to be hoped that some specimens of the characteristic car of the ordinary man in the 1950s and 1960s have been earmarked for the collection; a Mini-Minor is already here, sectioned.

The proper complement to this extensive display of road vehicles is provided in the side-gallery above, which is devoted to road-construction and bridge-building. The work is done entirely by models and dioramas. The Museum now includes an extremely important collection of models of Indian bridges, deposited by the India Office after it had shed its responsibility for such things in 1947. They are among the lasting monuments of the British Raj. The classic commentary on the triumphs and perils of their construction is the story that Kipling placed first in *The Day's Work*. Some of the recent long road bridges are well shown here, too, such as those over the Tamar and the Severn. The methods of road-building are clearly illustrated. A fine series of models of road-rollers makes up for the absence of a full-sized original of one of these unwieldy machines—if you are curious to see one, you must go to Birmingham.

The remainder of this Gallery, including the central part which forms a huge well, open through three floors to the roof, is given up to railways. This section demands a great deal of space: it includes some of the most famous exhibits in the Museum, which are also among the most bulky.

Two early locomotives are pre-eminent. *Puffing Billy* is one of the two oldest in the world. Its fellow is *Wylam Dilly*, now at Edinburgh (see p. 164). Both were built in 1813 to the designs of William Hedley of Wylam in Northumberland. The most celebrated of all locomotives is the *Rocket*, sketched, photographed, reproduced full-sized and in model throughout the world. All that remains of the original engine was presented to the Commissioners of Patents for their Museum in 1862, becoming in time part of the heritage of the Science Museum. Since the machine was altered during its life-time and is now incomplete, having been robbed of many of its parts before it arrived at South Kensington, a sectioned replica of the original has been made to go with it. A locomotive that competed with the *Rocket* at the Rainhill trials is also here, Hackworth's *Sans Pareil*; a third dating from the same year, *Agenoria*, is on loan from the Science Museum to the Railway Museum at York (see p. 157).

The next important railway engine is not a steam but an electric one. The City and South London line, opened in 1890, was the earliest electrically-operated tube railway in the world. For over thirty years it was worked by separate locomotives, not, like its modern successors, by multiple-unit trains with engines built into them. Here is one of the first batch of engines used on the line, built by Mather and Platt of Manchester. The York Museum has one of the 'padded-cell' cars it hauled.

The removal of the land transport collections into their new quarters has made it possible for the Museum to acquire and display two enormous modern locomotives of great historic interest. The first is *Caerphilly Castle*, built by the Great Western Railway in 1923. The Museum authorities must have given much thought to the selection of a single machine to represent the steam

37

locomotive at the zenith of its success in this country. They were restricted, of course, by what was still available; but even if that had not been so their choice might well have been the same. The 'Castles' had an exceptionally long run as passenger engines of the highest class: in the late 1950s they were still taking the principal express between Bristol and London to a schedule that is closely comparable to the best laid down for diesel locomotives today.

With the arrival of *Caerphilly Castle* at the Science Museum and of *King George V* at Swindon (though it cannot yet be displayed there) we are able to follow the evolution of the Swindon locomotive more completely than that of any other British series: from the 'Dean Goods' through the express engines to the last version of the 'pannier tank', built at the very end of the Great Western Railway's life in 1947.[1] This is just as it should be: because—through political accident, aiding the intelligence and foresight of the Company's engineers—Great Western designs were allowed to pass through a long process of evolution, continuous and uninterrupted, to the very end of the Age of Steam.

In line with *Caerphilly Castle* stands the prototype 'Deltic' diesel locomotive.[2] This was built by the English Electric Company in 1955 and tested extensively on British Railways, while remaining the property of its makers. For a long time it worked 700 miles a day (London–Liverpool–London–Crewe–London) on express service, besides undertaking special tests over the heavily-graded Settle and Carlisle line and elsewhere. Satisfied with its performance, the British Railways management ordered twenty-two machines of a closely-similar type for use on their East Coast main line out of King's Cross. It was a big investment, for they cost nearly £200,000 each; but since their introduction in 1961 they have justified themselves well, on a service that has steadily grown quicker and more exacting.

The decision to include this immense locomotive here is a bold one: for it occupies a great deal of valuable space, and it is no quaint antiquity but a machine of a type that is still in the highest class of service. That indeed is the point. One of the things that makes the Science Museum such an exciting place is that it is

[1] Cf. pp. 103.
[2] So called because its eighteen opposed-piston cylinders are arranged triangularly, more or less in the form of the Greek letter *delta*.

alert, moving, keeping abreast of the swift development of technology: the very reverse of the museums of the past, which confined their interest to what was already dead.

The remaining original vehicles here include a motor-car from a London tube-train, dating from 1929, and a Glasgow Standard tram of 1901 (cf. p. 171). In view of the very generous representation of Glasgow trams elsewhere—at Clapham, Crich, and Glasgow itself—one may perhaps question if this was the best example to choose.

One more large exhibit demands mention: the signal-box that has been erected in one corner of the great well, opposite *Caerphilly Castle*. This comes from Haddiscoe in Suffolk, where the line from Lowestoft to Norwich crosses that from Beccles to Yarmouth (now closed). It is a tall box, well suited to display the mechanism of the levers underneath; and a series of semaphore and colour-light signals have been set up near by to show something of the evolution of railway signalling in this country.

It was a happy thought to include here a Southern Railway booking-office, complete with all its furniture and equipment, and a waiting-room. Such things have not yet found their way into museums in this country (though the new Staffordshire County Museum at Shugborough is bringing one in from Gnosall), but they have been admirably managed in the Norwegian Museum at Hamar.

As everyone who has seen the railway material in the Science Museum in the past will remember, the models form a splendid collection. Some of them are very old: that of the broad-gauge engine *Ixion*, for example, standing on track of the original pattern with longitudinal sleepers. Some represent types of locomotive that we know very little about otherwise, like the tank engines built for the Dublin and Kingstown Railway in 1851 and for the North London four years later. Some illustrate machines built for railways abroad—a 4–6–0 for the Chemin de Fer de l'Ouest, a 2–8–0 for the East Indian Railway, a huge electric locomotive for the Spanish State Railways. The series extends to a group of shunting engines, including one of the pioneer diesel shunters introduced by the London, Midland and Scottish Company in the 1930s. There are some excellent models of railway coaches, and a really informative set of early signals. Could the Museum workshops find time to carry the series on throughout the semaphore period to the colour lights of today, to complement and enlarge the history of what is displayed in full size close by? This would be a real service to all students of railways. We are also offered here a sound and informative display of the components of railway track.

Some excellent dioramas have been made to illustrate the early railways in use—in conjunction with carriage by packhorse, for example; they stand against backgrounds painted with refinement and meticulous care by Hugh Chevins.

Finally, it should be mentioned that this section includes some notable models of tramcars, especially the Grantham steam car of 1871. It was designed to work either on roads or on rails, with two sets of wheels; and its mechanism was built into the centre of the vehicle, the smoke being discharged through a tall flue running up the centre of the car through the upper deck and the roof. It must have been fiercely hot in summer for the passengers sitting near the middle.

Another interesting model is that of a tram from Dewsbury, designed for use with horses but subsequently hauled as a trailer by a steam engine. The arrangement of windows on the lower deck still shows an affinity with that adopted in G. F. Train's first cars (see p. 204). The upper deck is reached by a spiral staircase; it has knifeboard seating and, unlike the Grantham car, is open to the weather.

The collections illustrating navigation and marine engineering are above, on the second floor. The design here is ingenious and attractive, with a central raised section resembling the deck of a ship. Along one side of it, seen both from above and from below, are suspended three original craft, including the Oxford Eight of 1829 and its Cambridge counterpart of 1934.

The central section contains models which illustrate shipbuilding from the Middle Ages to the nineteenth century. A sizeable number of them are contemporary, made for the Admiralty or prospective purchasers. Two splendid cases contain eleven of these: an early naval schooner, a sloop, two frigates, and five large men-of-war, the biggest of them H.M.S. *Boyne*, a 98-gun ship built in 1790. They are well displayed, with the help of mirrors and good lighting, to show the perfection of their craftsmanship from every angle: look at the bow of H.M.S. *Boyne* with its figurehead of

William III at the battle and the decoration below and behind him.

Next door is an East Indiaman of the early nineteenth century, perhaps the *Princess Amelia*: again a contemporary model, though rigged in the Museum. These were virtually men-of-war, though more broadly built and less heavily armed; the arrangement of the decks, too, was different. Other merchant ships include a Hooghly pilot boat, a half-block model of *Loch Torridon*, an Australian wool-clipper of the 1880s—incomparably elegant in its lines—and the iron-built *Arundel Castle* of 1864.

The outer walls of the central section are filled with models of small craft. Inland navigation is not forgotten. There is a well-constructed model lock (unhappily not a working model, as at Munich), containing a canal boat and a modern cruiser side by side. Coracles are well displayed, in all their main varieties. A great deal of sensitive invention has gone into the mounting of some of these little individual exhibitions. Look, for example, at the section demonstrating the Yorkshire coble. It includes two half-block models, one neatly superimposed on a photograph of Robin Hood's Bay; a complete model, rigged; a print from Walker's *Costume of Yorkshire* showing one of these boats being manœuvred, on a wheeled undercarriage, on the beach; and an excellent 500-word description. It is a perfect demonstration of the way this kind of thing ought to be done.

The models of steamships are adjacent. We begin with the pioneers of the Atlantic crossing, *Savannah*, *Sirius*, and *Great Western*; and close by is another *Savannah*, the American nuclear-powered ship of 1959. Besides the *Great Western*, Brunel designed two other steamships: the *Great Britain* of 1843 (whose hull is still extant in the Falkland Islands) and the *Great Eastern*. There are splendid working models here of the engines of both ships on a scale of 1: 12. *Britannia*, the first ship of the Cunard line (1840), can be compared here with *Scotia*, the paddle-ship built for the Company (1861)—a highly successful ship, too, which held the Blue Riband of the Atlantic for five years. She lost the title to the Inman liner *City of Paris*, which is also represented here. That ship was driven by a screw, and her success helped to induce the Cunard Company to abandon paddles.

The development of the Atlantic Ferry can be followed here through every important stage. Here is *Servia*, the first electrically-lighted Cunarder (1881) and the first large merchantman to be built throughout of mild steel; and the second Inman *City of Paris* (1889), the first Atlantic passenger liner to be driven by two screws—though unfortunately she is shown in her later form, when altered by the American line and renamed *Philadelphia*. The Allan liner *Virginian* was one of the very first ocean-going ships to be built with turbines. What the careful description here might have added is that she enjoyed an almost unequalled length of service on the Atlantic—forty-seven years out of her astonishing total of fifty. She was broken up only in 1955. The series is continued through *Mauretania* to the second *Empress of Britain* and the *Normandie* of 1932. The internal arrangements of the great liners are indicated by two sectioned plans, of the incomparably beautiful *Caronia* of 1904 and of the *Queen Mary*.

Small steamers used round the coasts of Great Britain are well represented in the collection. There is a contemporary model of the *City of Bristol* of 1827. Cross-Channel steamers include *Connaught* and *Rose* for the Irish service, the Newhaven–Dieppe steamer *Brighton* of 1878, and the handsome *Queen Victoria*, which went on to the Isle of Man run from Liverpool in 1887. These were all paddle-steamers. We arrive at the threshold of the modern world with the Midland Railway's *Londonderry*, one of the pioneers of the Heysham–Belfast service of 1904, which helped to demonstrate decisively the value of turbines in work of this sort. Now that the traditional passenger steamer of the Channel crossings is being rapidly edged out by the car-carrier and threatened by the Channel Tunnel, it is to be hoped that the Science Museum will acquire a good model of one of the last of a long and distinguished line: perhaps *Invicta*?

Dredgers and river-craft form an interesting section. It begins with a Dutch dredger, operated by a horse and in use around Amsterdam in the 1780s, and the first steam dredger, designed by Trevithick, which helped in the construction of the East India Docks. One of the first iron steamers to be built on the Thames was *Lord W. Bentinck*, for service on the Ganges. From forty years later comes another Indian steamer, designed to carry grain into districts stricken by famine; it is made in four water-tight sections, to be assembled on the spot. The use of the steamer in developing the economic life of tropical countries is illustrated again by *Maud*, built for service in Lagos Colony in 1897, and *Fabius*, which went into service as a train-ferry on the Niger in 1909. One of the prettiest decorative models in the whole Museum must be that of a Danube river-steamer of 1946. It stands on a wooden base with inlaid pictorial designs, including one of the launching of the steamer itself; it is supported by six stout giants, carved in ivory; and ivory is used again for the elaborate carving on the stern and for the funnel.

The Aeronautical Gallery, on the top floor, presents an amazing spectacle the moment you move into it. Structurally it comprises one single hall with an elliptical roof of light metal construction. Flying machines can be shown on ground level; they are also suspended from the principal transverse ribs or from the lighter members that run the length of the building. A raised catwalk zigzags down the centre to allow a good view of the machines on the upper levels. The colour-scheme is pleasantly cool, in aluminium and R A F blue, with touches of yellow here and there in the illuminated display-cases.

The assembling of all this material has been contrived with incredible skill. For ingenuity of arrangement the Gallery surpasses by a considerable distance anything else described in this book. In this one hall, large but not vast, the Science Museum has brought together twenty-three full-sized machines, over eighty aero engines, and more than twenty large and admirably designed cases containing models and small relics, besides innumerable miscellaneous exhibits: cockpits; propellers (on the east wall they are kept revolving, which gives a pleasant sense of motion and at least the illusion of a breath of cool air); wheels— look at the monsters fitted to the Beardmore Inflexible bomber of 1926.

The total effect is one of overpowering quantity, an overcrowding that may seem oppressive. On the other hand it must also be one of admiration for the minute care and forethought that have gone into the whole display, the effort that has been concentrated into showing as much material as possible. This proudly claims to be the National Aeronautical Collection. It deserves the title, beyond question. No other country in Europe can show anything to compete with it.

As with the collection of ships' models, let us pursue two or three separate themes, to exemplify what this splendid collection can show.

First, the prehistory of flying—that is, down to 1903. The balloon takes its natural first place, with dioramas showing the two earliest flights, from Paris in 1783, and models of other eighteenth-century hot-air balloons. Nor is the later history of the balloon forgotten, down to Piccard's of 1931–32 (the original gondola of his craft is here) and the barrage balloons of 1939.

Among the pioneers of the aeroplane, honour is rightly given to Sir George Cayley. His silver disc of 1799 is here, showing from the sketch he engraved on it that he already understood the principles of heavier-than-air flight. The work of W. S. Henson and John Stringfellow is well shown. The actual model of their aircraft, tried out in Somerset in 1847, is displayed, with the steam engine designed to provide its power. Though the machine did not achieve its object, the model may be described as that of the earliest powered aircraft built on principles that we should now recognize to be sound. Its failure discouraged Henson deeply, and he emigrated to the United States. Stringfellow continued his experiments, with another model, which is also at the Science Museum, together with the engine from the triplane he built for the Aeronautical Exhibition held at the Crystal Palace in 1868. If a critical examination of Stringfellow's achievements has now cut him down to size, he persevered and he played his part by inspiring other men to make progress more important than his own.

Sir Hiram Maxim's machine of 1894 presents problems to the psychologist that are more interesting than his contribution to the history of flight. It was a failure, abandoned prematurely, after an accident, by its inventor, who yet complacently believed that he had laid down the true principles of powered flight. With a totally distorted sense of his own importance, he presented the original engine, one of the propellers, and a 1: 12 scale model of the whole aeroplane to the Museum in 1896. They are mounted now in front of a comically pompous photograph showing the inventor and a group of spectators at the trial of the machine, many of them dressed in frock coats and top hats. The descriptive account in the case treats the whole business with solemn respect. Here—and here alone in this Gallery—one asks oneself if the exhibits deserve the precious space they occupy.[1]

[1] Sir Hiram Maxim's claims are subjected to a brief but devastating examination in one of the Museum's most distinguished publications, C. H. Gibbs-Smith, *The Aeroplane* (1960), 25–6, 206–7. Sir Hiram readily condemns himself by his own words.

Meanwhile another line of approach was being profitably developed, in the glider. One of the seven gliders made by Otto Lilienthal hangs here, next to a reproduction of Pilcher's *Hawk* (cf. p. 163), the machine in which he met his death in 1899.

The original relics of the Wright brothers' triumphant aeroplane of 1903 are, appropriately, in the United States, but there is a reproduction of it here, prominently shown and well described, together with a replica of the engine and a fragment of the fabric that covered its wings.

The time-scale in the development of successful powered flight is astounding. Only ten years and eight months separate the Wrights' achievement from the outbreak of the first World War. In the military operations of that war aircraft were employed from the very beginning—on a bigger and bigger scale as time went on, with more and more devastating effect. When it ended, aeroplanes had been produced that were reliable enough in performance over extended periods to make it possible to contemplate flight over very long distances. When in 1913 Lord Northcliffe had offered a prize of £10,000 for the first non-stop flight across the Atlantic, that had seemed hardly more than a gesture by a millionaire with more than a touch of megalomania. The challenge was taken up in 1919, first by the Americans, who achieved the crossing with a stop in the Azores. Only a fortnight later, on June 14–15, 1919, the prize was won by J. Alcock and A. W. Brown. The Vickers Vimy biplane in which they achieved the feat is the largest exhibit in this Gallery, and to many people it will be the thing they remember longest. The machine was a military one, designed for use as a heavy night bomber though never used as such in the war. This aeroplane is indeed one of the most important of all links in the chain of evolution of long-distance civilian flight. Within forty years the crossing of the Atlantic had become a commonplace of many performances a day: hardly more of an adventure than the crossing of the English Channel by steamer in the nineteenth century.

After its brilliant success over the Atlantic, this type of machine was adapted to everyday civilian use and served the Instone line on its routes between London, Brussels, and Paris. A model of one in this service appears here, together with a number of other civilian aircraft of the inter-war years: the Armstrong Whitworth *Argosy* for the Continental services of the new Imperial Airways in 1926, the big *Heracles* and *Hannibal* built by Handley Page in the thirties. The series is continued down to the present day (the latest model to be included at the moment is of a Trident of 1963). It is especially valuable since most unhappily no museum in Europe seems to possess any full-sized airliner. Here is a major deficiency. Will not our successors expect us to keep for them at least one or two of the smaller examples of the passenger-carrying aircraft? There would clearly be no room here for such things: indeed there will be room for very few additions of any kind without evicting things that have worthily earned their place. Can the Science Museum consider establishing an out-station for the purpose, where land is a little less valuable than it is in South Kensington—on the analogy of the Victoria and Albert Museum, which now has dependencies at Osterley and Ham? Otherwise we can look for no enlargement of space until the West Block of the Science Museum is built, which will require, at the rate of progress so far achieved, another quarter of a century.

A corner of the Gallery is devoted to the one serious rival that the aeroplane has met with so far in its development: the airship, which did for a time begin to challenge it in civilian service in the 1930s. Its origin goes back far into the nineteenth century, to such experimental machines as those of Giffard, one of which is shown here in model. As early as 1883—twenty years before the Wrights flew their first successful aeroplane—Tissandier was able to make an electrically-powered airship that flew at a speed of 7 m.p.h. In the years before the first World War it developed neck and neck with the aeroplane, principally at the hands of the Germans. Several of the airships—not only those designed by Count Zeppelin—are to be seen here in pictures, with the first successful British airship R34, largely modelled on the captured German L33. With its bigger and more famous successors R100 and R101, it was considered as a prototype for civilian as well as military operation. The disastrous crash of R101 near Beauvais in 1930 fatally discredited the idea in Britain, which resolutely adhered to the aeroplane thereafter. But it did not deter the Germans, whose *Graf Zeppelin* went into regular service between Germany and Brazil in April 1932. That service continued without interruption for five years, until *Hindenburg*, the fellow of the *Graf Zeppelin*, exploded in New Jersey and the service was abruptly terminated. *Graf Zeppelin*, however, carried all its passengers in safety from beginning to end.

The Science Museum has models both of R101 and of *Graf Zeppelin*. They represent the climax of a long process of invention tested out with the same courage and skill as the aeroplane, which in the long run proved the victor.

The helicopter and gyroplane are not properly to be seen as the rivals of the aeroplane, but rather as offering a service that is complementary to it, with the great advantage of not requiring an airfield for take-off and landing. They are represented here by one full-sized original (a Cierva) and a case of good models.

The Aeronautical Gallery concentrates on machinery. It does little to illustrate, save very incidentally, the uses to which the machines were put in ordinary service. Something of this is indicated by a modestly-presented exhibition—which no one should miss—near the entrance to the Gallery. This comprises a fragment of the most remarkable collection assembled by the Misses Penn-Gaskell of small curios and *objets d'art* connected with aviation and of items in the history of the air mail. They come from all over the world: some addressed to the two ladies, who lived—could any place be more improbable?—at Widecombe-in-the-Moor; others patiently collected by them and described with minutely careful annotation, written out in a clear feminine hand. We now take the air mail for granted—where would our daily business, our intercourse with friends, be without it? Here you can see it evolving: from the letters that came out of Paris by balloon in the siege of 1870 to the first air-mail service in Britain in 1911, the early days of the London–Paris service in 1919–20, and one of the earliest letters ever to cross the Atlantic by air (it came with Alcock and Brown). Here is one sent to Cardiff by the service operated temporarily during the General Strike of 1926, and some of the first letters sent experimentally by rocket in Germany and Britain in the 1930s.

Finally, up above, there hang four brightly-coloured posters to announce aviation meetings and competitions in 1909–10—at Reims, for example, and Nice. All of them are designed to appeal as much to women as to men. They take one's mind back very directly into that earlier world, where every flight was a gay and dangerous adventure.

No brief account like this can possibly do justice to the Science Museum. I have singled out only a very few of its treasures: fewer in proportion than those of any other museum described later, its collections being so extraordinarily rich. The quantity of material shown can easily induce a surfeit in the visitor if he attempts to gorge too much of the succulent plum cake he is offered. But this is a fault found only in the world's greatest museums and galleries. The authorities of this one have gone resolutely out to meet it: with a display that is varied and enticing, with a good lecture-programme, with written guides of exceptional merit.

In this last respect the Science Museum sets an example to all the thirty-three others that are described in this book. Its introductory literature begins with a threepenny guide and an admirable booklet entitled *50 Things to See*; the casual visitor is also offered an excellent series of postcards, in black and white and in good colour, of things he will wish to remember. The admirable *Handbooks* to the collections have already been mentioned. They are backed up in turn with a series of monographs issued by the Museum, many of which—like Mr Gibbs-Smith's study *The Aeroplane*—became standard works as soon as they were published. For the Museum exists to promote research, in the fullest sense. Its very extensive library, archives, and photographic collection are an invaluable instrument for scholars.

Perfection has not, indeed, been attained. (Can it ever be hoped for?) Disconcerting errors, inconsistencies, and false grammar occur even on the carefully-prepared descriptions attached to the objects that are displayed; there are some objects, like the Avro triplane in the Aeronautical Gallery, that have, unaccountably, no description whatever. More serious, the machines that are shown are too often regarded by those who have described them as self-contained entities, to be seen in the perspective of techno-logical development but not at all in relation to the economic purposes they were designed to serve. Why did this machine displace that? Was it cheaper to build—we are seldom told any-thing here about capital cost? Or cheaper to run? Or more pro-ductive—and if so, by how much? These are all questions that ought to be asked if one wishes to understand fully why the machine justifies its place in this national museum.

Such thoughts as these are prompted by the very excellence of the collections themselves and the information we are offered about them in such generous abundance. At a time when Britain is losing so much of the pre-eminence she formerly enjoyed, it is a matter of pride for an Englishman to feel that in the Science Museum he has one of the richest and best-run museums in Europe.

2

MUSEUM OF
BRITISH TRANSPORT
CLAPHAM

The British railways were nationalized on January 1, 1948. It is much to the credit of the British Transport Commission that even in the midst of immediately pressing problems concerning the present and the future it found time to think also of the past. It set up a committee to investigate the treatment of the relics and records inherited from the old companies. Its report, published in 1951, was comprehensive and far-sighted, laying it down as a guiding principle that the arrangements to be made for their custody 'should be founded on a clear appreciation of the wider social and cultural heritage of early transport development in many different fields'.[1] Furthermore, the committee indicated its view that the need was not confined to the preservation of what happened to survive from the remoter past; that the operation was a continuing one, involving 'the gradual bringing up to date of the collection from internal sources. . . . The Commission's museum policy should therefore provide for the retention of appropriate items for the collection while they are still readily available.'[2]

The chief recommendations of the report were accepted. On the museums side, a Curator of Historical Relics was appointed; and a standing committee was established to advise him and the Commission on the problems in the history of technology that arose. Under its auspices a list was drawn up not only of machines and equipment that were disused but also of those that were still in service and merited preservation. This enabled a carefully-

[1] *The Preservation of Relics and Records: Report to the British Transport Commission* (1951), para. 6.
[2] *Ibid.*, para. 8.

selected list of steam locomotives, for example, to be earmarked for preservation even when many of them were still in traffic.

The report of 1951 recommended that the existing Railway Museum at York, which had already been in existence for a quarter of a century, should be retained and that two—ultimately three—others should be established: a principal one in or near London, a second in Edinburgh, and a third, at a more distant date, in Cardiff.[1] For the housing of the London museum it proposed the old station at Nine Elms. That was an attractive suggestion, but it proved impracticable. It was only in 1957–58, after prolonged discussion and inquiry, that the problem was solved by making available for museum purposes a London Transport garage then falling out of use at Clapham. This comprised a rectangular main shed with workshops at the side, offering a floorspace of some 55,000 square feet and a two-storied administrative building with a sequence of rooms well suited to the display of small objects. The Museum was opened to the public in two stages: the small exhibits section in 1961, the main hall just over two years later.

There are several ways of reaching the Museum. To anyone who is interested in the history of what he is going to see, the journey there is part of the fun. The quickest route from most parts of London is by the Underground to Clapham Common station, which lies only a hundred yards away from the Museum. This line is historic: part of the City and South London, the earliest electrically-operated 'tube', or deep-level underground railway, in the world. It was opened from King William Street (by the Monument) to Stockwell in 1890, extended ten years later to Clapham Common, and hence to Morden in 1926.

Or you can go by bus by way of Vauxhall Bridge and Stockwell, traversing scenes familiar to all students of the history of the omnibus in London. This was the home ground of Thomas Tilling's vehicles, with their headquarters at Peckham. Many readers of this book will remember the Tilling-Stevens petrol-electric buses, with their distinctive radiators and emitting their no less distinctive noises, on route 36.

But my own favourite approach to the Museum is by train to

[1] *The Preservation of Relics and Records: Report to British Transport Commission* (1951), paras. 34–6.

Clapham station on the South London line. There is a half-hourly service from Victoria (in six minutes) and London Bridge (in about a quarter of an hour). You descend from the station into Clapham High Street, turn right, and the Museum is five minutes' walk down the road. The South London line has recently attained the centenary of its completion, on May 1, 1867, and even now it keeps a little of its mid-Victorian air: most of all, perhaps, at Denmark Hill, but also elsewhere, in tiny cottage gardens, bright with flowers, by the side of the railway and in the iron-work of some of the station buildings, notably East Brixton. It was on this line that Stroudley's famous 'Terrier' locomotives did their most valiant work: little ochre-coloured engines, puffing along busily with their close-coupled trains, a gay enlivenment to the drab landscape. In later years, this was the first surface line to be electrified in London (1909).

You will soon find your way in Clapham High Street by catching sight of a full-sized replica of the *Rocket* that has been mounted high in the entrance, its tall chimney thrusting up among the traffic and the shops to proclaim the presence of the Museum. You push open the large glass doors and find yourself at once in the main gallery.

The collections on display may be divided into three parts: 1. Railway rolling-stock; 2. Road vehicles; 3. Small exhibits. The first and second groups are all to be found in the big main hall and the courtyard behind it; the small exhibits are interspersed with them, and they also have a series of little rooms to themselves in the two-storied administrative block at the rear.

1. RAILWAY ROLLING-STOCK

Sixteen locomotives are to be seen here, all of them originals except the replica of the *Rocket* that has been mentioned already. The passenger coaches number thirteen, including five royal saloons; and there are a number of other miscellaneous railway vehicles.

The exhibits are not arranged in chronological order; their placing has been determined in large measure by their size. A boldly-lettered notice is, however, displayed above each locomotive and a description will, as a rule, be found beside it. There should therefore be no difficulty in locating the machines in the order in which they are discussed here.

The earliest original locomotive at Clapham is the Furness Railway's *Coppernob*, which has shown exceptional powers of survival, both in service and under preservation. It was already somewhat old-fashioned when it was built in 1846 by the Liverpool firm of Bury, Curtis and Kennedy. Such had been the locomotives provided for working the goods traffic of the London and Birmingham Railway on its opening in 1837–38: cheap and safe, but slow and weak—Bury himself admitted that as many as seven of them had been required to haul a train of forty-five wagons in a gale. This is the only extant specimen of the type. *Coppernob* had a working life of fifty-four years. When withdrawn from service in 1900, it was one of the oldest locomotives in the country, and the company decided to put it on show in a glass case on the station at Barrow-in-Furness. The case was blown to bits, together with much of the station, in 1941; but *Coppernob* stood like a rock. Now it stands here, a little dented and chipped from the air-raid but glowing in polished brass and the rich rust-coloured livery of the Furness company.

A few yards away stands a passenger engine that was turned out, in its original form, only a year later: the eccentric *Cornwall*, built to the designs of Francis Trevithick for the London and North Western Railway. At that time much thought was being given to the means of securing a low centre of gravity for locomotives, which it was thought would make them steadier at high speeds. Crampton tried to solve the problem in one way (cf. pp. 191, 252), Francis Trevithick tried another in *Cornwall*, giving the engine single driving wheels 8 feet 6 inches in diameter, with the boiler slung *beneath* the axle. In this form—though with four leading wheels instead of two—she was shown at the Great Exhibition of 1851. Seven years later John Ramsbottom reconstructed her drastically into her present form. Only a part of the outside frames and the centres of the wheels of the original engine survive in the one we see now. She had an even longer working life than *Coppernob*. For many years she worked fast, light trains between Liverpool and Manchester; then, after she had been taken out of regular service in 1902, she was used with the Chief Mechanical Engineer's inspection saloon until 1922.

Perhaps we shall do best to consider the remaining thirteen

locomotives by groups, according to the class of work they were designed to perform. Let us begin with one that stands out entirely on its own—the smallest of them all, and the first thing you see inside the barrier: the 18-inch gauge engine *Wren*. This was built in 1872 and employed for very many years in the Horwich works of the Lancashire and Yorkshire company. Not far from *Wren*, near the entrance, is a light engine supplied by Aveling and Porter of Rochester to the Wotton Tramway, in Buckinghamshire, in 1872. It is interesting as an example of the application to railway work of the firm's experience with traction engines. It has a single cylinder 7¾ inches by 10 inches, with transmission by spur gearing and chain drive to the wheels. Though its career on the Tramway lasted little more than twenty years, it continued in the service of a brickworks in Northamptonshire until 1940.

There are three tank engines, designed for suburban passenger work, all of outstanding interest. The oldest is Metropolitan No. 23, a 4–4–0 engine of the type that worked all the services on the London underground railways as long as steam lasted. It was built in 1866 and continued at work until 1948; like *Coppernob*, these engines were magnificently strong in construction. No. 23 is an abiding memorial of the first underground railway in the world. Opposite stands one of William Stroudley's fifty 'Terriers', built for the London, Brighton and South Coast Company from 1872 onwards. They were tiny engines, their weight kept down as low as possible (it was under 25 tons) in order to enable them to work over the East London line through the Thames Tunnel and over the South London line, both of which were laid with very light track. They too enjoyed a very long life—no fewer than sixteen survived to be taken into the stock of British Railways in 1948.

The third of these engines played its part in one of the most remarkable of all the achievements of steam locomotives: the 'intensive' suburban service introduced by the Great Eastern Railway in 1920. By that time the company was carrying over 100 million suburban passengers a year, most of them into and out of one station, Liverpool Street. Even if it had believed that electrification would solve its problems—and it did not—the Great Eastern could not afford to undertake any development so costly. The General Manager, the American Sir Henry Thornton, and his Superintendent of Operation, F. V. Russell, were confident that the steam locomotive, properly handled, could find a solution. The remodelled service they introduced in July 1920 did what was asked of it. The rush-hour service in the morning from Enfield and Chingford was augmented by 75 per cent; a train ran every ten minutes on both lines; the record of precision in punctuality was remarkable. And the chief burden of maintaining this service —with heavy trains, loading a thousand passengers and more apiece, up the incline at 1 in 70 to Bethnal Green—fell on the little six-coupled tank engines like No. 87, which is to be seen at Clapham. If ever a locomotive, like a horse, earned an honoured retirement, it is this one.[1]

Great Eastern engines were always distinguishable by their livery: to my own way of thinking, the most beautiful of all those worn by locomotives in this country—a royal blue, picked out in black and scarlet. Another, dressed the same, stands near by. This is a 2–4–0 for mixed traffic of class T26, a versatile type, working well not only in East Anglia, its home, but in later years on the long and arduous line from Darlington over Stainmore to Penrith.

The other six engines here were all designed for express passenger work. The London and North Western 'Precedent' 2–4–0 *Hardwicke* achieved lasting fame in the Race to Aberdeen in 1895 when—after a series of splendid performances all through July—she reached her climax on the night of August 22nd with a run over the 141 miles from Crewe, across the 915-foot summit of Shap, to Carlisle in 126 minutes. She was hauling a light train, but the feat of driving and firing so small an engine at such a high continuous speed was heroic; and only an excellently balanced machine, free-running and powerfully built, could have stood up to demands like these.

Two 4–4–0 engines from the railways south of the Thames are here: one from the London and South Western Company, No. 563 of class T6, with outside cylinders, designed by William Adams and built in 1893; the other No. 737 of H.S. Wainwright's class D for the South Eastern and Chatham Company (1901). Both have good records of long service. They can fitly represent the British express engine at the turn of the century, successfully tackling tasks that were becoming more and more exacting; and as for

---

[1] There is a good account of the remarkable Great Eastern service of 1920 in Ch. xv of C. J. Allen, *The Great Eastern Railway* (1955).

looks—they are incomparably handsome, Adams's engine at once lithe and stately, Wainwright's in the view of many people (including myself) the most graceful express engine ever built, the most perfectly proportioned in all its parts.

Two other machines of the same type, but much more powerful, stand near them: Midland No. 1000 and No. 506, *Butler Henderson*, of the Great Central. The Midland engine, which appeared in 1902 and was altered to its present form in 1914, represents the only really successful adoption of the principle of compounding—that is, the use of the same steam twice over, at high pressure and at low—on the railways of this country. On the Continent that principle became almost universal; here it was never liked. But the exception to this rule was a fine one indeed; engines of this Midland class continued to be built until 1932, when they numbered 240. They were used with success for high-speed work not only on the Midland system, but on services as diverse as the Euston–Birmingham two-hour expresses and the run over Beattock summit from Carlisle to Edinburgh and Glasgow. The Great Central engine was built in 1919,[1] to the designs of J. G. Robinson. It, too, represents a type designed for work in England (between Marylebone and Manchester) which was subsequently adopted for use in Scotland on the old North British system: the two-cylinder simple-expansion 4–4–0 engine at about the greatest possible size of its development.

And so, finally, we move into the 1930s, the St Martin's summer of steam on the railways: to Sir Nigel Gresley's 4–6–2 engine *Mallard* for the London and North Eastern Railway, which holds the world's speed record for a steam locomotive of 126 m.p.h., attained in 1938. Enclosed in its streamlined casing, vastly bigger than any other of the machines here, it seems to belong to another world than theirs. But if *Mallard* is one of the most powerful, complicated, and costly steam locomotives ever produced in this country, the essential features of its design can be traced back through the long series of engines exhibited here and at York and Swindon.

The passenger rolling-stock can be divided into two groups: the royal saloons and the rest.

The royal saloons number five, all from the London and North

---

[1] It was put into service on December 27, 1919 (G. Dow, *Great Central*, iii. 370), though the plate on the engine itself bears the date 1920.

5a National Maritime Museum: seal of the borough of Pevensey, Sussex, *c.* 1230, showing one of the earliest representations of ratlines, forming a rope ladder in the shrouds

b Munich: German *Ewer* sailing-ship *Maria Finkenwerder*

6a Lucerne: model of a French frigate of 1804

b Hull Maritime Museum: H.M.S. *Hector* under construction at Hessle on the Humber, 1743

7*a* National Maritime Museum: the East Indiaman *Northumberland*, painted in two positions off St Helena by Thomas Luny

b National Maritime Museum: model of the East Indiaman *Scaleby Castle* (1798).

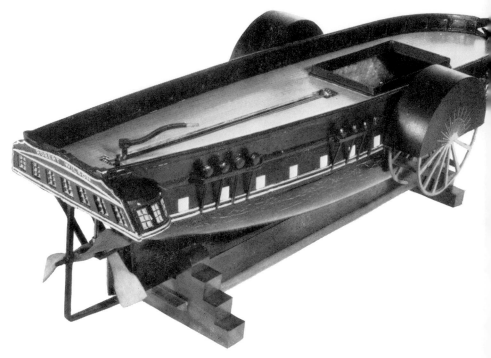

8a Royal Scottish Museum: model of the first steamer to make use of screw propulsion, demonstrated by Robert Wilson in 1828

b Newcastle: the original *Turbinia*

a Science Museum: model of Midland Railway's turbine steamer *Londonderry* for the Heysham–Belfast service (1904)

b Clapham: models of railway steamers. Left to right: S.S. *Dewsbury* (G.C.R.), P.S. *Rose* (L.N.W.R.), S.S. *Dinard* (S.R.), Dredger *Rhyl* (L.N.W.R.)

10*a* Stoke Bruerne: boatpeople's costume

b Stoke Bruerne: ironbound chest made for the Coventry Canal Company *c.* 1780

a Stoke Bruerne: decanter made for the Coventry Canal Company, showing a horse towing a canal boat, engraved on the glass.

b Stoke Bruerne: Measham teapot for a canal boat

Stoke Bruerne: reconstruction of the cabin of a narrow boat

12a National Maritime Museum: state barge made for Frederick, Prince of Wales, in 1732

   b National Maritime Museum: shipping on the Bristol Avon, by Jan van Beecq (1722)

Western Railway. First, the small four-wheeled carriage made in 1842 for Queen Adelaide by one of the North Western's parent companies, the London and Birmingham. Its body is of a dark claret colour with the Company's arms and monogram emblazoned by hand on the side panels. The door-handles are gold-plated, and in every detail the vehicle is superbly finished. But what gives it especial interest is that it is the only surviving example of the 'bed-carriage', the predecessor of the sleeping-car of today. The carriage comprises a coupé, two compartments, and a boot. This last is a relic of the horse-drawn mail-coach, now put to a new use. The backs of the seats against it can be lifted up on hinges, and a cushion put across the space between the seats in the compartment; the passenger can then lie down. Such carriages were not the exclusive prerogative of royalty. Ordinary passengers could secure accommodation of this kind on the London and North Western Railway until it introduced sleeping-cars of the modern type from 1873 onwards.

Queen Adelaide's niece Victoria took kindly and immediately to the new mode of travel when she tried it in this same year 1842, though she soon developed her own rigid notions about the ways in which it should be managed. A number of British railway companies built vehicles specially for her use[1]—a fragment of the Great Western saloon of 1874 is mounted on the wall behind. Her London and North Western carriage stands, intact in its glory, next to Queen Adelaide's. Originally there were two vehicles, built at Wolverton in 1869, a day and a night saloon, each running on six wheels. In 1895 they were joined together to form the single carriage we see now, mounted on a single frame with two six-wheel bogies.

The appointments of this vehicle are splendid indeed; sumptuous, yet never gaudy or over-ripe like some of its Continental counterparts—Ludwig II's saloon at Nuremberg, for example (p. 251), or Pope Pius IX's in the Municipal Museum in Rome. Mr Ian Nairn remarks that here is 'one of the loveliest sequences of rooms that the nineteenth century ever created'.[2] The silks of the day saloon are unforgettable, royal blue for the upholstery, quilted ivory for the ceiling above a gilt cornice. The Queen's bedroom is more subdued, in red; and at each end of the coach

---

[1] Cf. H. Ellis, *Railway Carriages in the British Isles* (1965), Chap. viii, and his delightful pamphlet *Royal Journey* (1953).   [2] *Nairn's London* (1966), 192.

57

are compartments for dressers and attendants. Both roofs and floors are double, to reduce noise, the floors filled with cork and covered in thick carpet and under-felt.

Adjoining this magnificent vehicle stand the two saloons built for King Edward VII and Queen Alexandra in 1903, together with a dining saloon of 1900 that was marshalled in the train with them. The old Queen never ate a meal on a train. On her journeys to Balmoral she dined at Windsor before she set out, had a substantial tea at Banbury, and breakfasted at Perth. She did not succeed in preventing electric light from being installed in the reconstructed royal saloon of 1895; but she insisted on the retention of the old oil lamps and made no use herself of the new-fangled equipment. Her son and daughter-in-law belonged emphatically to the twentieth century; the dining-car and the electric light were symbols of the change. These two saloons were refurnished, under Queen Mary's eye, during the first World War, when they were often used as a mobile hotel, and baths were installed in them.

The detailing of these coaches, inside and out, repays long and careful study, whether one looks at it as a student of engineering or of decoration or of social history.

With these royal vehicles may be grouped the saloon built, also by the London and North Western Railway, in 1899 to the orders of the Duke of Sutherland, for his exclusive use. This one coach provides a completely self-contained living unit, including a complete Victorian pantry fitted with an oil-stove for cooking. It has no corridor connections and could therefore be attached to the night train from Euston to Inverness without giving other travellers any chance to invade the Duke's privacy.

The other Victorian passenger vehicles here, for the use of more ordinary travellers, comprise two replicas of carriages used at the opening of the Liverpool and Manchester Railway, a composite coach of the Bodmin and Wadebridge company, possibly dating in part from the 1830s (one of a train of three, the other two vehicles being at York), and a six-wheeled directors' saloon built for the North London Railway in 1872. It is rather a pity that room has not been found here for a vehicle of more normal type dating from the last quarter of the century, to demonstrate how the private traveller was catered for; but there is an instructive mock-up of a Midland Railway third-class compartment, which shows the sort of accommodation that company offered when it took the bold decision to admit third-class passengers to all its trains in 1872.

Again, from the twentieth century the Museum lacks ordinary vehicles (apart from a mock-up of sections of British Railways standard stock of 1951); but the three it displays are all interesting. First, there is the Pullman car *Topaz*, built in 1914 for service on the South Eastern and Chatham system; to be compared with the only other Pullmans that are on show, in the Montagu Motor Museum at Beaulieu. How splendidly these twentieth-century Pullman cars rode the track! I never remember better travelling in Britain than I have had on some of them: from Edinburgh to Leeds, from Cardiff to Paddington.

From the same year, 1914, comes a very handsome twelve-wheeled dining-car built at Derby for the service between St Pancras and Glasgow (St Enoch). You can walk through this vehicle and see not only its layout and decoration (including the familiar tinted photographs of scenes on the Midland Railway) but a varied set of table appointments culled from a number of different railway companies. And out in the yard behind is a Great Western buffet car of 1934.

Several special vehicles, working commonly in passenger trains though not for the use of travellers, are also to be seen here: a replica of the first specially-constructed travelling post office, which ran on the Grand Junction Railway in 1838; an original West Coast Joint Service mail sorting van, built at Crewe in 1885; a Metropolitan Railway milk van of 1896; a dynamometer car, used for testing the performance of locomotives, from the North Eastern Railway, dating from 1906.

There are only two freight vehicles here, and they are an oddly-assorted pair: a chaldron wagon of the ancient traditional type from Seaham Colliery and (in the back yard) an oil-tank wagon belonging to Shell-Mex and B.P. It comprises a drum mounted on a four-wheeled truck, very modern in appearance; one is astonished to see, from the plate it bears, that it was built as early as 1889.

2. ROAD VEHICLES

The Clapham collection includes a representative group of the road vehicles that provided ancillary services to the railways:

a horse ambulance of the London and South Western Company, for example, a horse-breaking cart from the Caledonian, fire-engines from the Great Eastern and Great Western, several petrol-driven tractors and trucks. In the present display the eye is caught by a horse-bus in a yellow and black livery. It was attached to Tenterden (Rolvenden) station and belonged to the Kent and East Sussex Railway. This must be one of the last horse-buses ever to be acquired by a railway company; for the line did not reach Tenterden until 1900, as the Rother Valley Light Railway, nor pick up its later title, displayed on the side panels, until 1904. Very small and very old-fashioned, it was an appropriate adjunct to the company that owned it and to Tenterden itself.

In line with this quaint little vehicle stand three others that illustrate the development of the horse-bus in London. To begin with, there is a replica of the first that ever worked there, introduced by George Shillibeer. It ran five times a day between Paddington and the Bank in 1829. The patterns on which Shillibeer based himself were French.[1] The vehicle was drawn by three horses and seated twenty passengers, all inside; the fare for the whole distance was a shilling—dear, but competitive with the established modes of transport, the short-stage and the hackney coach. Though the journey was scheduled to take an hour, it was often accomplished in forty minutes. Shillibeer's experiment was an immediate success, partly owing to its novelty and its *chic* French origins, but more from the real advantages it offered. Though it did not bring him a fortune himself (he did better when he became an undertaker in the City Road), it led directly to the establishment of the bus as a London institution. There were over 600 buses in London in 1839; more than twice that number by 1850. By that time they were beginning to grow bigger, many of them accommodating passengers on a 'knifeboard' seat running the length of the roof.[2] An original vehicle of this period is to be seen at Clapham: one of Thomas Tilling's, dating from about 1851.

The horse bus reached the apogee of its success in the last quarter of the nineteenth century. By 1891 the London General Omnibus Company was operating nearly 1,100 buses, the London

---

[1] The best account of the introduction of the omnibus into London by Shillibeer is given in T. C. Barker and M. Robbins, *A History of London Transport*, i (1963), 17–30.
[2] *Ibid.*, i. 37, 59.

Road Car Company and its other rivals nearly 600. Throughout the eighties the LGOC was paying dividends to its shareholders that varied between 10 and 12½ per cent.[1] And all this in spite of the competition of underground railways and trams.

The final phase of the horse-bus is well represented by the latest of these vehicles at Clapham: a General bus of 1895. By this time the design of the vehicles had changed a little—but only a little. On the roof the passengers were now accommodated on pairs of seats facing forward—'garden seats' as against the old 'knifeboard'. But the size of the unit had hardly increased, for there was a strict limit to the weight a pair of horses could draw, in the exacting conditions of London traffic.

Few horse-buses now survive, even in museums. Their decline and fall came very suddenly with the emergence of the electric tram and the motor-bus in the opening years of the twentieth century. The last belonging to the LGOC disappeared in 1911. Nearly 800 still remained in London then, operated by other proprietors. The last of all in regular service were Tilling's, on the route from Peckham Rye to Honor Oak. It symbolized the ending of an age—in this as in greater matters—that they were taken off on the first evening of the Great War, August 4, 1914.[2] Though some of them survived, lifted from their wheels, to serve as huts or hen-houses—like the old coaches of the 1830s and 1840s, like some railway carriages—most of them were broken up, systematically and at once.[3]

Horse-trams, too, are rare. Not one from London seems to survive complete. The two at Clapham come from Douglas and Chesterfield. The Douglas car—built in 1883 at Birmingham, by the Metropolitan Carriage and Wagon Company, and bought second-hand with five others in 1886—is a double-decker, and it continued in service until 1947. The Chesterfield car appeared in 1897, and it had only a very short life, for it was withdrawn when the system was electrified in 1904. It is a modest little single-decker, with sixteen seats.

[1] *A History of London Transport*, i. 252–3.
[2] C. E. Lee, *The Horse Bus as a Vehicle* (1962), 24.
[3] An atmospheric photograph of the process is reproduced in my book *Transport* (Visual History of Modern Britain, 1962), plate 221. The caption there is mistaken in stating that 'today no General horse bus survives' (I had not then seen this one at Clapham), and the Star bus, mentioned there, has since been withdrawn from the Museum at Maidstone.

But though the horse and steam tram made a stalwart contribution to urban transport in the later nineteenth century, the electric tram brought with it something like a revolution. Successful experiments with electric traction on a small scale were made in Northern Ireland and at Blackpool, Brighton, and Ryde in the 1880s. The urban electric tramcar made its first appearance in this country at Blackpool in 1885 and at Leeds six years later; by 1900 it was also established in a dozen other towns, from Bradford to Plymouth, from Coventry to Dublin. But not yet in London. No regular electric tram services ran there until 1901. The LCC, which became the biggest operator in the capital, adopted electric traction only in 1903.

Once it had proved itself, the electric tram shot ahead at a dizzy speed, to enjoy a supremacy in urban transport, not only over the horse-bus but also over the steam-operated railway. As this was exemplofied in one great city after another, it became clear that the railway's best answer to the electrification of the tramways must be the electrification of the railways themselves. Some were quick to draw this conclusion, and to act on it. The Tyneside Tramways and Tramroads Company, for example, opened its line from Gosforth to North Shields in the autumn of 1902. The North Eastern Railway lost ground to its new competitor so fast that it quickly decided to electrify thirty-nine miles of its Tyneside system. The whole circuit between Newcastle and Tynemouth, via Wallsend and Whitley Bay, went over to electric working in 1904. Similar stories come from other towns: from Manchester and Liverpool, from London itself. Where the railway company could afford the great capital outlay required for electrification, it could hope to recover much of the ground it had lost to the tram; but where it could not, or would not, the tram was usually the victor.

It penetrated into quarters that no railway touched. It was brisk and clean, and quite as comfortable as most suburban third-class trains. Politically, too, the tram had behind it the formidably strong interest of the municipalities, which were naturally anxious to see the utmost use of the current that their power-stations were generating.

But if the triumph of the electric tram was spectacular, it was also brief. Even before 1914 the motor-bus had come through its growing-pains—less protracted than the tram's, though equally intense—to challenge its older rivals. When the first World War was over it shot forward in favour, and by the 1930s the tram was in retreat: not only before the motor-bus, but before the hybrid trolley-bus too. By the end of the second War electric trams were on the way to extinction in this country. In 1962 the last of them ran in Glasgow, leaving Blackpool as the only town in Britain to retain them.

It is a piece of singular good fortune that has preserved for us one of the original cars that operated the first service at Blackpool; and here it is at Clapham, lent by the Tramway Museum Society. In its original form it was powered by a motor driving the two axles by chains and taking up current through a slot from a live rail underground. It was converted to overhead traction, and given new trucks, in 1899.

Next to it stands another tram from the Isle of Man—No. 1 of the Douglas Southern Electric Tramways Company. It is a double-deck vehicle, with toast-rack seating below and garden seats above, built by the Falcon Works at Loughborough, running on a truck designed in Baltimore, in 1896. It was not withdrawn from service until 1939.

Three cars represent the noontide of tramway development in Britain, the years just before the first World War. Two of them come from London, from the LCC and West Ham, the other one was in service in Llandudno. The LCC car is No. 1025 of Class E/1, built in 1908; one of the largest single type the LCC ever owned, representing the very best practice of its time.

Six of the boroughs in eastern London owned separate tramway systems. They were apt to guard their independence jealously and to emphasize it by adhering to some practices different from their great neighbour's. They remained faithful to the four-wheeled vehicle, for instance, long after the LCC had adopted bogies: as in the car belonging to West Ham Corporation (the biggest of this group of operators), which is now here at Clapham. It ran from 1910 to 1938; it was then withdrawn from service and spent fourteen years in store. Then it was refurbished at the Charlton repair works by London Transport, in 1952—only some three months before the running of the last tram in London. It is interesting as a vehicle in itself, and as a reminder of the quite peculiar pattern taken on by transport in our capital, with its multiple outlying municipalities. Nothing of the same sort is to be seen, for example, in Paris.

Car No. 6 of the Llandudno and Colwyn Bay Electric Railway worked first at Bournemouth from 1914 to 1936. Like some other seaside resorts, Bournemouth considered the open-top tram an attraction to visitors in the summer and it retained them to the end. This car, with nine others, was then sold to the undertaking in North Wales. Towards the end of their life in 1956, these were the only trams with open tops left in England and Wales.

Of the three remaining trams, two may be said to belong jointly to London and Leeds. They are almost exact contemporaries— the Feltham car of 1931 and the LCC No. 1 of 1932. Both were of steel construction throughout. The Feltham car was the product of a long exercise in research into potential improvements in tramcar design, using the techniques and materials that had by that time become available: a gallant effort to avert a change that —as we can now see looking back—was already inexorably on its way. The same may be said of LCC No. 1. It was designed specifically to win traffic through the Kingsway Subway, which had been enlarged to take double-deck cars in 1931. This splendid vehicle— quite as comfortable as any bus of its time, smoother-riding, quieter, and above all odourless—stands with the Kingsway Subway itself as a sad monument of missed opportunity.

All the Feltham cars and LCC No. 1 were bought by the Corporation of Leeds, and worked there until the system was closed in 1959. No. 1 appears at Clapham in its Leeds livery.

End to end with No. 1 stands a Glasgow 'Cunarder', No. 1392, the last completely new tram built for its own city, and one of the last double-deckers to be built anywhere in the world. This was Mark II of the Coronation type, one of which is to be seen in the Transport Museum at Glasgow (see p. 173). It seated seventy passengers, had folding platform doors, a separate cab for the driver—all the latest refinements. By the time it was built, in 1952, even Glasgow was considering the abandonment of the tram, though on a gradual basis that would perhaps have left them running into the 1970s. In the event, this vehicle had only ten years of active life, until the change-over to buses was completed in 1962.

One instrument in the downfall of the tramcar in this country has been the trolley-bus, which shares its great defect, depending on electric current transmitted by wires overhead, yet is more flexible, since it does not run on rails. The trolley-bus has the added merit—peculiar to itself among all powered transport machines—of running almost silently. The experimental stage of the trolley-bus, in this country and abroad, lasted a very long time, reaching back to 1881. Some of the vehicles produced in the course of these experiments were extremely weird: one that emerged in Leeds in 1921 has been characterized as 'looking for all the world like a tramcar that had had a collision with an ancient battery-electric dustcart and carried away a watchman's hut in the process'.[1] The first really satisfactory trolley-buses were evolved by Wolverhampton Corporation in 1926. Before that year was out two other towns, Darlington and Ipswich, had decided to abandon trams in favour of trolley-buses.

The two trolley-buses at Clapham both represent the vehicle in the prime of its success. One is a single-decker built by Ransomes, Sims and Jefferies Limited of Ipswich for the Corporation Transport Department in that town in 1930: a strangely primitive and clumsy-looking vehicle beside its fellow, a big double-decker built only a year later for London United Tramways, to run in the Kingston area. During the next nine years trolley-buses replaced trams on almost the whole of the London system north of the river, as well as in the Tooting, Sutton, and Woolwich districts. London eventually had nearly 1,800 trolley-buses, the largest number operated by any undertaking in the world.

But the heyday of the trolley-bus proved even shorter than that of the tram. It too is on its way out in this country—it disappeared from London in 1962—defeated just as clearly by the motor-bus.

The story of the emergence of that vehicle is a curious and fascinating one, which awaits the extended treatment it deserves at the hands of a competent historian.[2] Experiments began as far back as 1889, but no reliable and economical vehicle emerged from them for some time to come. In 1903 the Corporation of Eastbourne led the way in securing Parliamentary powers to operate motor-buses, and in the same year the railway companies began

---

[1] C. Klapper, *The Golden Age of Tramways* (1961), 270.
[2] Meanwhile, Mr Charles Lee's pamphlet *The Early Motor Bus* (published in 1962 in the series for which the Museum at Clapham is responsible: see p. 280) is an excellent introduction to the subject.

to employ the new vehicles in connection with their exisiting services in rural districts. It was not until 1904 that permanent motor-bus services began in London, through the enterprise of Thomas Tilling Limited and Birch Brothers. At the end of 1905 there were 230 motor-buses on the London streets; just over two years later there were over a thousand.

But though the motor-bus by now had plainly come to stay, it remained noisy, cumbrous, and unreliable. The new General Company was still searching for a satisfactory design, and it decided to go into the business of manufacturing buses for itself. The first result was the 'X' type of 1909; the second, based on the experience thus gained, was the 'B' of 1910—one of the outstanding technological developments of the early twentieth century. For here, at last, was a motor-bus that could be depended on in the exacting conditions of London traffic and multiplied as a standard type in a way that had never been previously dreamt of. Nearly three thousand of them were built in all.

What strikes one most about the 'B' bus, looking at it today, is its simplicity and its small size. The simplicity was a great virtue: the first cost was low (the chassis worked out at less than £300), and the vehicle was easy to maintain. It seated thirty-four people, sixteen inside longitudinally and eighteen on the garden seats of the upper deck. The driver was entirely exposed to the weather at the front and sides. Glass side-screens were provided for a time but removed as a danger to his vision in 1913; the Metropolitan Police declined to sanction a windscreen or a cab of any sort until 1929.

The 'B' bus exhibited at Clapham is one of the last of its long line, built in 1919. In that year the General Company put out the first of its class 'K', one of which is to be seen here too. In the 'B' type the body was narrow and pitched high above the wheels, still on the lines of the horse-drawn vehicle. The 'K' was lower, squarer, sturdier; and its broad body could provide forward-facing seats for all the passengers, inside as well as out. It accommodated a third as many of them again: forty-six, against the thirty-four of the 'B' type. The 'S' of 1920—an improved version, of which an example is also at Clapham—provided yet another eight seats.

The next steps were to roof the upper deck and to improve the riding of the bus by substituting pneumatic for solid tyres. These moves were accomplished in 1925–26, and they are exemplified in a vehicle of the 'NS' type here dating from 1927. The series of London buses is rounded off, for the present, by examples of two types introduced in 1929—the 'ST' and the six-wheeled 'LT' —and a Green Line coach of 1931.

The provincial motor-bus was represented here by one example only: an Eastern National double-decker of 1939. It looks rather forlorn, standing in the back yard, as if it had been pushed out by its cousins from town. Though, in a severely restricted space, there is much to be said for displaying related machines—all built for the greatest, and on the whole the most advanced company in Britain—in sequence, it would be no less interesting to be able to compare closely the London and the provincial bus and to observe the points at which differing standards prevailed. These vehicles are easily moved. Could the Eastern National bus be brought inside sometimes, say in place of the London 'ST'? This would have the incidental advantage of allowing it to be compared not only with London buses of the same time but with an Ipswich trolley-bus that was its own competitor.

Here, for the present, the exhibition stops. The Museum has preserved a number of other motor and trolley-buses, both from London and from the provinces, of a later date; but it is not yet possible to display them.

3. SMALL EXHIBITS

The small exhibits relating to road transport are chiefly to be found in the Tram Annex to the left of the entrance and on the back wall, behind the motor-buses. In the Tram Annex there are some good models and a set of nearly seventy framed photographs that are of great interest, making an appropriate and informative background to the original vehicles that are on display. They illustrate the development of the tram, mainly though not exclusively in London, from 1880 to 1952. Among them are pictures of the Highgate Hill cable tramway (1884); the North London steam tramway, which operated from Finsbury Park to Ponder's End for five or six years and then reverted to horse traction in 1891; the first electric trams in the London area; a Grimsby tram of 1903—the first to have the top deck wholly enclosed; an LCC petrol electric tramcar of 1913.

A similar sequence of photographs is mounted behind the buses. They demonstrate particularly well the expansion of London and the ancient, the perennial, problem of traffic congestion in the great city. See, for instance, the excellent series along the top showing the development of Piccadilly Circus from about 1880 to 1934.

On the ground floor of the smaller building behind, across the courtyard, there is a room containing other exhibits bearing on the same problem: a series of Underground and bus posters—rightly given a place here, because for fifty years now they have been of a high standard, and many of them have been a true and delightful decoration of London's public places. The Underground fought vigorously and imaginatively for its traffic. Here is a poster, for example, depicting a street under repair with the Underground beneath, proclaiming '*Our* Road is Our Own'; and another announcing that 'Mr Pennyfare came back January 1925'. (Alas, he has vanished again, and he does not seem likely to make a second reappearance now.)

Up above, on the first floor of this building, there is a varied display of small railway exhibits. It is treated unsystematically, as a miscellany, and that is an excellent idea, for it helps to make plain how infinitely multifarious were the tasks the railways performed. On the landing at the head of the stairs we are brought back again momentarily to royal journeys, with a display of some of the exquisite engraved glass produced for Queen Victoria's service, part of the Limoges enamel toilet set that graced her retiring rooms at Perth, and a series of the timetables printed specially for journeys made by her and other royalty. Here, for instance, is that for the Princess Alexandra—'Sea-kings' daughter from over the sea'—when she travelled up from Gravesend to Bricklayer's Arms on the last stage of her journey from Denmark to marry the Prince of Wales in 1863; and another, in her widowhood, for her journey back to her home country in 1911, in the company of the Empress of Russia. Some of these documents are very elaborate, giving a complete plan of the train and naming the occupants of every coach.

The next room is dominated by a series of portraits: the famous one of John Ellis painted in 1858, with a railway scene, including the Glenfield tunnel on the Leicester and Swannington line, in the background; another, lively and of quite good quality, of John

68

Ramsbottom of the London and North Western; a third, coarse and unattractive, of Sir Edward Watkin.

In Gallery 5—the rooms take on numbers, for some unexplained reason, at this point—the miscellany shows its true breadth and scope. More glass and some silver-ware, to start with, including an electric kettle and saucepan made for Queen Victoria's North Western saloon after its reconstruction in 1895. (Can the Queen have known that she was drinking infusions prepared with water heated in this unseemly way?) Among the many models is one, very fine and large, of a North Union passenger coach, made in the Company's workshops at Preston in 1842. It shows very clearly the experimental arrangement of placing the buffers on a bow-shaped spring outside the headstocks that was favoured also by by the Manchester and Leeds Company at the same date. This is one of the finest and most instructive models of an early railway carriage to be seen in this country. At the far end of the room is a group of ships from railway service, attractively mounted in a style like that to be met with at Lucerne (see p. 224). They have been shrewdly chosen, to show not only a variety of types— a Holyhead paddle-steamer of the 1870s, a dredger, the Great Central's *Dewsbury* of 1910 (the first steamship to sail out of Immingham)—but also some interesting features of construction. Here, for example, is the paddle-steamer *Sandown*, built for the Southern Railway's Portsmouth–Ryde service by Denny's of Dumbarton as late as 1934, with a cruiser stern but in other ways hardly distinguishable from one of her predecessors of, say, fifty years earlier.

Some fine railway notices are here: the South Eastern and Chatham's well-known threat to 'skylarking' cabmen; one from the Cheshire Lines ordaining that the lavatories were for the use of passengers only and excluding from them 'workmen, cabmen, fishporters, and idlers'; a Great Northern timetable reflecting the Methley Junction row of 1849.

The next gallery, 6, is a small one, showing an assortment of prints and water-colour drawings of railways: a good series, which was until lately reduced to the level of mere pretty pictures by the want of explanatory labels. It was as if the Museum's interest had stopped, suddenly and quite arbitrarily, at this point, leaving the visitor to shift for himself. Now, however, they are adequately described. They include two notable water-colours of the 1860s:

one of Southampton, with a train skirting the shore to the west, the town walls intact and visible; the other of Charing Cross bridge before the Embankment was made.

Beyond, on the staircase descending from the far end of this gallery there is another interesting miscellany of pictures and notices. We are always told, in general terms, that the Great Exhibition of 1851 did much to popularize travel by excursion train. An advertisement of the Lancaster and Carlisle Railway announces 'Exhibition Trains' from Carlisle and other towns on the line to London, allowing for a stay of seven to fourteen days, at fares, from Carlisle, of £3 first class, £2 second, and 30s third. Here is a notice of the 'London Road Car Company's (Hornsey Depot) Drivers and Conductors Walking Competition (Fancy Costume)' of 1903, with echoes of other sports too: an excursion to a wrestling match at Haydon Bridge on the Newcastle and Carlisle Railway in 1845, a demand by the London, Brighton and South Coast Company that the dogs to be conveyed by its trains should be muzzled, with the careful postscript: 'This notice does not apply to packs of hounds or greyhounds for sporting purposes in charge of a competent person.' And Awful Warnings continue, like this one from the Edinburgh and Glasgow Railway: 'Caution. John Whitton, sailor, belonging to H M Ship *Jackall*, charged with being drunk and disorderly in the 2 p.m. train from Edinburgh to Glasgow on Saturday the 4th July current and with annoying and assaulting his fellow passengers. He had to be taken from the train at Falkirk station, and was brought before Sheriff Sconce, and fined in the sum of 5 shillings, or eight days imprisonment.'

This fascinating series of railway miscellanea is continued on the walls of the main gallery. Among them on the far wall, behind the royal coaches, is a great rarity, the *Railway Calendar* for 1839.[1] This is a single sheet published by the *Railway Times*, combining a map of the whole system, timetables, information about the companies, and notes on legislation—the simple ancestor of George Bradshaw's two famous publications, his timetables and his *Manual* for railway shareholders. Among the railway notices are some that are of great interest. Here, for example, you read of a cheap trip from Leighton Buzzard to London in 1843, with a tempting additional inducement: 'It is also proposed to take an

---

[1] It can fairly be described as a great rarity since Mr George Ottley's *Bibliography of British Railway History* (1965), items 418–19, lists only the issues of 1840 and 1841.

Aquatic Excursion up the River Thames . . . in a S P L E N D I D S T E A M
V E S S E L .' And here too are the embers of the violent quarrels and
fights of the past—a group of handbills bearing on the controversy
over railways between London and Portsmouth in 1846. The
Manchester and Leeds Company comes in for a savage attack in
an ironical broadsheet purporting to announce the Company's
policy:

'. . . We intend to continue (as far as in our power) our customary
and well-known incivility to all passengers. . . .

'We promise to increase our speed of travelling, so that the
above parties, who have presumed to run coaches in opposition to
our railway (disregarding our known wishes on the subject) may
perform the journey in not more than a quarter of an hour shorter
time than we or our agents. But as this will augment the charges,
and increase the number of casualties, we have arranged . . . that
cemeteries shall be immediately erected at each station, and plans
of such cemeteries deposited for passengers previously to starting,
to book a place in, by payment of a small charge, so that when
the accidents happen there will be no confusion or unpleasantness
in the arrangement or burial of the bodies. A dissecting room will
be attached. Our fees for maiming and killing are as follows. . . .'

The critic ends up with a comprehensive assault on the brakes
and axle-trees of the Manchester and Leeds coaches, on their dirt,
on the dangerous state of the Littleborough Tunnel, and on the
length of the stoppages of the trains at stations—except where they
are intended for refreshments, when they are perversely made too
short.

On the wall immediately adjoining the main entrance, facing
Hardwicke and the Great Eastern 2–4–0, and in its small side-
rooms are some models and pictures of stations: a model of
Euston in its pristine condition, to be compared with the original
sketches of the building of the station and railway by J. C. Bourne,
which are mounted on a screen not far away, and then a set of
more than twenty photographs showing the demolition of the old
station in the 1960s. A jolly composition in blue tiles shows a
North Staffordshire train passing the Bridge Inn, Hanley;
it comes from the inn itself. And everywhere around and above are
fragments of the engaging bric-à-brac left by the railways: notices

to trespassers, number-plates attached to bridges (the figures on those of the London and Birmingham superbly cast), the maker's plates from railway ships and engines. Here is the name-plate of one of the Great Western broad-gauge express engines, *Sultan*, incorporated into a fire-screen. And interspersed with the rolling-stock runs a series of over a hundred name-plates borne by loco-motives of all kinds and sizes, from the little tank engines of the Isle of Wight Company, the Lynton and Barnstaple and the Dundalk, Newry and Greenore to the last express train engines, taken out of service in the 1960s. They are a subject for a whole essay in themselves, with their associations, the overtones they carry. Royal names occur, of course, from *King George VI* and *Queen Elizabeth* back to *King Arthur*; great public men are com-memorated—*Clive of India, Michael Faraday, Rudyard Kipling*; railway men too, *Hackworth, G. J. Churchward, Sir William Stanier, F.R.S.*—not forgetting *Lord Hurcomb*, first Chairman of the British Transport Commission and a benevolent sponsor of this Museum.

But the most moving is the series of twenty-four simple, curved plates mounted in one great row behind Queen Victoria's saloon. They are taken from Sir William Stanier's 'Jubilee' class, built for the London, Midland and Scottish Company in the 1930s. There were once 190 of these excellent engines, and they are affectionately remembered by many travellers in the Midlands, North Wales, and Lancashire. The names they bore were drawn from three different sources: the Commonwealth, the Royal Navy, and the locomotives serving on railways a hundred years before they were built. So here is the old British Empire—*Bombay, Uganda, Trini-dad, Straits Settlements, New Zealand*. Then come the ships—*Warspite, Orion, Agamemnon, Polyphemus, Camperdown, Hogue*—and the admirals—*Kempenfelt, Wemyss, Cochrane, Drake*. And finally, reaching back to the dawn of the railway as we know it, *Atlas, Samson, Novelty*. This is part of the very stuff of the history of Great Britain.

When you walk round this splendid Museum, you will find it fascinating to turn your mind away from time to time from what you have been looking at and absorbing yourself to watch the faces and listen to the comments of your fellow-visitors. There will be children, of course: more and more astonished, with every year that goes by, at these strange steam locomotives and trains, the like of which they have never seen in their world. But the middle-aged and the elderly will be there too, and sometimes you will see simple people deeply moved: for they recognize these great vehicles as a part of their daily lives that has now vanished for ever. As for the locomotives, Mr Nairn is right when he remarks that they 'represent man's ingenuity and self-respect at one of its highest levels'. He sums up pithily: 'The far-away look in those other visitors' eyes holds something more than nostalgia. Like *Quattrocento* architecture, Jacobean poetry, German baroque sculpture, this was It.'[1] That claim is not pitched too high.

[1] I. Nairn, *Nairn's London*, 192.

3

NATIONAL MARITIME MUSEUM
GREENWICH

The quickest way to get to the National Maritime Museum is by train from Charing Cross to Maze Hill station, from which you can walk to the Museum in five minutes: an interesting little journey, for it takes you over the line of the London and Greenwich Railway, the first to be opened in London (1836–38), built on a continuous $3\frac{3}{4}$-mile viaduct from London Bridge to Greenwich, still the longest in England.

A slower but more attractive way is available in the summer months by motor-launch from Westminster Pier to Greenwich. This is one of the classic journeys through the cities of Europe, like that of the No. 11 bus here in London or the 21 in Paris or the Circolare Destra and Sinistra, which follow closely the Aurelian Walls of Rome. For the river-boat gives you an unequalled view of the heart of London: with St Paul's, still presiding with infinite majesty over the clobber of third and fourth-rate buildings that have risen up around it since the second World War; London Bridge and the Pool; the Tower, guarding the approach to the city from the sea; the whole system of docks, from the very first Greenland Dock of 1697; and then, on the last curving sweep of the river, Wren's Naval Hospital at Greenwich. As you draw into the bank, three tall masts catch your eye: those of the sailing-ship at rest in dry dock here, the original *Cutty Sark*.

The origins of the National Maritime Museum go back a long way. The Commissioners of Greenwich Hospital brought together what was intended to become a 'National Gallery of Marine Paintings' from 1823 onwards; and the Royal Naval College, which came to occupy Wren's buildings after the Hospital was closed in 1870, assembled a Naval Museum that included exhibits transferred from South Kensington and from naval stations in Britain and overseas. The idea of enlarging these collections to form a national museum of the sea was pressed energetically by the Society for Nautical Research, which was founded in 1910. The task would not have been achieved on this splendid scale even now if it had not been for the munificence of one benefactor, the Glasgow shipowner Sir James Caird (1864–1954). He had already put up most of the money for the restoration of H M s *Victory* and purchased for the nation the Macpherson Collection of maritime pictures, one of the most valuable ever assembled anywhere; now he found, first and last, more than £1¼ million to equip the National Maritime Museum. None of the other museums considered in this book has known so ample a benefaction; few museums of any kind have seen anything like it in the twentieth century, outside the United States of America. With this bountiful assistance and the goodwill of the Government, which made available to it the historic Queen's House and the adjoining buildings of the Royal Hospital School at Greenwich, the Museum was opened by King George VI in 1937. It was substantially extended in 1951.

This is primarily a museum of the Royal Navy, of maritime war. As I have explained in the Preface, this book is primarily concerned with commercial transport in peace. This chapter concentrates almost—though not quite—exclusively on the mercantile marine, as its history is treated at Greenwich. But with a very few exceptions, the exhibits of outstanding importance there are naval, and though nothing can be said of them here, no visitor should fail to see such things as the Van de Velde drawings and paintings of the Dutch Wars or the wonderful display of the relics of Nelson.

The collections are arranged mainly in chronological order. Those relating to the sixteenth and seventeenth centuries are in the Queen's House, the remainder in the Caird Galleries that flank it on either side.

There is, however, one important exhibit that reaches back further in time: the display of casts of seals depicting ships. Most of these were given to the Museum by a well-known expert in the subject, Mr H. H. Brindley. They are to be found in a small room by the entrance to the Library, near the catalogue stall in the West Wing. It leads off a panelled octagon, designed by Lutyens, with a sculptured head of Sir James Caird in the centre.

Seals provide one of the most valuable sources we have for follow-ing changes in the form of medieval ships and their equipment. The first known representation of the rudder in the form in which we are familiar with it today appears on the seal of the borough of Ipswich early in the thirteenth century. The reefing-points on a sail are to be seen for the first time on the late twelfth-century seal of La Rochelle; ratlines in the shrouds appear at Pevensey about 1230. From Dunwich (? 1199) and Poole in the thirteenth century comes evidence of the early development of the forecastle and the poop. And so on, through the municipal heraldry of dozens of ports along the European coastline, from Scandinavia to Spain. A special case is devoted to the fascinating sequence of ships, from about 1200 to 1789, on the seals of one city: Paris—almost the only one of them that lies away from the sea.

Of the exhibits in the Queen's House the pictures are outstand-ing.[1] They begin with a painting of the first half of the sixteenth century, attributed to Cornelis Anthoniszoon, of Portuguese carracks—the earliest full-rigged ships, of a type evolved in the Mediterranean but familiar by this date in northern waters—lying off a port on a rocky coast. Several of the paintings illustrate the development of trade in remote seas: the arrival of four Dutch East Indiamen at Amsterdam in 1599, the departure of an English one (signed by Adam Willaerts and dated 1620); the port of Archangel, the main point of entry for English trade into Russia, painted in 1644. The crossing of the narrow waters to the Continent is illustrated several times—though always on state occasions, when larger and more comfortable ships were used than the ordinary passenger could command. Here, for instance, is the Elector Palatine embarking at Margate with his new bride in 1613; and William of Orange returning to Holland after his fateful wedding to the Princess Mary in 1677. An interesting section here deals with the Thames in these years, with a painting

[1] It is not easy to indicate the exact whereabouts of individual exhibits in the Queen's House, since, although every room bears a number indicated on the plan, only one (14) displays that number anywhere. This is a maddening trick, especially as many of the rooms are small and the sequence in chronological order is not an obvious one. Occasional plans on the walls, marked 'You are here', are no adequate substitute. Many of the rooms in the Museum have been most agreeably redecorated in recent years; perhaps another fiver could now be found to put this anomaly right? The rooms in the Caird Galleries bear a fresh set of Roman numbers, over their doors themselves as well as on the plan—though in the current *Short Guide* to the Museum these figures are translated into Arabic.

of the East India Yard at Deptford about 1670, showing several of the very big ships required for that trade on the stocks; another of Greenwich some ten years later, looking down from the hill, with Charles II's palace under construction and the river higher up crowded with shipping; and finally Canaletto's picture of Wren's superb building, seen broadside on from the river, the Thames watermen magically transformed into gondoliers.

Of the long and fine series of ships' models, the oldest—one of a ship of some fifty guns—was made in the middle of the seventeenth century.[1] There is a modern model of the first English royal yacht, *Mary*, which was built for the Dutch East India Company and presented by the Admiralty of Holland to Charles II on his Restoration; and two large contemporary ones of other yachts of the late seventeenth century. Though it is impossible at this date to draw any firm line of distinction between the man-of-war and the merchantman, it can fairly be said that very mearly all the eighteenth-century models are of warships. Yachts provided an exception: like that of the Lord-Lieutenant of Ireland, the *Dorset* of 1753. A 'cat' or 'bark' of the middle of the century is here, used for transporting coal from the Tyne to the Thames; *Endeavour*, which carried Cook on his first voyage, was a ship of this type. There are Dutch and French East-Indiamen, of 1723 and 1764, but no English East-Indiaman before the *Scaleby Castle* of 1798. This is a point on which one might hope to see some change at Greenwich in the future. Would it be possible to group together a set of exhibits illustrating the maritime history of the East India Company, which became so immensely important to Britain in the eighteenth century and the early ninteenth? There are a few already, in different parts of the Museum: a painting by Thomas Luny of the East-Indiaman *Northumberland*, seen in two positions off St Helena; another by Francis Holman of the Blackwall Yard, where so many of these ships were built; one or two paintings and prints of actions in which they were engaged with the French. A more comprehensive presentation of this great subject, illustrating Sir Evan Cotton's fine study *East Indiamen*, would be very welcome here indeed.[2]

[1] They are all admirably described by a great authority, Dr R. C. Anderson, in the Museum's *Catalogue of Ship-Models* (1952, with a supplement of 1958).

[2] There is a great deal of material for it in the Print Room of the Museum. Life on the Indiamen figures prominently in one of the Museum's most attractive publications: E. H. H. Archibald, *Travellers by Sea* (1962).

But if models of merchantmen of these years are scarce, the Museum can boast four splendid original state barges from the Thames. They are accommodated together in a room specially built for them beside Neptune's Hall—the former gymnasium of the Royal Hospital School, in the west wing of the Caird Galleries. The earliest is the shallop, an open barge rowed by ten oarsmen, made for Queen Mary in 1689. It is simple and unadorned, not out of character with the Queen herself. At the other end of this gallery, in strong contrast, is the state barge made for Frederick, Prince of Wales, in 1732: for a crew of twenty-one, with a cabin to seat nine people at the back, and ornamented in the finest taste of its time to the designs of William Kent, the carving executed by James Richards (Grinling Gibbons's successor as King's Carver), the painting and gilding by Paul Pettit. It is a dazzling display of craftsmanship, from the dragon and the six glorious sea-horses at the prow to the richly-painted ceiling of the cabin and the exuberant dolphins at the stern. The series is completed by two barges, one open and one with a cabin, for the Commissioners of the Navy. They are, as it is appropriate they should be, plainer, and they exemplify very well the type of craft that was still plentifully used under the Georges for the conveyance of persons of importance up and down the river, such as one sees in the Thames paintings of Canaletto and Samuel Scott.

There are other things, too, of the eighteenth century that linger in the mind. One of the earliest paintings of the Avon, in its gorge below Bristol, is here: Jan van Beecq's of 1722, which shows the river crowded with tall ships. As one comes upon scenes of arrival and departure, one is often surprised to find how little the ports have changed. Look at the paintings of Charles Brooking, for example, of a two-decker and a frigate arriving at Harwich, of a merchant ship and a royal yacht off Dover—exactly, in essentials, what one sees today, leaving for Calais or Ostend. The elaborate views of the royal dockyards, by Nicholas Pocock and others, have a great deal to tell us about the construction and repair of ships of all kinds; and anyone who is interested in the purposes that ships were actually made to serve will be delighted with the model, admirably detailed, of a section of a naval transport, carrying horses and ammunition over to Germany for the British troops operating there in 1759.

The achievement of Captain Cook in the Pacific is magnificently commemorated in a gallery of its own (VI). His original journals are here, the fine portrait of him by Nathaniel Dance, and many relics of his three voyages. Among the most remarkable of them is the series of sketches and paintings by William Hodges, who accompanied Cook as draughtsman on his second expedition in 1772–75. He was the first European to attempt to render in paint the grandeur and richness of the Pacific world—its strangeness, too, in his unforgettable picture of the weird figures of Easter Island. He revealed to Europe a whole new world, of vision and thought and feeling, in just the same way as the explorers who had made their way across the Atlantic and into the Indian Ocean in the fifteenth and sixteenth centuries.

Another relic of Cook's voyages, of high importance, is to be found in the Navigation Room. This is the chronometer that he took with him on both his last expeditions, which served him perfectly under tests that could hardly have been more stringent. It was the work of Larcum Kendall, a duplicate of one designed and made by John Harrison. Its three predecessors, on which Harrison worked for nearly thirty years (1729–57), are all shown here, together with the brilliantly-successful fourth and the duplicate so thoroughly proved by Cook. All are at work—thanks chiefly to the patient labour of Lt-Cdr R. T. Gould, who devoted twelve years to their restoration.[1] They are an abiding memorial of Harrison's intelligence, craftsmanship, and pertinacity. Though the modern chronometer does not descend from Harrison's work, but from that of Leroy and Berthoud (which can be studied in the Arts et Métiers Museum in Paris), these are a wonderful demonstration of the stages by which the problem of finding longitude at sea was solved: an achievement of fundamental importance for all modern navigation, and the sea-trading that depends on it.

The Navigation Room also contains a fine display of charts, beginning with the medieval portulans—the earliest of them dating from 1456; of manuscript and printed maps; of sextants, compasses, and navigating instruments of all kinds. They are amply and carefully described.

The transition from sail to steam is illustrated in two places: in Neptune's Hall, chiefly by means of models, and in the galleries of the East Wing. The display in Neptune's Hall is, to be candid,

---

[1] Cf. his *John Harrison and his Timekeepers*, a reprinted lecture on sale at the Museum.

rather confusing: for the models are not shown in any clear order, either chronological or by type, many of them are poorly labelled, and the visitor is given little indication of the reasons why these particular ships have been chosen for exhibition. The paddle-boats include an early Thames steamer, *Belle* (in a case behind the Prince of Wales's state barge); the historic H M S *Rattler*, which demonstrated the advantages of the screw over paddles in a contest with H M S *Alecto* in 1843; the first of the British royal yachts to be propelled by steam, *Victoria and Albert*, commissioned in the same year; the General Steam Navigation Company's *Taurus*, employed largely in the livestock trade with the Continent. *Taurus* was built in 1866 at Preston, and we are often usefully reminded here of the multiplicity of small shipyards that existed—some of them exist still—up and down the country, often in quite small places. Here, for instance, are two trawlers built in recent years at Beverley and a lightship built for Trinity House at Dartmouth in 1937.

There are some models of ships of a pioneer type or unusual design: *Great Eastern*, as one would expect; *Euplectela*, built at Newcastle in 1894, as an oil-tanker convertible at will for the carriage of other cargo; *Nonsuch* (1906), one of the turret-decked ships built by Doxford's of Sunderland from 1891 onwards. A special interest attaches to the model of *Elderslie*: for when she appeared in 1884 she claimed to be the first ship equipped with refrigerating plant for the frozen-meat trade, and the model belonged to Sir James Caird, for whose firm, Turnbull Martin and Co., the ship was built. He had other models here of ships with which he was connected. His firm managed for the Elderslie Company, or, as it later became, the Scottish Shire Line, and here is a sequence of its ships from *Elginshire* of 1891 to *Argyllshire* of 1911, which was one of the earliest merchant-ships to carry defensive armament in the first World War.

The passenger ship is shown here unsystematically and rather inadequately. The Clyde services are represented alone by *Columba*—one of MacBrayne's vessels that enjoyed a very long life, from 1878 to 1935; the Channel by the South Eastern and Chatham Railway's *Biarritz*, which was not completed until after the first World War had broken out and was at once requisitioned by the Government, to enter normal service only in 1921. The earliest passenger liner here is the *Gloucester Castle* of 1911,

3a Maidstone: general view of the carriages on the ground floor

b Belfast: road vehicles

14*a* Maidstone: Italian gig, late seventeenth century

b Science Museum: Sir George Armitage's phaeton, *c.* 1770

followed by the much larger *Andes*, which had an interesting and varied career. She became an armed merchant cruiser in the first World War, reverting afterwards to the River Plate trade, then (under the new name *Atlantis*) being turned over in 1930 to the new and profitable occupation of cruising. In the second War she served as a hospital ship—the guise in which she is represented here; when it was over, she carried emigrants out to Australasia until she was broken up in 1952. Among the big ships of the inter-war years here are *Mooltan*, *Normandie*, and *Orion*; together with two merchantmen that are remembered for heroic actions in 1939–40, *Rawalpindi* and *Jervis Bay*.

The second of these fights is commemorated in a fine painting by Norman Wilkinson; and it should be said that the Museum has a really distinguished series of pictures by the artists commissioned by the Government in the second World War, such as Charles Pears's of the sinking of the *Tirpitz* by Barracudas and several by Richard Eurich—his 'Dunkirk', for example, and his poignant painting of H M S *Revenge* steaming out of Portsmouth on the morning after an air-raid.

This is indeed our national gallery of marine painting. Its holdings are very large: over 3,500 oils, nearly 30,000 prints and drawings. The Museum includes not only pictures of ships and the sea but a noble collection of portraits: Nicholas Hilliard's miniature of the Earl of Cumberland, the set of twelve half-lengths of the commanders in the Battle of Lowestoft against the Dutch in 1665, painted by Lely and highly admired by Pepys, the portrait of Commodore Keppel with which Reynolds first established his fame. Many of the portraits, and some of the most famous of the pictures of historical scenes, came from the old collection assembled at Greenwich by the Commissioners of the Hospital; but the great majority of them, and of the rest of the exhibits as well, have been brought together, by gift or purchase, especially for the Museum as we see it now. It is the youngest of our major national museums. But it is the most splendidly housed; and, taken all round, its contents are worthy of their magnificent accommodation.

If the Museum itself does, as yet, less than justice to the mercantile marine, that is due in large measure to its history, for it is the legatee of collections designed solely to illustrate the development of the Royal Navy; and something of the balance is redressed by *Cutty Sark,* laid up in dry dock only a few minutes' walk away; for the ship can show much that cannot possibly be managed in a museum.

Built as a tea-clipper in 1869, she attained her greatest success in the Australian wool-trade under Captain Richard Woodget in 1885–95.[1] She passed under the Portuguese flag, until in 1922 Captain Wilfred Dowman bought her back into English ownership and began the task of restoring her to her original condition. Through his devotion and his widow's generosity, aided by private well-wishers and public authorities, the ship was eventually brought to her present home and opened to the public in 1957.

Cutty Sark was not a large ship—her gross tonnage was a little under 1,000—but she was extremely swift. Her first three homeward passages under Captain Woodget were made in an average of sixty-nine days, an unsurpassed record. In 1888 she overhauled the new P. and O. steam liner *Britannia* (no sluggard, for she had herself made a record passage from Brindisi to Adelaide in the previous year) off the Australian coast, sailing triumphantly into Sydney harbour in front of her. No ship—unless it were her great rival *Thermopylae*—could therefore more fitly represent the mercantile marine in the closing years of sail. Visit her now, and you get the true sense of scale and proportion that very few photographs can suggest: the great height and span of the rigging, the broad decks with their low headroom, the minute living-quarters in which her officers and crew, numbering about two dozen in all, were accommodated. The methods of stowing the tea and wool cargoes are well shown on the ship today. She is admirably displayed in working order, not at all as a dead museum.

She contains a most interesting exhibition relating to her own past and that of her contemporaries. On the lower deck is the superb Long John Silver collection of ships' figureheads, illustrating the techniques of maritime wood-carving in the Victorian age to perfection. Some of them represent living worthies of the times— Florence Nightingale, Garibaldi, Gladstone, Gordon; others mythical figures like Hiawatha or Sir Lancelot; others again abstractions, like the magnificent Hunter, for a wooden barque

---

[1] For the history of the ship see B. Lubbock, *The Log of the Cutty Sark* (1924); *Mariner's Mirror,* xxv (1939), 279–85; A. Villiers, *The Cutty Sark* (1953); and F. Carr, *The Cutty Sark and the Days of Sail* (n.d.).

built in 1854. Among the relics associated with *Cutty Sark* herself are a log and journals of her voyages and a long series of photographs illustrating her career in different forms under the British and Portuguese flags. (To our great advantage, Captain Woodget was a keen amateur photographer.) Here, from the eighties, is a group of the ships' apprentices, taken with Captain Woodget himself at Shanghai; there an evocative picture of Sandridge Pier at Melbourne.

On shipboard—even in the simplest terms, as on a cross-Channel steamer—you always get a powerful sense of stepping into a narrow, enclosed community, a separate world of its own. How much more in a ship like this, accustomed to running for a couple of months and more on end, across the China Seas and the South Atlantic or round Cape Horn and through the Roaring Forties, with every yard of sail stretched to beat a rival whose progress, before the days of wireless telegraphy, was quite unknown. There is no finer memorial than this of the daring, the enterprise, and the peculiar skills that once gave Britain her pre-eminence in the world.

4

TYRWHITT-DRAKE
MUSEUM OF CARRIAGES
MAIDSTONE

This museum owes its origin and development chiefly to the man after whom it is now named, Sir Garrard Tyrwhitt-Drake (1881–1964). He formed the collection and vested it in the Corporation of Maidstone, which owns the building it is housed in and accepts responsibility for its custody and maintenance.

The building itself is a remarkable one: a two-storied range, with a fine external staircase, formerly the stables attached to the Archbishop of Canterbury's manor-house. It is an entirely appropriate place for a museum of horse-drawn vehicles, and those assembled here are worthy of their distinguished setting.

Sir Garrard has given us his reasons for forming the collection. Horse-drawn vehicles were being driven off the roads by mechanized traffic, and though many had been stored in coach-houses, more and more of those were being cleared and their contents destroyed, under the relentless pressure of increasingly heavy taxation. 'Thousands of fine examples of the coach-builder's craft,' he writes, 'have been broken up since the end of the first World War, and I am satisfied that within a very few years the only examples in existence will be those in museums, such as this.'[1] The work of building up the collection was undertaken indeed just in time. Nobody who started on the task now, even if he were backed with very large funds, would be able to bring together a collection of the quality of this one at Maidstone.

---

[1] *Museum of Carriages: Official Illustrated Guide* (4th ed., 1959), 2. In the current edition of the *Guide* (6th ed., 1964) this introduction by the founder of the Museum has been replaced by an admirable note defining the different types of carriage, and a short bibliography.

Its scope is very broad indeed, embracing any kind of vehicle that is not mechanically propelled. It thus includes bicycles, sedan chairs, sledges, even a costermonger's barrow and the parish bier of Cranbrook; but its main attention is given to the coachbuilder's art.

The majority of the large vehicles are on the ground floor. The series includes a travelling chariot of George III, dating from the end of the eighteenth century: a splendid object, though disfigured by a subsequent application of dark paint—the earlier gilding and coloured decoration that have been overlaid can still be detected. There are two dress coaches of exceptional grandeur. One was built for the Duke of Buccleuch in 1830; it is resplendent still in yellow paint and copious brass-work. The other—a dress chariot, for two passengers—is a little later. It belonged to the Marquess of Lansdowne, and lay figures of a coachman and footman in his livery are mounted outside. This gives a good impression of a nobleman's carriage in working order for the road. Queen Victoria's semi-state landau (with a hood, in two sections, that can be taken down), heavy and handsome, was built by Messrs Hooper of St James's Street and has been lent by the firm to the Museum; older visitors will remember their showrooms at the top of the street, with a very large bay-window—still there, though the premises have now passed into other hands—in which a yellow carriage was normally exhibited as late as the 1930s. By that time Messrs Hooper had long ago turned over to building coach-work for motor-cars. It is interesting to trace such changes, by following through the history of these firms of coachbuilders, where it is continuous. There are other famous names of the eighteenth and early nineteenth centuries still in the motor-car business today, such as Mulliner's of Northampton. Here, at Maidstone, is a wagonette, designed by the Earl of Lonsdale for his own use in driving to race meetings and built about 1890 by Messrs Hamshaw of Leicester—today one of the best-known motor engineers in that city.

Several of these carriages have interesting associations, and stories attached to them. Here, for instance, is a chariot that belonged to Count Walewski, Napoleon I's bastard son. He served for a short time as French Ambassador in London in 1851. In the early nineteenth century a large number of the very richest Europeans had their carriages—like their clothes—made in

England. The travelling coach built for the 12th Earl of Moray about 1840 has a melancholy history. It was made for the Earl's honeymoon, when he was engaged to a daughter of the Earl of Elgin; but the marriage did not take place and the coach remained, never used, in the stables at Darnaway Castle until the present Earl of Moray gave it to the Maidstone Museum in 1951. Next to it stands a hansom cab that belonged to H. M. Stanley, the African explorer; and, close by, one of the sober brothers of the hansom, an unpretentious four-wheeled 'growler', the standard type of London cab in the late nineteenth and early twentieth centuries. This is an admirable example, in apple-pie order. Its simple, clean lines give it a dignified air appropriate to the age of the Forsytes: an air wholly foreign to the modern taxi, and its occupants.

The series is well rounded off with examples of two other types of vehicle: a private omnibus, dating from about 1898, and a hearse, made at Margate and used at Faversham. This is a more florid counterpart of the Scottish one preserved at Glasgow (see p. 175); the windows surrounding the coffin are decorated with designs in ground glass and silver-painted flowers.

The display on the upper floor is more varied in character. The wheeled vehicles here include some that are older than those downstairs. The earliest is a light Italian gig, said to date from about 1675. The character of the decoration, elegant and refined, seems to suggest the early eighteenth century rather than the seventeenth; but the Museum is probably justified in claiming that this is one of the earliest carriages in existence. Next to it stands a four-wheeled French cabriolet of Louis XVI's reign: high and stately, very much a piece of the old aristocratic world before the Revolution. It rubs shoulders, in the impersonal democratic fashion of museums, with an Irish jaunting car. The two-wheeled vehicles include a curricle, drawn by a pair of horses, one on each side of a central pole, and two gigs, one a *sjees* from Friesland, dating perhaps from the eighteenth century, the other driven by Sir Garrard Tyrwhitt-Drake when he was Mayor of Maidstone in 1926. Among the larger carriages of the late nineteenth century are a Victoria (that type, introduced into England from Paris almost a century ago, can still be seen on the streets of its native city), a landaulet, a mail phaeton, and a dog-cart.

The ladies' small carriages and the children's vehicles here include a delightful group made for, or presented to, Queen Victoria and her family: a droshky given to her by Tsar Nicholas I in 1850—very pretty, with the seats covered in blue silk standing out against the black frame; a Japanese rickshaw and a carrio (a very light high single-seat vehicle), both given to the Princess of Wales, later Queen Alexandra, in 1875; a tiny pony carriage used by Queen Victoria's children; and two of the low garden chairs in which the old Queen herself perambulated the grounds of Osborne in the closing years of her life. The other children's vehicles include a fascinating four-wheeled baby carriage of the early nineteenth century that formerly belonged to the Ashburnham family—reputedly built by sailors under the command of one of that family on the Indian Station; a Friesland child's cart, gaily painted on the sides, to be drawn by dogs, and an English one to be drawn by goats; a perambulator for two children, of about 1870.

There are some other miscellaneous vehicles: a group of sledges, kept in the small room over the porch, a sedan chair, and—a great rarity—a *brouette*, which was in effect a sedan chair mounted on a pair of wheels and so drawn by one man, in place of the two required for a chair. Needless to say, this sensible invention was staunchly opposed by the chair-men, who saw redundancy ahead of them, and though it was introduced into England from France as early as 1678, it was never allowed to catch on here.

Besides the vehicles, the Museum contains some interesting smaller exhibits. Perhaps the most remarkable are those that come from the great London coachbuilding firm of Barker: a frame of water-colour drawings of carriages constructed by them, their repair book, showing work undertaken for their rich clientele in 1788–97. Two coloured panoramas by J. R. Cruikshank show a long sequence of road vehicles of all kinds. A number of advertisements give a good idea of coach services in Kent. Some of them survived well into the second half of the nineteenth century, to fill in gaps in the railway service. Here is Thorpe's London and Sevenoaks coach, for instance, in 1856, starting from the Spread Eagle, Regent Circus, at 10 a.m. and picking up passengers at Lewisham station off the 11 a.m. train from London Bridge; Sevenoaks did not get its railways until 1862–68. Finally, on your way out, you may care to notice downstairs a door torn from a carriage by rowdy Radicals at Rotherhithe during the general election of 1885.

This Museum, though its equipment is modest, is steadily being improved. New exhibits are being taken in. A good many are on loan, and some—like the remarkable two-horse bus which plied between Brixton and Camberwell—are occasionally reclaimed by their owners. A small illustrated catalogue is available, and the main exhibits bear numbers corresponding to the descriptions in it. Anyone who wishes to get a clear idea of what conditions of travel in this country were like before the railway and the internal combustion engine revolutionized them should go first of all to this Museum at Maidstone.

5

BRIGHTON MOTOR MUSEUM

The Brighton Motor Museum is housed in a part of the Aquarium building, close to the Palace Pier and, appropriately, to the finishing point of the annual London–Brighton run for veteran cars. It comprises a single large hall, below the level of the ground but well lighted by natural means and conveniently adapted for moving the exhibits in and out from the road. This is important, because exhibits are sometimes exchanged between this and the other Montagu Museum at Beaulieu.[1]

At the foot of the entrance staircase, in front of the main doors into the Museum, is a late example of a stage-coach. (Having a hand-brake, it is thought to be dated after 1848.) When it ceased to perform its proper function it was used for a time to advertise Seager's gin; it then lay in a shed off the Gray's Inn Road, where it was discovered in 1957.

Some forty cars, twenty-seven motor-cycles, and five bicycles are exhibited here—not to mention a bath-chair with a wicker body, which gave many years' service to invalids on Brighton front. Some of the cars have striking historical associations. Here, for example, is the staff car, a Humber Super Snipe, used by Lord Montgomery during the final European campaigns of the second World War, from Normandy to the Baltic (H8).[2] The Royal Sussex Regiment has lent the staff car of General von Arnim, captured by the 1st Batallion of the Regiment together with the General himself near Zaghouan in Tunisia in May 1943; it is an Austrian machine, a 30 h.p. Steyr (S14). More interesting still is Goering's Mercedes (M11): an appropriately bloated vehicle,

---

[1] The Brighton museum was closed in 1968, while this book was passing through the press. I allow my description to stand, however (see the Preface).

[2] These numbers refer to the *Pictorial Guide to the Montagu Motor Museums*, where technical descriptions of the individual vehicles will be found.

weighing well over four tons and heavily armour-plated. Such 'Grosser' cars, of 45 h.p., were specially built by the firm for eminent clients of this kind, including not only Nazi leaders but the Emperor of Japan, President Salazar, and Field-Marshal Mannerheim. They could exceed 100 m.p.h. even when fully loaded.

Two British royal cars offer the sharpest imaginable contrast, both to these vehicles and to each other. Queen Mary's 50 h.p. Daimler Double Six of 1935 (D17) is as stately as the Queen herself. She acquired it only a month before her husband George V died; and nothing could symbolize more plainly the sudden transition to the new régime of her son Edward VIII than the Buick he used (B16), which stands a few yards away. Its curvaceous styling seems intended quite deliberately to proclaim that it is designed for speed. It played its part in the abdication crisis, conveying Mrs Simpson to the coast on her embarkation for France, and it was retained by the Duke and Duchess of Windsor until 1938. These two cars should surely be displayed side by side or in line. It is hard to believe that they were built within a year of each other: they represent two wholly different social and political worlds.

The majority of the cars exhibited here are, as they should be, of more normal types, designed for steady service on the road in the hands of plain citizens—or, in the case of some of the earlier vehicles, their chauffeurs. Among the older small cars is a Brushmobile 6 h.p. of 1904 (B6), one of a short-lived series built by the Brush Electrical Engineering Company of Loughborough and priced as low as £140; and a Singer 10 h.p. of 1914 (S2). This is an interesting model, for when it was launched on to the market in 1912 William Rootes, a motor agent in Maidstone, contracted with the manufacturers to buy the entire output of the first year. The Rootes Group, established by that motor-agent's son, eventually engulfed the Singer Company in 1956.

Most people know that the Nuffield empire originated in Mr William Morris's cycle shop in Oxford. It is useful to be reminded that other great names in the motor-car industry have emerged from similarly modest beginnings. John Dennis, for instance, began life as an ironmonger and then turned to the selling and making of bicycles in Guildford. With his brother

Raymond he went on to the production of powered tricycles, quadricycles, and cars. As early as 1904 they built a delivery van for Harrods, and they moved increasingly into the production of commercial vehicles, until in 1913 the firm decided to concentrate on them exclusively. They made a special reputation by their fire-engines, the first of which they built for Bradford in 1908, and here (D11) is a sturdy example of one of them, dating from twenty years later.

An interesting stage in the evolution of the Rover Company is represented by its 4 h.p. tri-car of 1905 (R5). The firm originated with J. K. Starley and W. Sutton, who began to make bicycles in Coventry in 1877. The partnership broke up seven years later, and Starley went on to become one of the chief pioneers of the 'safety bicycle', with the diamond frame and chain drive on to the rear axle. His Rover Cycle Company became one of the leading cycle-manufacturers in the country. This led it on to motor-cycles in 1903 and so to tri-cars, like the one exhibited here, and to four-wheeled motor-cars, in which the firm established its reputation securely by 1912.

Of the motor-cycles shown at Brighton, the earliest is an interesting German machine, an N S U of 1906 (NN6). This was presented by its manufacturers to Lord Montagu; it has been completely renovated and is in perfect working order.

Two of the classic designs of internal combustion engine are mounted for inspection here, both of them made by Rolls-Royce: a Silver Ghost of 1914 (Y23) and a Merlin aero-engine of 1948 (Y20). This is the last version of a design that goes back as far as 1935; the one that powered the Hurricane and Spitfire fighters in the Battle of Britain, and the Lancaster bombers.

Two cars may perhaps be singled out in conclusion: a Frazer Nash of 1930 and a Lanchester of 1910. They represent two strongly-contrasted types of elegance. The Frazer Nash (F8) is a light sports car, fitted with the remarkable chain transmission perfected by its designer: not cheap—£425 was a substantial price to pay for a car of this kind at that date—but good value for money. The *Guide* calls its bodywork 'stark'. That is a harsh epithet. Rather, it may be suggested that the whole job is outstandingly neat, and it prompts a reflection on the age that produced it. In most fields of design, especially in Britain, the late 1920s were the very reverse of distinguished. These were the years of cloche hats and jazz architecture, years characterized by formlessness and vapid ornamentation. Yet when those who know their minds set out to make a machine they eschewed ornament and achieved a form, in such a car as this one, that had a classically inevitable quality. Something very similar is to be seen eighty years earlier, at the Crystal Palace in 1851, in the contrast between the aimless decoration of the art metalwork and the spare elegance of the machinery.[1]

The Lanchester (L3) is an example of the first six-cylinder model that the firm produced: a seven-seater limousine, to be driven by a chauffeur. Everything about it proclaims it as an aristocrat among cars, truly worthy of its designer, an 'engineer-artist, apt for the discovery of scientific knowledge and of new and practical ways of applying it'.[2] The brasswork (attended to, of course, by the chauffeur) is rich, not gaudy; so is the colour-scheme—umber, lined out in red and black; the square-fronted bonnet, recessed between the wheels, adds to the impression of lithe strength. The Edwardian age often seems to us, in many of its aspects, vulgar and overblown, but in the production of some machines it attained a final, balanced perfection: on the sea, for example, in the Cunarders *Caronia* and *Carmania*, which went into service in 1905; on rails the D class express engines of the South Eastern and Chatham Railway (1901);[3] on the road these cars and the more famous, though scarcely more handsome, Rolls-Royce Silver Ghost of 1907.

Within the limits of space allotted to it, this is a varied and comprehensive exhibition. As a general survey of mechanized road transport, it could include with advantage two or three more commercial vehicles; among the motor-cycles it would be good to see a side-car combination and a scooter; the bicycles are inadequately displayed and described. But these are minor criticisms. Anyone who will look at the collection with the *Guide* in his hand will be able to pass a pleasant and instructive afternoon.

[1] I have developed this argument further in *Britain and the World* (1965), 115.
[2] Kingsford, *F. W. Lanchester*, 54.   [3] See pp. 55–6

6

MONTAGU MOTOR MUSEUM
BEAULIEU

This Museum was founded, the present Lord Montagu tells us, in 1952 in memory of his father, the 2nd Lord Montagu, 'one of the pioneers of motoring in Britain, and the first Parliamentary champion of the motorists' cause'. The 2nd Lord was interested in everything to do with transport. He was trained as a railway engineer and many years afterwards assisted the London and South Western company by driving trains for it during the strikes of 1919 and 1926 (a photograph of his locomotive hangs framed in Palace House at Beaulieu). In his later life he became much interested in aviation and devoted a great deal of his energy to promoting its development. Above all, he took a leading role in securing acceptance of the motor-car as a safe and convenient machine, a necessary part of the life of the country. It had a harder battle to fight in Great Britain than it did on the Continent; and if it was to win, the condition of politics and society at the turn of the century required that it should find vigorous and respectable sponsors, not cranks or tricksters. As a Conservative MP from 1892 until he succeeded his father in the peerage in 1905, as a trained engineer who yet came of a ducal family, and as a politician with a real talent for imaginative publicity, Lord Montagu was excellently placed to influence Governments and Parliament. He took full advantage of his opportunities, and everyone who drives a car in Britain today is in his debt. Something of his spirit has carried itself over into the Museum established by his son.

The permanent collection at Beaulieu does not include a single motor-car dating from the nineteenth century—though there are at present about half a dozen here deposited by their owners, one hopes on long loan. But then this Museum has been in

93

existence barely fifteen years, and its most rapid expansion is quite recent. Such very ancient vehicles—the incunabula of motoring—are now so rare as to have become virtually unobtainable, even at a prohibitive price. Taking it all round, the Beaulieu collection represents a broad catholic view of the development of the internal-combustion engine as applied to road transport in this country in the first half of the twentieth century.

The nineteenth-century cars that are here on loan include the first of all Wolseleys, a tricar of 1895 (W1),[1] an 8 h.p. Benz (B4), the unique Pennington tricar of 1896 (P1), and a Beeston quadricycle (B1) dating from two years later. In the history of motoring, however, one of these vehicles stands out from all the rest: the Coventry Daimler made for the 2nd Lord Montagu in 1899 (D1). It was the first four-cylinder car manufactured by the company, and the first British-built car to race on the Continent. It was also the first car to be driven into New Palace Yard and so to display itself to Members of Parliament. Lord Montagu took the Prince of Wales out in it; the Prince liked motoring and as King Edward VII helped to make it a fashionable pastime. The car was later converted into a shooting-brake and used in this form on the Beaulieu estate. Then in 1919, with a true sense of history, its owner gave it to the Science Museum. Now, by a graceful gesture, it has been lent back to this museum, established in its original home.

Like her husband, Queen Alexandra was willing to experiment with the new mechanical traction, and in 1901 she acquired a small Columbia electric car (C3) for driving in the park at Sandringham: an American machine, made at Hartford, Connecticut.

Among the other very small vehicles of these years is a Sunbeam of 1901 (S5), in which the driver and his passenger sit in line ahead, facing outwards on to the road in opposite directions—this was intended to reduce the danger of skidding, but it produced a most unstable car; and a Vauxhall (V1), made in 1905. Its engine has three cylinders, and it was regarded as notably reliable, when reliability was still a rare and conspicuous virtue in a motor-car.

[1] These numbers refer to the *Pictorial Guide to the Motor Museums*. It may be added that the vehicles are displayed approximately in chronological order by classes: motor-cars, commercial vehicles, racing cars; then bicycles and motor-bicycles in a separate gallery.

Somewhat larger, but still quite small, are the three Allday and Onions cars, lent by Mr G. J. Allday. The earliest of the trio (A1 of 1907) is a single-cylinder machine accommodating four passengers; access to the *tonneau* at the back is given through the front seat, which splits and opens for the purpose. The other two cars are somewhat larger: a 2-cylinder 10–12 h.p. model of 1909 (A2) and a 4-cylinder 12–14 h.p. of 1913 (A3).

Two or three of these cars were designed for motoring on the grand scale. Here, for instance, is a French Lorraine-Dietrich of 1903 (D13), with a hood like that of a Victoria. It belonged to Sir Joseph Robinson, the South African gold magnate, who left it in London when he returned home in 1910. There it remained until the 1950s. It has now been sumptuously restored.

But perhaps the most complete reflection of the luxury of motoring in the pre-war world comes from the 26 h.p. 6-cylinder Delaunay-Belleville of 1911 (D10). It has a landaulette body, complete with every comfort for the passenger that was possible at that time. By means of a series of buttons at his (or her) right hand, the driver could receive a large number of instructions, indicated on the dial: to go faster or slower, or—doubtless valuable when a round of afternoon calls proved too fatiguing—'home'.

Two other vehicles of a different sort dating from these years must also be mentioned. One is an early Unic taxi (pp. 35–6); the other is now a fire-engine (G2), though it began life in 1907 as a private car. It is of a French make rarely seen in this country, the Gobron-Brillié, which was distinguished by a notable and stubbornly-maintained eccentricity. Mr Nicholson exaggerates only a little when he remarks that the Gobron-Brillié engine 'was rotated by the same fuel, but there its resemblance to most other petrol motors practically ceased'.[1] Its oddity consisted in the use of pairs of opposed pistons in each cylinder. This car became a fire-engine in 1913 for work on a private estate, by the addition of a Merryweather steam pump and the other necessary equipment. To bear the extra weight it runs on solid tyres. It consumes petrol at the rate of 3–4 miles to the gallon

And finally, from these early years, there is the handsome Vauxhall 'Prince Henry' of 1914 (V2), one of the first sports cars ever produced as such. It seats four (a two-seater version of the

[1] T. R. Nicholson, *European Cars, 1885–1914* (n.d.), 28.

95

same car is also here, V5) and it has put up good performances very recently in vintage-car rallies as far afield as New Zealand.

The 1920s are well represented here by motor-vehicles of almost every type, from the bus to the racing car. There are several notable commercial vehicles: a Maxwell charabanc of 1922 (M1); a model-T Ford bus of 1921 (F5), which continued at work in Wales until 1950; a van of the same type dating from five years later (F12), carefully restored by its owners, Messrs T. Wall and Son Ltd; and a pair of the vans used by Bass, Ratcliffe and Gretton to advertise their beers, comprising a huge Bass bottle lying horizontally on a Daimler chassis (1921 and 1924, D4 and D5).

The Citroen-Kegresse of 1926 (C5) is a car in front and a tractor at the rear. A vehicle of this pattern made the first crossing of the Sahara in 1922. This one was supplied to the French army and subsequently served as a shooting-brake in this country. Two other eccentrics of these years are the quaint little German Phanomobil three-wheeler (P4) and the Stanley steam-car (S15). This, dating from 1920, comes towards the end of the long line of steam cars that firm had been building since 1897. The boiler is placed under the bonnet and the radiator acts as a condenser. It is surprising at so late a date to find that the frame of the chassis is made of wood. Though these steam cars were difficult to drive and required very careful maintenance, they had outstanding virtues in their smooth and silent running.

The ordinary man's car of the twenties is well represented by a Morgan three-wheeler of 1927 (M9) and two family cars, a Morris-Cowley of 1924 and a Jowett of 1927; both tourers, seating four and selling respectively at £225 and £150. These are important vehicles, illustrating the process by which motoring ceased to be a diversion for the eccentric and the rich and became instead part of the normal routine of living in England.

The student of this aspect of the motor-car, which may well be thought the most important of all, will unfortunately find little else to interest him at Beaulieu. There is an Austin Seven Swallow of 1931 (A8)—it seems curious to think of four people cramming themselves into that bulbous little lozenge; and then nothing in the cheap popular class except a Volkswagen of 1953 (V9), one of the first of those cars to be imported into this country commercially.

Phaeton latter part of 18ᵗʰ century

Barouche latter half of 19ᵗʰ century

5 Maidstone: water-colour drawings of carriages by Barker and Co.

16a Hull: sedan chair forme[rly] owned by the Corporat[ion] of Huntingdon

b Maidstone: *brouette*, a se[dan] chair on wheels

c Science Museum: the orig[inal] brougham

The sports car is much better represented: by two Alfa Romeos, one of 1929 (A18)—look at the beautiful opposed curves of its lines from the side—the other of 1933 (A11), which belonged to Leslie Hawthorn and his famous son, Mike; the Jaguars of 1950 and 1954 (J1, 2); and the pair of Aston Martins (A16, 22), which offer an instructive comparison between the styling and design current in 1931 and in 1956.

The racing cars, in the full sense of the term, begin with three dating back to the early years of the century. Huge battleships they appear to us: an Itala of 1907, an Austin of the following year, and a Sunbeam of 1912 (I1, A5, S7). The 120-h.p. Itala is still capable of running at more than 100 m.p.h. The Austin represents a short-lived and unsuccessful attempt made by the firm at that date to enter the racing business. By contrast, the Sunbeam stands in an historic line of brilliant machines. This was one of five built to compete in the Coupe de l'Auto race for 3-litre cars at Dieppe in 1912; they swept the board, with first, second, and third places. Several of its successors are also in this collection. S9 broke the world speed record three times in 1922–25, taking it eventually to just over 150 m.p.h. In the enormous S11 (with two 12-cylinder aero engines, developing 1,000 h.p.) Sir Henry Segrave took that record for the first time over the 200 m.p.h. mark, at Daytona Beach in 1927.

That record was raised to 231 m.p.h. only two years later, again by Segrave; and the 'Golden Arrow' car he used for that feat is also here (G3). In earlier editions of the guidebook to the Montagu Museums it was described as 'probably the most beautiful record-breaker ever built'. No one should quarrel with that judgment.

Among the later racing cars two have personal associations of great interest. One is 'Romulus', the E R A that belonged to Prince Chula of Siam and was driven by his cousin Prince Bira (E1); this is shown with the original pit equipment standing beside it. The other (R7) is the Riley in which Mike Hawthorn won the Ulster Trophy in 1951. That was the start of his brilliant career as an international racing driver; he retained an affection for the car and restored it himself not long before he met his tragic death in 1959. Finally—memorial of a protracted and bitter controversy—here is the B R M 1½-litre car of 1952 (B5).

Near the entrance to this section of the Museum is a little

exhibition commemorating the 2nd Lord Montagu. It includes the summons served on him for exceeding 12 m.p.h. through Basingstoke in 1902, an offence for which the magistrates fined him the swingeing sum of £5; a striking sketch of the London–Birmingham trunk road that he proposed in 1921—which was nearing completion forty years later as the M1; the first number of his magazine *The Car Illustrated*, together with some of the working models of parts of cars that were produced in association with it. The display epitomizes in a small space something of his vision and achievement.

The bicycles and motor-cycles are for the most part housed in another gallery, though a few early ones are to be seen with the cars, notably the biggest 'ordinary' or 'penny-farthing' ever built (X9)—one of those made by Starley of Coventry with a front wheel 7 feet in diameter, instead of the normal 4 feet 6 inches to 5 feet. At the entrance to the motor-cycle gallery are two exhibits illustrating the development of the sparking plug and the speedometer, presented to the Museum by Lodge Plugs Ltd and Smith's Motor Accessory Division. Both are well designed, well lighted, and well explained.

The motor-cycles stand packed very close together, and it is not always easy to inspect them closely. More space is evidently needed here, and for lack of it many of the bicycles are at present in store—though it is good to see a Michaux boneshaker (X3), dating from 1867. A De Dion motor-tricycle of 1898 (DD2), produced under licence at Aachen in Germany, represents the first phase of the successful application of mechanized power to cycles of the older form. The earliest Triumph motor-cycle known to exist now is here (TT1). It dates from 1903 and is followed by three others (TT2, 6, 8) representing the development of this famous make over the next forty years. An historic racing machine of the pre-1914 period is the 1912 Norton (NN4), which achieved 112 national and international records; it can still travel at more than 70 m.p.h. By way of contrast is the BAT of 1913 (BB1), a comfortable family vehicle with an ample sidecar—it might almost be described as a basketwork and leather armchair, slung well clear of the cycle itself.

An interesting series of motor scooters includes a very early American Autoped of 1916 (AA7), two British machines dating from 1919 and 1921 (AA1, 6), and one of the first two Lambrettas to be exported to England, made in Italy in 1948 (LL3).

This gallery also includes some exhibits of other kinds. Round its walls runs a wonderful series of photographs of the Isle of Man TT race from 1907 to 1959; and beneath them, on stands, are a number of engines, including examples of the Anzani and Gnome aero engines (Y5, Z1)[1] and a cylinder-head from the engine of the airship R101, few relics of which seem to have survived its tragic end in 1930. Two glass cases in the middle of the room contain a varied assortment of small relics of motoring: the tool-kit for a De Dion car of 1903; a gradient gauge of 1905, like a spirit-level; petrol ration documents from both World Wars; a foot-warmer of the twenties—we are apt to forget that the heating of cars has become common only within the last twenty years; headlamp masks from the second War.

Outside stand two large public-service road vehicles: a stately Newcastle Corporation electric tram of Class F (1902) and a Portsmouth trolley-bus, in service from 1934 to 1958. These are on loan from the Tramway Museum Society and will go to Crich in due course for restoration to working order. There is a show-man's engine by Burrell's of Thetford (1913), now happily being brought back to its original splendour, the brass barley-sugar columns shining in the sun. The Sno-Cat built for Sir Vivien Fuchs on his Antarctic expedition of 1956 is here. And at the back of the site, tucked shyly away, is an important railway exhibit: a 4–4–0 of the 'Schools' class from the Southern Railway (No. 928, *Stowe*), together with three Pullman cars, making up together a miniature version of the Bournemouth Belle. The engine has been repainted in an amateur style in the wrong shade of green—neither the rich olive, lined out in orange and black, with which it began life nor the hideous 'malachite' adopted in the 1930s—and the lettering on the tender is imperfect; a semaphore signal mounted alongside comes, incongruously, from the Great Western. It is no fault of the Museum that the engine's nameplate has to be a plastic replica, or that the number is painted on to the side of the cab instead of appearing on an oval brass plate: for these things were stolen by some maniac thief. These defects are trifling in compari-son with the positive merit that here—*and in no other museum in Britain*—is an original steam-hauled train to be seen complete.

[1] Neither of them listed in the *Pictorial Guide*. The cataloguing in this section is less accurate than that of the motor-cars.

The Museum at Beaulieu seems oddly ashamed of this fine exhibit. The train secures no mention whatever in any edition of the *Pictorial Guide*, and no photograph of it is on sale.

This complex exhibition is accommodated, out of doors and in pleasing prefabricated timber buildings, immediately behind the Palace House, in the angle between it and the parish church of Beaulieu. The work has been cunningly carried out, in a very restricted space. It is almost incredible that in 1965 it should have proved possible to receive 600,000 visitors. As a museum this stands out from nearly all the others described here in that it is a private venture; and one is conscious all the time that it has to pay its way, and do more. But before anyone is tempted to speak slightingly of the Museum's 'commercialism', he should remember two things. Like the most academically-respected of its fellows, like the Science Museum itself, it maintains a library, and its staff spend much time in answering questions put to them, both personally and by correspondence. And of all the museums discussed in this book, only four others—those at Maidstone, Old Warden, Newcastle, and Utrecht—produce an item-by-item catalogue of their main exhibits, comparable with that at Beaulieu and Brighton. The guide-book is crisp, informative, clearly arranged—a characteristically efficient product of this notable museum.

Even when you have seen all this, there is another pleasure awaiting you—if you still feel strong enough—in the little Maritime Museum at Buckler's Hard, three miles down the river. Buckler's Hard is itself a memorable place. It consists of a single broad grass-verged street leading down to the water, lined with small eighteenth-century houses: all that was built of an intended port founded by the Duke of Montagu in 1724. Though the port never developed, a shipbuilding yard was established here, which is known to have constructed over seventy men-of-war and merchant ships between 1745 and 1822—among them Nelson's *Agamemnon*. The Museum (which is part of the Beaulieu organization) is housed in what was once an inn and recreates something of this vanished life, especially of the work of Henry Adams, overseer of the yard during the second half of the eighteenth century. Some of his draughts of ships are shown here, together with models, prints, charts—not to mention a drawing and a poster that illustrate the earliest history of steam navigation in the Solent.

7

GREAT WESTERN RAILWAY
MUSEUM, SWINDON

This museum was opened in 1962 through a joint effort by the British Transport Commission (as it still was then) and the Borough of Swindon. The local authority made the building available, which was adapted for its new purpose by the Borough Architect, and it is responsible for the day-to-day running of the Museum; the Commission provided most of the exhibits, and its Department of Historical Relics undertook the task of displaying them. This partnership has worked admirably, to produce one of the most entirely delightful new museums to be found in the English provinces.

The building itself is of interest to the student of railways in their social context. It was erected as a model lodging-house for employees of the railway works, who arrived in the town in substantial numbers and found it difficult to secure accommodation. But it was not a success—the scale of employment in the works fluctuated and it soon transpired that the men preferred to live in separate houses, either provided by the Company or privately built. (The Company's housing at Swindon is worth study: it is to be observed in the streets immediately adjoining the Museum on the east and south sides.) These premises were sold to the Wesleyans in 1869, who used them as a chapel; when the chapel was closed down, the trustees in whom it was vested conveyed it to the Corporation, and the way was then open for converting it to its present use.

The conversion has turned out admirably. The main hall is occupied by the locomotives and other large exhibits; the galleries to the left of the entrance accommodate the smaller things on two floors, beside and above.

The Museum makes a most forceful impact on you at the very moment you arrive. Turning in from Faringdon Road, you are suddenly confronted by a display of dazzling magnificence. Here are five of the Great Western's engines in the very pink of external condition, glowing in their rich green livery with its copper and brass ornamentation, disposed across the hall with a splendid amplitude. The sight hits you hard in the solar plexus. You are never likely to forget it.

This is the Churchward Gallery, named after George Jackson Churchward, the Great Western's Locomotive, Carriage, and Wagon Superintendent (later Chief Mechanical Engineer) from 1902 to 1921 and one of the outstanding locomotive engineers in our history. A biographical note on the wall emphasizes, very properly, that he was not only a distinguished engineer but also an active citizen of Swindon. When the town was incorporated in 1900 he was its Charter Mayor, he was made an honorary freeman of the borough in 1920, and throughout his life he took a keen interest in the development of education.

On your left as you enter is the broad-gauge engine *North Star* —not the original, which was broken up in 1906 after being refused as a gift by the Science Museum, but a replica incorporating some original parts, made for the Railway Centenary celebrations in 1925. What a scale it is built on! All the leaders of a party could address a political meeting from its driver's footplate. Is it not possible—one is bound to think as one walks round it—that we made a mistake in allowing Stephenson's gauge to prevail over Brunel's, with such important consequences for us and for the rest of the world?

In front of it stand the 8-foot driving wheels of *Lord of the Isles*, one of Gooch's famous express engines: all that now remains of it, alas! For it, too, survived the extinction of the broad gauge in 1892 and then was condemned by Churchward—a truly great man, but not much interested in the past—as he thought it occupied too much space in Swindon Works.

A pair of goods locomotives stand next in line. The first is one of Dean's 0–6–0 tender engines built in 1897. It is astonishing that this is at present the only example to be seen in any museum in England (though there is now one in Scotland, at Glasgow) of the standard British type of goods engine, first evolved in 1848 and built continuously for more than 100 years. This makes one realize how often locomotives have been preserved for their picturesque or eccentric qualities rather than for their intrinsic importance. A total of 260 of these engines were built between 1883 and 1899. Far greater numbers of the type were in use on other lines: the London and North Western and Lancashire and Yorkshire Companies had a total of 943 of the DX class, the Midland class 3 extended to 482 engines, class 4 (including those built by the London, Midland and Scottish Company) to 772. For most English railways (though the statement is not quite so true of Scotland and Wales) this became the normal jack-of-all-trades freight engine. It has been elbowed out by the diesel locomotive only since the War.

Behind this 'Dean Goods' is a six-wheeled tank engine. It dates from as late as 1947 and is one of the very last to be built for the Great Western Railway. One feature of its design is highly characteristic of Great Western practice: the square side 'pannier' tanks, pitched high so as to give easy access to the inside cylinders and motion. A very large number of these useful engines, to the same general design but incorporating successive improvements, were built. Many people will remember them as the engines that brought trains of empty coaches into Paddington; they were used for shunting, for general goods work, and sometimes for passenger trains. After the railways were nationalized they moved all over the system: I have seen a squad of them in use as banking engines on the steep Folkestone Harbour branch, another at The Mound Junction in Sutherland, patiently waiting with the train for Dornoch (it contained one passenger, asleep).

The other two locomotives here were both designed for express work. One is *City of Truro*, which dates from 1903 and is among the most celebrated of all British railway engines, the first to reach a well-authenticated speed of over 100 m.p.h. Beyond it stands *Lode Star*, one of the class that may be called Churchward's masterpiece, at least as far as passenger engines are concerned: a four-cylinder 4–6–0 built in 1907 and in service for forty-four years. All the chief characteristics of mature Great Western design are here, most notably in the tapering, domeless boiler (pressed to 225 lb. per square inch) rising up to the high crown of the Belpaire firebox. The performance of these engines of the 'Star' class was superb, and they have influenced all subsequent express locomotive design in this country.

Though the locomotives dominate the Churchward Gallery, there is much else in it that is worth seeing too. (It is much to be regretted that the great engines are not seen as truly as they should be owing to the placing of a number of models in glass cases around them. Some of the models themselves are excellent, such as that of the Dean single *Majestic*, and no one would wish the silver-plated coffee-pot, made in the form of an engine, that was used in the Swindon station refreshment rooms to disappear: but they clutter up a splendid exhibition and another place should be found for them.) Near the entrance stands a group of broad-gauge signals, including one of the well-known disc-and-crossbar pattern and an interesting lattice-post semaphore. This last was of a type made by Stevens of Worcester from 1863 onwards and continued in use at Bledlow on the Watlington branch until 1959. All these signals call out loudly for adequate labelling. Round the walls is a fascinating miscellany: to the right, a well-prepared display of successive types of carriage door-handle, showing the care and ingenuity that have gone into solving the problem of keeping the passenger in his carriage and letting him get out in safety; high up on the left-hand wall a ventilating grid from Newton Abbot station bearing the initials of the South Devon Railway, removed when the station was reconstructed in 1924–25; a long series of photographs and diagrams of rolling-stock, together with some amusing cartoons—notice Dick German's neat comment on the amalgamation of 1923 with its Great Western porter jumping up and crying 'Hurray! Never even blew me cap off!'

Moving upstairs to the Gooch Gallery, you pass some interesting material in the passage: one of the rare early travelling charts, for the section of line from Paddington to Southall, a series of water-colour drawings of broad-gauge locomotives of 1857, time-tables and rules for the Taff Vale and Rhymney Railways in 1857–59. But the outstanding exhibit here is a set of satirical ink sketches of railways in the 1840s. So far as I know they are all unpublished, and here no attempt whatever is made to identify or explain them. They seem to bear the initials 'C. A. S.'. It is tempting to think that they might represent doodles by the Great Western Company's first Secretary Charles Alexander Saunders; but alas there is no evidence that he had such talents, and sprightly satire would hardly have been seemly in a staid senior railway official. Who, then, drew them?

The Gooch Gallery is admirably laid out. The colour-scheme is pleasing. The walls are grey and white, and the cases, which are very well lighted, supply a touch of colour, their contents appearing against yellow, red, and purple backgrounds. The exhibits are of a miscellaneous character; their one common feature is that they are small. Here is a sample of them, taken nearly at random.

Among the items especially connected with Gooch himself are his letter applying to Brunel for the post of Manager of the Engine Works of the Great Western Company at Bristol in 1837. It sets out his career and qualifications; what it does not give is the applicant's age—twenty. Here are the original bills from Robert Stephenson and Co. of Newcastle for locomotives supplied to his orders in 1840–41. From the years of his reign as Chairman comes an illuminated address from the Company's workmen, thanking him and his fellow-Directors for the introduction of the 54-hour week in 1871. Some fine lithographs are displayed, both of towns and general railway scenes and of important engineering works, like that by W. Dowson of the Slade viaduct on the South Devon Railway in 1848, showing off to perfection its lightness and grace. The models include one of the Gooch express locomotive *Emperor* made by J. G. Robinson, at that time (1883) an apprentice at Swindon and later a distinguished Chief Mechanical Engineer of the Great Central Railway, and a fine one of *The Great Bear*, the work of Crewe apprentices in 1959. In the long series of companies' seals is a very early one of the Gloucester and Cheltenham Railway, dating from 1809 and showing a ship and a horse-drawn train. One panel shows a number of the instruments used at level crossings and for warning men working on the line of approaching trains. Close by are staffs for working single lines, most of them bearing evocative names from Cornwall—Little Trevisco, Treamble, Tolcarne Junction.

It must, however, be said that not everything here is satisfactory. The selection of locomotive models could well have been better—why include a 'Dean Goods', when the original type is to be seen downstairs? Again the models of signals could be of great value, but they are scarcely explained at all, and in no way related to the full-sized specimens to be seen in the Churchward Gallery. This is an important branch of railway engineering in which, it is only too evident, the staff neither of this museum nor of its parent at Clapham has any interest at all.

In descending to the Brunel Room you again traverse a corridor hung with exhibits in frames. They include a notable series of photographs of motor-buses operated by the Great Western Railway in the early years of the twentieth century. The Company was one of the most energetic pioneers of this form of transport, as a feeder to its own lines, beginning with the service it instituted between Helston and the Lizard—the first run by any main-line railway in Britain—in August 1903. As these pictures demonstrate, the Great Western services spread quickly, from Cornwall to Wiltshire, and extended also to the carriage of light freight. But they were not developed as fully as they could have been; and the opportunity, once lost before the first World War, was not recovered in the 1920s.

The Brunel Room is small, and devoted entirely to the great engineer himself. It is presided over by J. C. Horsley's well-known portrait, with which are associated some of the remarkable photographs of him taken in the last years of his life, while he was at work on the *Great Eastern* steamship and on the Tamar Bridge at Saltash. That bridge figures prominently here in a series of contemporary prints and photographs, reminding us not only of the unique design of the whole but also of the unprecedented magnitude of the operation of sinking its central pier in the bed of the river and raising the structure from it. The last of his famous timber viaducts in Cornwall disappeared in 1934, though others remained in use as late as 1947. There were altogether sixty-four of them in the West Country, together with many others in Berkshire, Gloucestershire, and South Wales. The model of four bays of the Ponsanooth viaduct (half-way between Truro and Falmouth), shown here, affords perhaps the best opportunity we now have of understanding the construction of these marvels of timber engineering and of appreciating their authentic distinction.

No British engineer has designed bridges in forms so widely different as Brunel. For it must be remembered that his work was not confined to railways. In 1831, when he was still a very young man under the shadow of his eminent father, he produced the winning design in a competition for the Clifton Suspension Bridge. Its completion was laid aside, for lack of funds, in 1843, and it was not finished until after his death; but it remains one of the memorials of his genius. Here are some of his drawings for it, executed in sepia wash, of the utmost delicacy, like all his work of this kind.

He was indeed a refined artist as well as a great engineer. This room contains some highly personal relics of him: some of his instruments, made to a most exacting standard; his drawing-board—preserved, with a fitting respect, in Swindon Works. Like all truly great men, made on the heroic scale, he experimented and committed costly mistakes. The most spectacular of them, the atmospheric system, is commemorated here by a section of the iron tubing used on the South Devon line. But they were noble mistakes, the mistakes of an eager pioneer, feeling his way, with astonishing versatility of mind, to solutions to half a dozen major problems simultaneously, any one of which could well have formed the life-work of one of his fellow-practitioners. The Great Western Railway is his chief monument, and an abiding one. Something of the essence of his work and personality can be felt quite distinctly here, in this small room at Swindon.

In social and economic terms, Swindon presents an interesting study.[1] In origin it was a market town, existing quietly in its own right, with less than 2,000 people in 1840. It was then transformed, by the decision to build the Great Western Railway works in the plain below the hill on which it stood, this work involving in time the construction of a new town adjacent to the old and socially, in large measure, independent of it. By 1900, owing primarily to this development, it had grown into a town of over 40,000 people. Then in the mid-twentieth century the new town, in its turn, lost much of its occupation with the drastic reduction in the scale of the railway's business, so that fresh economic activities have to be sought instead. In recent years Swindon has, in some aspects of culture and education, become a very much more lively place than it was in the past. But aesthetically it remains somewhat drab, curious rather than inviting. By the development of this excellent museum, in partnership with the nationalized transport industry, the borough has worthily commemorated what gives distinction to its past history and provided for itself an outstanding 'sight' that no intelligent tourist in Oxford or the Cotswolds or Wiltshire should miss.

[1] There is no adequate history of the town. Useful sketches appear in L. V. Grinsell (ed.), *Studies in the History of Swindon* (1950); the Great Western Railway Works are dealt with by D. E. C. Eversley in the *Victoria History of Wiltshire*, iv (1959), 207–19. See also K. Hudson, *Industrial Archaeology of Southern England* (1965).

8

SHUTTLEWORTH COLLECTION
OLD WARDEN

This is a different thing from any of the other museums described here. It began as a purely private collection of aircraft, motor-cars, and bicycles, formed by Richard Ormond Shuttleworth of Old Warden in the years between the wars. He was a descendant of Joseph Shuttleworth, of the well-known firm of Clayton and Shuttleworth, builders of steam engines and agricultural machinery at Lincoln, who bought the Old Warden estate from the last Lord Ongley in 1871.[1] Richard Shuttleworth was killed in a flying accident while serving in the RAF in 1940; and in 1944 his mother, Mrs Frank Shuttleworth, OBE, formed a Trust in his memory, to establish an educational centre 'for the teaching of the science and practice of aviation and of afforestation and agriculture'. Her son's collection passed under the administration of the Trust, to become the nucleus of the present exhibition, which is accommodated in four hangars on a small airfield on the edge of the Shuttleworth estate at Old Warden.

Alone among the institutions we are considering here, this one

[1] Though it has no bearing on the main subject of this book, I cannot forbear adding a note on Old Warden: for anyone visiting the Shuttleworth Collection whose interest is not confined to transport should spare time to look at the village and its neighbourhood. As it stands now, the whole place is a monument to the last Lord Ongley. It is a 'model village', surviving intact from the mid-Victorian age and showing what beauty can be achieved—and maintained even in the 1960s—by the imposition of firm standards of picturesque planning and taste. As for the surrounding countryside, it is still unravished: as quiet as you can imagine, even though it is only forty-five miles from London and within three of the Great North Road, wooded, gently rolling, and from the edge of the low escarpment to the north (for example, at Mox Hill, by Deadman's Oak) offering an astonishing sweep of a view over the broad plain of Bedfordshire. There, right in front of you, are the huge hangars of Cardington, the base of R100 and R101, among the last memorials of the airship surviving today in Britain.

is not called a museum. The use of the term 'Collection' to describe it is a happy one. For one thing it emphasizes the personal link with Richard Shuttleworth, the collector in whose discernment and enthusiasm it originated. But even more important, it makes clear that this is not a museum in the conventional sense of the word at all. For though the visitor on normal occasions sees these machines grounded and at rest, it was a leading idea of the founder that every one he acquired should be capable of being put to work as it did when it was first produced. In token of that he himself drove some of the cars to Old Warden from the places where he found them— the ponderous Arrol-Johnston, for example, all the way from Dumfries in 1931; the aircraft can, and do, still fly. Indeed, the Collection claims to include every aeroplane in this country constructed before 1926 that remains capable of being flown. In the summer there are open days at Old Warden, at which these machines are demonstrated in action.

The earliest original aircraft here are two important machines from France, a Blériot Type XI of 1909 and a Deperdussin of the following year. A good many of the machines at Old Warden were unearthed in obscure places: the founder had the passion of the collector, and his true instinct for nosing out what might interest him. These both came from a garage at Ampthill, where they had been stored for some twenty years. Their owner had picked them up in 1912–14, repaired them and flown them himself, and then had put them away early in the first World War, until Richard Shuttleworth bought them in 1935.

The Blériot is identical with the famous aeroplane that carried its designer across the Channel in 1909 and is now in the Arts et Métiers Museum in Paris (see p. 193): with this important difference, that the Shuttleworth machine is in working order and has often flown during the past thirty years. It has its original 25 h.p. Anzani engine, whereas other Blériot XI aircraft, also surviving across the Atlantic, have modern replacements. To take this machine, with its very small engine, across the Channel was a remarkable feat, even when every due allowance has been made for the weather, which was exceptionally favourable. Not surprisingly, the Blériot XI became popular—it was offered for sale at the Aero Show at Olympia in 1910 at £480. It was employed by flying schools (this particular machine is thought to have been one of those used for this purpose at Hendon) and produced in substantial numbers, continuing in service down to the outbreak of war in 1914.

The Deperdussin is the 'Popular' model of 1910, identical with that in which W. H. Ewen made his historic flights in Scotland (see p. 164). Its design was largely modelled on Blériot's, but it was developed so as to take on characteristics of its own. The Deperdussin monocoque of 1912 was the first aeroplane with a stressed-skin structure; it set up a world's speed record of 108 m.p.h. at Chicago in September of that year, and an improved version took that record to 127 m.p.h. at Reims in 1913.

There are two other machines here designed before the first World War began. One is a replica, of the Avro Triplane of 1909 —but a replica with a curious history. It includes one original element: the 9 h.p. JAP engine (much like that of a motor-cycle) that powered it. The Science Museum possesses an original Avro Triplane—lacking only its engine. So that the two could be put together to constitute one machine entirely in its first state. This sort of thing has always been particularly liable to happen with aircraft, more than with any other transport machines: the engine was so readily detachable from the rest of the structure, and experiments were so constantly being made with different types of engine, of varying power, that many such substitutions took place.

The last of these early pioneers is a Blackburn monoplane of 1912, a development of Robert Blackburn's 'Mercury' of 1910, fitted with a 50 h.p. Gnome rotary engine. It was built to a private order, put into store in 1914 and forgotten so completely that when it was found in 1938 it was partly covered by a haystack, its engine dismantled and the pieces put away in a barrel. Reassembled now, it flies admirably and has often taken part in displays. Blackburn met with many setbacks and disappointments in his early work. This was one of his successes—a precursor of what became a long and famous line of military aircraft.

Four famous types of British aeroplane from the first World War are here. The Avro 504 of 1915 (this is a machine of Series K which dates from 1915 and has a Le Rhône engine substituted for the original) claims two functions: three of the type made the first of all planned bombing raids, on the Zeppelin works at Friedrichshafen in November 1914, and it came to be used as a training machine by many of the world's air forces. In this capacity it continued to be used by the RAF until 1930, when it was replaced by another Avro: the 'Tutor', an example of which is also to be seen at Old Warden.

The other three aircraft of this date are all 'scouts', or fighters: a Sopwith Pup, an S.E. 5a, built by the Royal Aircraft Factory at Farnborough, and a Bristol 52b—one of the most brilliantly successful fighters ever built. It had a speed of 115 m.p.h. at 10,000 feet, and could attain double that height. This Bristol is fitted with the oldest Rolls-Royce aero engine that is still in working order.

Among the aircraft of the inter-war years there are two that were used in historic flights: Jean Batten's Percival Gull VI and the D.H. 88 (Comet) that won the international race from England to Australia in 1934.

A Gull machine had already been used by Kingsford-Smith on his Australian flight of 1933. The Mark VI appeared in 1935, and this one was used by Jean Batten on her solo flights to Brazil (1935) and to and from Australia and New Zealand in 1936–37. The flights involved vast sea-crossings—of the South Atlantic and the Tasman Sea—and both brought very substantial reductions in the times to and from Australia.

The design and production of the D.H. 88 represented an extraordinary achievement, for it was all concentrated into a period of nine months. No less than three of the type participated in the competition, with its alluring prizes, for which they had been built. The winner, which is to be seen here, reached Melbourne from Mildenhall in just under seventy-one hours, flown by C. W. A. Scott and Tom Campbell-Black. Evolved in this way, the type went on to become the basis of the Mosquito, one of the most versatile of all the aircraft used in World War II. This machine is a fine monument both to the skilful fortitude of British aviators and to the intelligence and dynamic hard work of which the British aircraft industry was capable.

The other military aeroplanes here include a Gloster Gladiator, a Hurricane, and a Spitfire. These are, of course, most important exhibits. But the choice of them does emphasize the bias, indeed the imbalance, in the Collection. It does not include a single representative civilian aircraft. Clearly it would not be practicable at present to accommodate even one huge air-liner of a modern type. But even a little Flamingo or a Heron would be welcome, to show something of the conditions in which ordinary passengers travelled in the air, in the years just before or after the second World War.

The aero engines begin with what is easily the oldest piece in the whole aeronautical collection: a 5 h.p. steam engine from an ornithopter designed by E. P. Frost about 1870—too heavy and clumsy, doubtless, to enable the machine to stay in the air. The others include duplicates (available for separate inspection and study) of the Anzani and Le Rhône engines installed in aircraft that are exhibited here—the Anzani was picked out of a window in a garage at Billericay; and a couple of the Napier Lion engines that drove so many different types of aircraft in the twenties, including two Schneider Trophy winners, as well as power-boats and several contenders for the speed record on land.

One aircraft accessory is of outstanding interest: a 'starter' devised by B. C. Hucks. This consists of the chassis of a Model T Ford with a shaft mounted on it, which could be fitted to the aeroplane's propeller; the engine of the car could be disengaged from the transmission, to supply instead a drive for the shaft, which could generally be expected to start the aeroplane engine after a couple of revolutions. Other miscellaneous exhibits include a series of photographs of winners of the King's Cup air-race between 1922 and 1957, with their machines; a set of programmes of the London Aviation Meetings at Hendon in 1912–14; and the board describing the history of Croydon aerodrome from 1915 onwards, which was placed there to commemorate the opening of the new buildings of the Airport in 1928. The airfield at Hendon now stands empty, that at Croydon is being built over: these are important memorials of the early history of public flying in England.

Richard Shuttleworth's interests were not confined to aviation. He assembled a representative collection of early bicycles and some motor-cars of importance.

Among the cycles a rarity is a ladies' hobby horse, of the type that became momentarily the rage in 1819; the rage did not last doubtless in part because the machines were so heavy, usually weighing 60 lb. and more. Another is a quadricycle, made by the Starley firm of Coventry, with two large wheels, operated by pedals, side by side and a pair of small ones in the front and rear. This was designed for two riders, sitting abreast; but it could be turned into a tricycle for one by removing one side of the frame

The Kangaroo of 1884 is an interesting variant of the 'ordinary' or penny-farthing type, with the front wheel much reduced in size, the pedals placed below the hub and driving by a vertically-moving chain. And it is good to see here a distinguished local product, made by Dan Albone at Biggleswade, less than three miles away. Albone was an agricultural engineer, who interested himself in cycle racing. His 'Ivel' cross-framed racing machine of 1886 captured a number of speed records; in the same year he built, in association with A. J. Wilson, the earliest practical tandem bicycle; he was also one of the pioneers of the ladies' 'safety' bicycle, and here is an example of the perfected machine, dating from 1901. A man's Lea Francis of 1903 ends the sequence—except for a Moulton of 1965, to show the first substantial advance that has been made on the diamond-framed safety cycle since its development in the 1880s.

The motor-cars include some built before the end of the nineteenth century, an English Daimler of 1857, a Panhard, a Benz, and a Mors 'Petit Duc'. The Panhard belonged to Lord Rothschild. Its present body was mounted on it in 1901, and in this form it was driven by King Edward VII at the Ascot meeting of that year. Richard Shuttleworth drove it from London to Brighton in 1929.

The Arrol-Johnston of 1901 has already been mentioned: a six-seater dog-cart with a two-cylinder engine generating 12 h.p. The Locomobile of the same year was among the first American steam cars to be imported into England. It retains its original single-tube tyres. The Baby Peugeot of 1902 (5 h.p., with one cylinder) is characteristic of the small car of its time. It is still game enough: it made the London–Brighton run no less than sixteen times between 1929 and 1963.

A splendid French racing car, of a make little represented in this country, is the Cottin et Desgouttes, built at Lyons in 1911. It is a very impressive machine with much copper and brass-work about it (excellently maintained), weighing well over a ton, with a 10½ litre four-cylinder engine, giving a top speed of 100 m.p.h. It has two contemporaries here, of very different types: a six-seater Crossley, of the sort that was most widely used as a staff car in 1914–18 and is familiar in so many photographs of the Western Front; and a Morris Oxford of the earliest pattern, which began to appear in 1912.

The series ends—for the present—with a group of racing and

sports cars of the years 1927–34; two Bugattis (one of which Richard Shuttleworth himself raced in the thirties), an Alfa Romeo, an Aston Martin, and a Frazer Nash.

Finally, it should be mentioned that the saddles and other horse furniture from the Shuttleworth family stables are here; and it is typical of the care given to explaining the exhibits that a diagram showing the place taken by all these items of equipment on the horse itself is shown beside them.

The Shuttleworth Collection is unpretentiously housed, on the edge of a quiet village, in the workaday premises used by aeroplanes, which are its chief concern; its administration is economical. The Trust has thought about its priorities, and got most of them right. Its main effort has gone into getting the machines in, repairing them and maintaining them, labelling them clearly and carefully for visitors and bringing the description to a point in an admirable catalogue. In the foreword to it Air-Commodore A. H. Wheeler indicates the developments that he and his fellow-Trustees wish to see ahead. He adds modestly, 'We are aware that many things are still lacking in the display and facilities we now provide for the public', and welcomes ideas for their improvement. In token of this, a suggestions book is kept at the counter of the publications stall. I have ventured to offer here one suggestion myself for improving the balance and widening the scope of the Collection. If I were to offer another criticism, it would be that the Collection is insufficiently publicized. My final comment, however, would certainly not be one of criticism, but of deep admiration for the vision and public spirit that prompted the formation of the Trust and has informed its work. It is a notable monument to Richard Shuttleworth himself and to the outstanding bravery and skill of the men and women who conquered the air.

9

WATERWAYS MUSEUM
STOKE BRUERNE

Of the four museums that are run under the auspices of the nationalized transport undertaking in Britain, three are concerned wholly with land transport, by road and rail. This one, the fourth, is devoted exclusively to inland navigation. Here is something unique, not only in this country but in Europe too. There are maritime museums in plenty, but their attention is given to the sea; some of the large transport museums—at Lucerne, Munich, and Nuremberg, for instance—offer a single room, or a few exhibits, to illustrate the history of inland waterways. Nowhere but at Stoke Bruerne is there a museum that concentrates on that history alone.

It was a happy inspiration to site it here, on a main artery of the English canal system. Stoke Bruerne was a place of importance on that system, as it grew up in the late eighteenth and early nineteenth centuries. It stands at the south end of the Blisworth tunnel and at the head of a series of half a dozen locks that lift the Grand Union (formerly Grand Junction) Canal out of the valley of the Ouse and its tributary the Tove. The Grand Junction Canal was authorized in 1793, to run from Braunston in Northamptonshire to Brentford on the Thames. By 1800 it was complete, with the sole exception of the stretch from Blisworth to the foot of the projected locks at Stoke Bruerne. Though the tunnel had been begun early, it had been abandoned in 1796. It was agreed that a new tunnel should be built following a different course, but the Company was in financial straits and could not contemplate the heavy additional expenditure that would involve. For the moment it bridged the awkward gap between Blisworth and Stoke Bruerne, first by a road over the top of the hill and then, in 1800, by a double-deck horse tramway. The gap was not closed, by the

115

completion of the locks and the new tunnel (3,075 yards long), until March 1805.[1]

All this can still be studied on the ground today. The tunnel remains open—it is the longest now in use by British Waterways. Relics of the tramway can still be traced; some of them are in the Museum. The locks continue in use.

The Museum itself is established round the basin at Stoke Top Lock, the highest of the series. It would have been hard to find a better site for it: in the very heart of England, easily reached by road and by bus from Northampton, on the main line of one of the chief canals in the country, with the tunnel a quarter of an hour's walk to the north and the six locks in quick succession to the south. It is a pleasant place in itself, and ideal not only for the study of the subject but for learning to appreciate something of the canals' very atmosphere. And as if to emphasize more strongly the quiet and stillness of the waterway you can hear, only a mile or two off, the electric express trains tearing through Roade at 90–100 m.p.h. on the line of the London and Birmingham Railway— the Grand Junction Canal's arch-competitor, which scooped up the greater part of its business in the later part of the nineteenth century.

The basin is an inland port in miniature. The canal broadens out here, to accommodate boats waiting to pass through the tunnel on one side and the locks on another. Two locks were formerly provided, side by side, though one has now been filled in. On the little quays are a warehouse, half a dozen cottages with a ropewalk behind them, and an inn, 'The Boat'.

The filled-in lock now serves as a dry dock, holding a canal boat, *Northwich*, of 1898—a typical narrow boat, save that it has a cabin forward as well as aft. It is cradled in a big iron weighing-machine, formerly at Cardiff, the property of the Glamorganshire Canal. And at the bridge end of the dry dock have been mounted a pair of cast-iron lock gates from Welshpool on the Montgomery-shire Canal (1832): a great rarity, for these gates were almost always constructed of timber. The engineer's name, G. Waugh, is carved in handsome bold Regency lettering on the stone sill of the entrance. It is instructive to compare these gates with a pair of the usual timber ones that stand beside them on the other lock

[1] For the construction of the Grand Junction Canal and its branches see C. Hadfield, *The Canals of the East Midlands* (Newton Abbot, 1966), 106–16.

The iron tophamper is so much neater and smaller by comparison (even making due allowance for the narrower gauge of the Welsh canal) that one is tempted to wonder why the use of iron for this purpose should be so uncommon. Telford employed it on the Ellesmere and Caledonian Canals—and that suggests part of the answer to the question: for he was working on them relatively late in the Canal Age. The majority of the British canals were built before cast-iron had come into general use, when no material other than timber was considered reliable.

The indoor exhibits are housed in a former warehouse, on three floors. They illustrate the building of the canals, their management, and the life and work on them. They are arranged with an agreeable informality, not to any rigid system—one famous print of the Paddington canal basin, indeed, turns up three times over. It is convenient to discuss them by topic, but hardly necessary to indicate the location of the exhibits, since the whole collection is not large.

The building and administration of the canals are illustrated chiefly by pictures and documents. The earliest is an interesting draft from John Partington to Sir Thomas Johnson, M P, concerning the Weaver Navigation in 1715. The prints and water-colours include some fine views: one of a lock and lock-keeper's house near Lechlade—the house a castellated tower; several striking drawings of the Regent's Canal; a photographic reproduction of a remarkable painting that shows the making of locks at Worcester as late as 1845. There are some good photographs of more recent work: an excellent series of the Manchester Ship Canal under construction, another of the widening of Hatton Locks in 1934, several of modern canal occasions, like the trip made by the Duke of Edinburgh and his children with the Crown Prince of Sweden on the Caledonian Canal in 1962—one of a long series of such royal excursions reaching back to Queen Victoria's first, on the Crinan Canal in 1847.

There is a good deal of material here bearing on the construction of the canals—though I think the informal arrangement of the display, which in general is most happy, is in this instance a mistake. It would have been fascinating to follow through, with documents, maps, and relics, the whole process of the construction of a canal, from the start of the idea to its realization. As it is, much less than justice is done here to the magnitude of the achievement the canals represent. The visitor is not really shown how difficult the work was, the new thinking and the new techniques it called forth in the eighteenth century, many of them fundamental to the subsequent development of economic organization and civil engineering.

Nevertheless, a good deal of this can be picked up at Stoke Bruerne. First come the documents—the prospectuses, deposited plans, Acts of Parliament, share certificates (there are good examples for two of the lesser known English canals, the Oakham and the Wey and Arun). The construction of the canals themselves —apart from the later examples just mentioned—is not very well represented here, and it is admittedly difficult to depict in detail: the canals, alas, found no one to do for them what Bourne did for the London and Birmingham Railway (cf. pl. 41b). Stone sleepers and a length of rail remind us of the tramroad that ran over the hill from here to Blisworth in 1800–5. The great works are shown in sets of photographs: there is a good series of the Marple aqueduct, for instance, taken in 1963–64.

Once the canals had been built they had to be maintained, and here the Museum has much to show that is interesting: the engineers' tools, a hand-operated pump, a tube with a glass end for inspection under water on the Kennet and Avon, the bell and shipbuilder's plate from the Crinan Canal's ice breaker, *Conway*. The interior of the long tunnels required constant inspection. When steam tugs appeared they corroded the low brick tunnel vaults with soot. The first crude remedy was to drag a hawthorn bush through (there is a picture of a barge here thus primitively equipped); later the bush was succeeded by specially-constructed wire brushes, one of which is in the Museum.

The craft used on the canals are shown in a variety of ways: by a series of models—extended to include such things as a Humber keel—as well as by pictures. The set of photographs of the Lancaster Canal packet boat, *Duchess Countess*, in her final state before she was (most unhappily) broken up, reminds us of the contribution the canals made to the conveyance of passengers as well as of freight. That practice lingered longest in Scotland. The Forth and Clyde Canal operated coaches of its own, which provided a service between Stirling and Glasgow. The Museum has a copy of two of the flysheets advertising it. There is a photograph of one of the steamers that plied on the Caledonian Canal and a poster of 1887 prohibiting 'children and others' from running along the Crinan Canal banks after the passenger steamers, requesting the passengers not to encourage them by tossing money to them and warning children not to throw flowers on board.

From the middle of the nineteenth century onwards the canals made some efforts to catch up with the railways by mechanization. One of their methods was to adopt steam haulage; and here is the engine fitted in the 1890s to the Worcester and Birmingham Canal Committee's boat, *Little Sabrina*. The Swedish Bolunder semi-diesel engine—an example of which is shown alongside— pointed the way to a more successful future. The two most famous mechanical lifts in the country are well represented: the Foxton inclined plane, which had a very short life in the early part of this century, by a series of clear photographs; the Anderton lift (which is still in use) by a working model.

The greatest effort of the Museum has been concentrated on illustrating the life of the men and women who worked on the canals. They formed a quite distinctive element in English society. Once the boatmen's profession had been established it was rare for any of them to marry outside it. They went their own way, keeping themselves to themselves on the water, rarely inviting anyone not of their own fraternity on board the boats, at least for any social occasion. In short, their life was as separate from the lives of other men and women in Britain as that of the gypsies.

They wore a special dress—not a uniform, which implies uniformity, but clothes that allowed a free play of fancy in colour and design, within certain clearly-defined conventions. These clothes are excellently shown at Stoke Bruerne; the men's sober corduroys, with a touch or two of brightness in shirt or neckcloth, the women's and children's clothes gay and full of colour, their best silks for high days and holidays very pretty indeed. Their headgear—white bonnets and broad black soft hats—remained quite distinctive, utterly impervious to all changes of fashion on dry land.

They decorated their boats no less distinctively than their persons. Various opinions have been expressed about the origins and development of the canal people's 'style'. Mr Rolt has argued cogently that it descends from the gypsies; Mr Hadfield will have

119

none of that.[1] The most elaborate of all the exhibits here comprises a full-sized reconstruction of the cabin and rear part of a narrow boat, *Sunny Valley*, registered at Daventry and owned by the Samuel Barlow Coal Company of Birmingham. The famous 'roses and castles' decoration is well exemplified. No chance is lost to adorn any available surface in strong, clear colours. All the characteristic equipment is here, too: the horse's tail on the rudder, a cooking-stove with its copper kettle, a painted water-can and a brass oil lamp, pretty plates showing a design of fruit and open-work rims, pottery dogs, a bird-cage, and a fine melodeon— a 15-keyed instrument that once sang under a boatman's fingers across the water in the evening.

There are a few good photographs showing a little of the social life these people led—of a christening party, for example, in 1913. But such pictures are necessarily very rare, for the men of the boats did not readily share their private lives with strangers.

Several of the best original objects shown here came, as it happened, from a single Company, the Coventry Canal. Among them is a manually-operated fire-engine and an iron chest for the custody of documents, protected with a marvellously intricate system of locks. It is interesting to see how, as late as 1780, a Company like this should still be using for security an instrument so old-fashioned—of a kind that many churchwardens had used for centuries past to contain the records of the parish. This chest must indeed have held valuables, for the Company attained an extraordinary prosperity, paying dividends that averaged 31 per cent for forty years (1804–43). No wonder the directors could adorn their board-room with fine glass-ware specially made for them. The decanters show canal boats hauled by horses. These are among the most elegant things in the Museum.

One comes back to reflecting on the management of the canals as one looks at the portraits that are hung here. Among them are oil-paintings of the first Chairman of the Grand Union Canal, the banker, William Praed, and of the first and last Chairman of the Grand Junction Company, R. F. de Salis, one of a family whose members had been shareholders in the two concerns since 1795. And close to the entrance is a framed photograph of Sir Reginald Kerr, Chariman of British Waterways from 1955 to 1962, 'to

[1] T. C. Rolt, *The Inland Waterways of England* (1950), 174–77; C. Hadfield *British Canals* (2nd ed., 1959), 73.

17*a* Hull: barouche built for Sir Christopher Sykes of Sledmere

b Science Museum: the Earl of Caledon's dress chariot, 1891

18a Science Museum: mail coach of the 1820s

b Lucerne: coupé-landau of the Swiss Post Office, which plied over the Alpine passes from 1880 to 1920

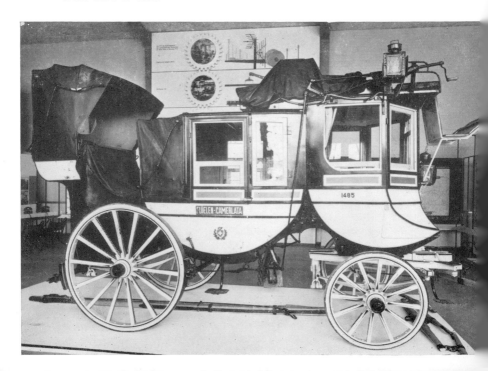

19*a* Science Museum: model of Sir Goldsworthy Gurney's steam mail coach

b Birmingham: steam roller by Aveling and Porter of Rochester (1892)

20*a* Science Museum: ladies' hobby horse (1819)

b Science Museum: Michaux bicycle (1865)

c Beaulieu: the largest 'ordinary' or 'penny-farthing' bicycle ever built: a Starley model with a 7-foot front wheel

21a Birmingham: wooden bicycle made in Nyasaland in 1900

b Science Museum: Raleigh tandem bicycle (1897). The gentleman sits in front, the lady at the back

c Beaulieu: the oldest surviving Triumph motor-cycle (1903)

22a Science Museum: an early scooter, the Skootamota, designed by Granville Bradshaw (1919)

b Birmingham: Saltley-Villiers motor-cycle (1921)

23a Munich: Karl Benz's first motor vehicles (1886)

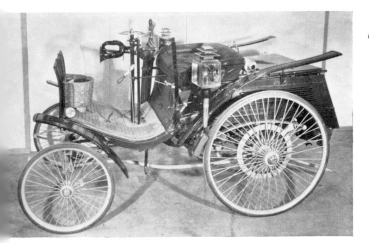

b Birmingham: Benz motor dog-cart (1900)

c Shuttleworth Collection: Arrol-Johnston motor dog-cart (1901)

24 Glasgow: th
stages of the w
on an Argyll mot
car of 1900: the
in its original st.
as received by
Museum; the proc
of restoration;
finished product

whose initiative the establishment of this Museum is due'. It is to be hoped that he has seen it as it now is, developed and in working order. If so, he has cause to feel proud to have taken part in establishing something that is unique not only in Britain but in Europe too.

10

TRAMWAYS MUSEUM, CRICH

The origins of this Museum go back roughly twenty years. It was already clear then that trams were on their way out in Britain—though no one would have expected that by 1962 they would have disappeared from every town in the country but two. They had their devoted admirers, and in 1948 a group of them bought a particularly interesting Southampton tram, to save it from destruction. This led to the acquisition of six more trams, and the establishment of a Museum Committe to devise means for giving them a permanent home and showing them to the public. A Tramway Museum Society was formed in 1955 which assumed responsibility for the cars that had already been acquired. Four years later its long quest for suitable premises ended, when it leased land and buildings at Crich Quarry in Derbyshire. Track was laid down there, and the cars gradually brought in.

From the outset the Society was determined that this should be not a static display but a live museum, in which the trams should work, performing their proper function of carrying passengers. Stage I of this operation may be said to have been completed on June 2, 1963, when a horse-tram from Sheffield was put into service on a line 200 yards long. Stage II followed a year later, on July 5, 1964. An electric service then began to operate.

Crich Quarry[1] lies six miles south-east of Matlock, whence there is a bus service (every half-hour at weekends during the summer), close to the A6 road from Derby to Manchester and not far west of the M1. Admission to the Museum is free, but a small fare is charged for a tram-ride.

Nothing could be less like the conventional idea of a museum than this one: out in the open air, over 600 feet up in the splendid limestone landscape of Derbyshire. Trams belong essentially

[1] 'Crich' does not rhyme with 'itch'; the 'i' is long.

to towns, and it is startling, at a sudden bend in the road, to come upon the trolley-pole and upper deck of one peering over a bank in open country. But no town, having once banished them, could now re-admit them to its streets; if we are ever to see them at work at all, it must be in rural conditions like these.

The Tramway Museum Society owns over thirty vehicles. Not quite all of them are here at Crich. One, from Newcastle, is on loan to the Museum at Beaulieu; Blackpool No. 1, the oldest electric street tram in Britain, is at present in the Museum of British Transport at Clapham. Of those that are kept at Crich many are dilapidated, awaiting restoration. The work is done with meticulous care, almost entirely by members of the Society at weekends, and it inevitably takes a long time. But to watch the progress of work on a particular car—say Leicester No. 76, one of those in hand at the time of writing—is to see the application of a craftsmanship that grows constantly rarer in our time.

The Museum comprises a group of large sheds, which house these tall and bulky vehicles, a few very small ones—barely more than huts—and a stretch of track running parallel with the cliff face in the vast quarry. This is at present some 700 yards long, though plans have been made for a future extension to Wakebridge, about as far again. Along this track the Society operates one tram, and sometimes more, at the weekends between April and October. It is an odd experience to travel on, for instance, a Glasgow tram through this remote countryside, reminded sharply of earlier days by the conductors (members of the Society) issuing tickets to the accompaniment of the well-remembered ting of the Bell punch machine, with all the peculiar noises of the tram in motion—the squeak and hiss of the trolley on the wire, the click of the wheels on the track. No static museum, which merely exhibits the vehicles at rest, can ever re-create the past for us as effectively as this simple little journey, of a few minutes out and back, along the Cliffside at Crich.

The vehicles preserved here exemplify almost every phase of tramway development in Britain. Almost, but not quite: unhappily they do not include a cable car—for no one ever thought to rescue one from Edinburgh, or even from Matlock nearby when that small undertaking came to an end in 1927. Nor is there an example of those enormous double-deck cars built to be hauled by steam engines, like those of very happy memory that served on the

Swansea and Mumbles line until it was electrified in 1929. The collection is, however, remarkable enough as it stands.

It illustrates most completely the development of tramways in our big towns. The largest contributors are Blackpool, with seven vehicles, including two from the long-distance Fleetwood line; and Glasgow, which also has seven if one reckons among them a car from Paisley, taken over when the Paisley District Tramways Company was bought by Glasgow Corporation in 1923. Next come Sheffield and Leeds, with five cars each, and Gateshead with two. London and seven other provincial towns supply one apiece. The remaining three come from outside Great Britain: from Dublin, Oporto, and Johannesburg.

Some such distribution as this might perhaps be expected. Blackpool is the only municipality in Britain today that still makes use of trams. They are to be counted, indeed, among its attractions for holiday-makers, and the administration has shown itself very ready to collaborate in schemes of preservation. Glasgow was the last of our great industrial cities to retain its tramways. Until they went out of fashion, largely through the rapidly-mounting pressure of motor traffic in the streets, they were reckoned a cause for civic pride: for the great distances they travelled—the through service from Renfrew Ferry to Milngavie was the longest in the British Isles—the cheapness of the fares, the brisk facility with which they moved their enormous crowds of passengers. When the trams ceased to operate in Glasgow in 1962 the city behaved handsomely in establishing a museum, largely in order to commemorate them; and it was not difficult for the Tramway Museum Society, by then well established at Crich, to acquire examples of some of the types it wanted. The tram also survived late in Leeds and Sheffield (respectively until 1959 and 1960). The Corporation of Leeds was the first in Britain to operate electric tramways of its own, in 1897. Towards the close of the second World War it adopted a plan for drastic modernization of its tramway system in the centre of the city, on Continental lines, using single-deck cars in subways. Then policy changed, and Leeds fell into line with other British towns in going for the bus alone. The Museum at Crich now has the distinction of possessing two of the cars that were to be the instruments of this abortive revolution. As for Sheffield, it seemed that the dominion of the trams there was as unshakeable as in

Glasgow. What bus, it was continually argued, could move up those fearsome hills with a full load of passengers in the snow and ice of a Sheffield winter? The tram alone was sure-footed enough to get through. Down to the 1950s that argument prevailed, and with good reason: for the motor-bus did not attain until then the peak of its achievement. But when it could be demonstrated convincingly that the bus could do the work of the tram, so peculiarly exacting in Sheffield, its triumph arrived. The last tram ran in the city on October 8, 1960. Nowhere was the change more conspicuously commemorated. Car No. 510, emblazoned with scenes of tramway life and the words 'Sheffield's Last Tram', was driven by the Lord Mayor on the last day of service. It now reposes, fittingly, at Crich.

Some two-thirds of the trams that the Society owns, then, come from these four towns. They include some of its most highly-valued possessions. The only horse-tram here is a Starbuck car built for Sheffield and used there from 1874 until the system was electrified in 1902. By a fortunate decision, it was then turned into a service vehicle. When the Sheffield Transport Department, which was justifiably proud of its own record, celebrated its jubilee in 1946, this car was refurbished and put back into service. It figured there again in 1961; but by that time it had passed into the hands of the Tramway Museum Society. It inaugurated operations at Crich, hauled by Bonny, a mare from a farm nearby, in 1963.

The early years of electric tramways operation are well represented by a grand toast-rack car running on bogies, built for the opening of the Blackpool–Fleetwood line in 1898 by Milnes of Birkenhead and in continuous service until 1939, and by one of the single-deck four-wheelers that inaugurated electric traction in Sheffield in 1899. Glasgow No. 812, which dates from 1900, belongs to the exceptionally long series of Standard trams constructed for that city.[1] Like most of its fellows it has been subsequently reconstructed, so that it looks more modern than its fellow No. 22, which retains its open balconies on the upper deck but was in fact built only in 1922.

Of all the early vehicles here the most striking, however, is the Blackpool Dreadnought (No. 59 of 1902), with its straight double staircase and steps of full width at each end of the car:

[1] The evolution of the Glasgow Standard tram is discussed below on p. 172.

an ingenious design to enable holiday crowds to surge on and off at the highest possible speed. This is a notable mammoth, able to seat eighty-six passengers—a larger number than any other tram here, or than any modern bus. But for all its size there is nothing bloated about it: the vehicle has just that perfection of amplitude which came naturally, for a short time at the turn of the century, to the designers of large machines used for transport.

Two other cars dating from the early years of electric traction come from Southampton and Leicester. Few electric trams were designed with knifeboard seating on the upper deck; the garden seat was an improvement that came to stay in the later years of the horse-bus. But Southampton had a peculiar difficulty to meet, in running its trams through the medieval Bargate. If double-deck cars were to be operated at all, this was the only practicable kind of seating. Even so, passengers had to be warned not to stand up while the car was passing through the Bargate, and they were firmly instructed that they 'Must Not Touch The Wire'. The Leicester car is one of the second batch delivered to the Corporation in the year in which electric traction began in the town, 1904, and it remained in service until 1947. The Museum's *Handbook* rightly draws attention to the restrained care bestowed on the decoration of the tram's interior. In this it reflected a tradition well established in the town during these years.

By 1904 the electric tram was secure in Britain, still on its way to fresh conquests in urban transport at the expense of the railway. The challenge of the motor-bus did not become serious until the 1920s. For about a quarter of a century—say from 1905 to 1930—the electric tram stood at the apogee of its success. Among the representation of this central period at Crich is an open-topped double-decker from the Cheltenham and District Company—the sole surviving tramcar from anywhere south-west of Birmingham. It was built in 1921 and had only nine years of life. The body alone has been preserved. Since the Cheltenham trams were built to a 3 foot 6 inch gauge, it will need to be re-mounted before it can run again. The two single-deck cars from the Gateshead and District Tramways Company (a subsidiary of British Electric Traction) both date from the 1920s. The earlier, No. 52 of 1920, worked the Teams branch, one of the shortest tram-routes in the country. When the system went over to buses in 1951 the car was bought by a former tram-driver, Mr William Southern, who later presented it to the Society: a generous gesture, and one more testimony to the affection the tram inspired. The other Gateshead car, No. 5, enjoyed an extra ten years of working life, for it was bought by the British Transport Commission for use between Grimsby and Immingham and continued in service there until 1961. Finally, from 1926 comes a Leeds tram (No. 399) fitted with compressed-air brakes for use on the steep Beeston route.

From the early thirties onwards it became increasingly clear, in Britain though not on the Continent, that the tram was on the way out. But it fought some stiff rearguard actions. New types of tram were developed by those operators who still had faith in them, and some remarkable examples of this last phase are to be seen at Crich: a Coronation and a Cunarder from Glasgow; two of the cars produced for the revolution that failed in Leeds; Sheffield No. 510, already mentioned, which was built as late as 1950. The only London tram at present in the hands of the Society is a remarkable vehicle of 1930, built experimentally for the Metropolitan Electric Tramways Company; one of the prototypes from which the all-steel Feltham cars evolved. This one remained unique and was sold to Sunderland in 1937.

The three 'foreigners' are all interesting. One is from Ireland: an open-top double-decker bult for the Hill of Howth line, near Dublin, in 1902 and fitted up so as to enable its passengers to enjoy the splendid scenery of the line. It does not seem to have been a success, however. It was little used, and this accounts for its unusually excellent condition today. The Johannesburg car dates from 1905 and still bears all its notices to passengers in English and Afrikaans.

But to many people the oldest thing in the whole collection will remain the most memorable: the Starbuck car built for Oporto in 1873. In the course of its very long life it was hauled first by mules, then by steam engines, then by electric cars, to which it served as a trailer. The Starbuck cars were indeed very stoutly built: the one from Ryde that is now in the Museum at Hull (cf. p. 146) worked continuously from 1867 to 1935. It is good that the Oporto car has now been repatriated to the country of its birth.

A steam tram engine is available here to haul it: one built by Beyer Peacock to William Wilkinson's patent for New South

Wales. Its running costs there were found to be heavy, and by some unknown process it was returned to its makers in Manchester. They then employed it as a works shunter for half a century, finally agreeing to deposit it with the Society on permanent loan.

To anyone interested in tramways it is natural to make a comparison between this Museum and the one at Schepdaal in Belgium, described in Chapter 24. They have one important feature in common. Both were established and both are maintained by amateurs of the tram, who give their service as volunteers: cleaning, maintaining, and repairing the vehicles, manning the bookshop, preparing publicity and writing the literature. But there all resemblance ends: the two Museums are both admirable in their way, and they are as widely different as the rocky heights of Derbyshire from the flat Belgian plain. Each reflects naturally the characteristic uses to which the tramway was put in its own country: the long-distance inter-urban and rural services of Belgium, catering for small numbers of passengers at a time; the intensive short town routes of Britain, heavily used in rush hours and needing therefore far bigger vehicles, with two decks—the largest single unit it is practicable to construct. Again, economic and social conditions in rural Belgium made for the surivival of the steam tram, running along the public road, long after its English counterparts—at Alford, at Wantage and Wisbech and Wolverton —had disappeared, or had ceased to carry passengers. Even now the *vicinal*, the country tram, survives in Belgium as a living thing, whilst in Britain the tram itself has vanished from normal commercial operation, save at Blackpool and Douglas. It finds its last stronghold in museums, and pre-eminently this one at Crich.

To those whose interest is not confined to tramways, who see them in their perspective of economic and technical change, a visit to Crich is exceptionally rewarding. For the parish was transformed by the Industrial Revolution: first through the establishment of the cotton manufacture at Fritchley in 1793, then through the great development of the quarrying of limestone, here on this very site. The parish had long been a centre of mining—the Wakebridge lead mine, which had been in use for centuries, was one of the richest in the Midlands. Limestone of a high quality was worked in this Crich Cliff, much of it being dispatched by the Cromford Canal to London and Manchester. This was on a small scale, however, until in 1841 George Stephenson, with three partners—one of them George Hudson the Railway King—bought the Crich quarries, linking them by a narrow-gauge tramway (worked by cable and horse) with Ambergate in the valley below. There the limestone was burnt in a series of twenty kilns, which could produce up to 25,000 tons of lime a year, and distributed to all parts of the country by the Stephensons' new North Midland Railway, running alongside. It was one of George Stephenson's best-conceived industrial ventures and contributed substantially to the fortune he left behind when he died in 1848.

If you descend from Crich to Matlock your road will lie through Cromford. There you will pass the mills established by Richard Arkwright. Derbyshire is indeed inspiring country for the industrial archaeologist. Here, in the very centre of the country, you can see milestones of the progress that made Britain, for a time, pre-eminent in the economic life of the world.

11

MUSEUM OF SCIENCE
AND INDUSTRY, BIRMINGHAM

The Birmingham Museum of Science and Industry is a Department of the City Museum and Art Gallery, established in the former electro-plating factory of Messrs Elkington. This was an agreeable classical building, probably dating from the 1840s. It was demolished in 1966, to the great detriment of Newhall Street, in which it stood. The Museum had by then moved sideways out of the original building into adjacent premises on the north side. A new building is to be erected for it on the site of the old one. The position of the Museum is excellent, close to the centre of the city and facing on to a branch of the Birmingham Canal.

The first thing that strikes you on entering the Museum is a bustle and subdued noise. For it is its policy to try as far as possible to keep its machines alive. A click and hum greet you at once, and possibly something very much louder, for at certain fixed times, announced in the hall you come into, some of the machines are set to work—among them the remarkable Orchestrion steam-organ from Blackpool, whose musical performance is an experience to be remembered. All through the day some machines are at work, like the 'semi-portable' steam engine in the entrance hall, which dates from the 1820s and demonstrates very clearly the mechanism by which such stationary engines worked.

This first hall is devoted chiefly to prime movers. It includes some transport machines, two of them really notable. The first has been famous for a long time, and rightly. It is the model steam locomotive built by William Murdock at Redruth in 1784 and subsequently demonstrated to Matthew Boulton and James Watt in Birmingham. That Watt discouraged Murdock from carrying the idea any further seems to be established; but whether that

130

was because he dispassionately judged it to be unproductive or whether he was moved by the interest he was himself taking in similar machines at the time, we cannot tell. From whatever cause, this machine of Murdock's proved to be a dead end; but nevertheless here is the second oldest steam locomotive, model or full-scale, to survive in the world, junior only to Cugnot's in Paris (see p. 194). A silver plate on the little model records that it was bought from Murdock's great-grandson in 1883 by Richard and George Tangye, Cornishmen who had established their great engineering business in Birmingham in 1855. Examples of their own products are to be seen elsewhere in the Museum—a steam engine for factory work, for instance, in the next hall, dating from the 1890s.

The other outstanding transport machine here is a steam-roller built by Aveling and Porter of Rochester in 1892 and used in the construction of the City Road in Birmingham. This is a quite regal machine, nobly proportioned, resplendent in brass-work and green paint. Close by it stands a traction engine by Burrell's of Thetford, of 1924; a 12 h.p. portable steam engine built about 1894 by Ruston's of Lincoln; and a Shand Mason horse-drawn fire-engine of 1898.

Next door is the main Transport Hall, which is—most properly in Birmingham—devoted principally to the internal combustion engine. There are twenty cars here, and almost as many motor-cycles. The cars begin with a series of motor dog-carts, dating from the very end of the nineteenth century. With a touch of real imagination, the Museum displays a true dog-cart, complete with a dummy horse, between a pair of these motor vehicles, to show the evolution of the type. The dog box under the seat at the back is the key to it; the ventilating louvres for the comfort of the dogs being retained to permit the escape of gases and fumes from the engine. The two oldest of these vehicles both have Benz engines; but next to them stands a Clément-Panhard dog-cart of 1901. These are not, however, the oldest motor vehicles here; you will find a tricar by Léon Bolée a little further down the line.

To turn to the cars of 1901 that are here is to find yourself suddenly jerked forward a long way towards the motor-car as we know it today. Both are of great historical interest: for they are among the earliest production models to be turned out by two of the most famous of the early British manufacturing firms—Lanchester and Wolseley. The Lanchester has the light springy grace that characterized so much of its designer's work; the Wolseley (primarily the work of Herbert Austin) is heavier, with a tonneau body. Both cars were produced in the Birmingham suburbs, the Lanchester at Sparkbrook, the Wolseley at Adderley Park.

There is a group of four cars belonging to the years just before the first World War. Three are English and quite small (including two more by local firms, BSA and Alldays), the fourth is a Benz 'grand touring car' of 1912. It is a huge, not to say overblown, machine: an appropriate possession, one might feel, for some fleshy, strong-jowled tycoon of that day, eternally smoking the thickest of cigars.

Two commercial vehicles here, also dating from this time, are of interest: the chassis of a 20–30 h.p. Renault of 1908 and a Dennis fire-engine of 1911. The inter-war years are represented by a 10 h.p. Singer coupé of 1920, an early Austin Seven, and three cars of 1935: a Riley Imp, for competition work, and two saloons, a 2-litre Triumph and a 17 h.p. Armstrong-Siddeley.

The outstanding post-war exhibit is the Railton racing car in which John Cobb took the world's land speed record to 394·2 m.p.h. on Bonneville Salt Flats, Utah, in 1947. The interest of this spectacular machine is much enhanced by the designer's recorded commentary on it, available at the push of a button, in which he explains very coolly and clearly its evolution and achievement. The series ends—for the present—with a Jaguar of the famous type XK 120, which was in production from 1949 to 1954.

Of the series of motor-cycles, all but two belong to the years 1913–29. The only earlier machine is a Belgian FN of 1907. A motor-scooter of 1921 is here: one of the ABC 'Skootamotas', which were among the most successful, both technically and commercially, of their kind and date. Again, local firms are well represented, with BSA, Velocette, and—reaching out an arm as far as Wolverhampton—Sunbeam; the Saltley-Villiers is a rare locally-built machine, dating from 1921.

The ancestry of the motor-cycle is well displayed in a series of pedal bicycles and tricycles to be seen in a room leading off the Aircraft Gallery upstairs. An interesting early machine is a tandem of about 1870 with the seats placed back to back, the front rider pedalling. One of the earliest of James Starley's Coventry lever tricycles (first produced in 1876) is here: an important design, which may be said to have put the tricycle on the way to commercial success. The modern bicycle can be seen to be emerging in the Singer of about 1885; it is a pity that the series of bicycles then breaks off (apart from a couple of interesting freaks) until 1957, though very recent history is well represented by a Moulton machine of 1964. The freaks comprise one of the bamboo-framed cycles developed for a short time at the close of the nineteenth century, with the main object of reducing weight to ease the handling of the machine by ladies; and a remarkable home-made bicycle constructed in Nyasaland about 1900. The frame and wheels are made entirely of wood, the chain of thongs of knotted leather. It is a splendid piece of improvisation, transforming one's thoughts about a machine completely by forcing one back to first principles; its construction has been achieved without the use of a single one of the materials normally considered indispensable for it.

The central place in the main gallery adjoining is occupied by two aeroplanes—two of those that did most to save us all in the second World War, a Spitfire and a Hurricane. The Spitfire is of Mark IX, built in outer Birmingham at Castle Bromwich in 1944; the Hurricane a Mark IV of 1943. Both are displayed standing on the floor, with a view of the cockpit given from a platform raised on steps. Within these severe restrictions of space, which would make it out of the question to put an air-liner or a bomber on show, this was a good choice of exhibits, and it is supplemented, here and in the main Science Gallery downstairs, by a series of aero engines, together with the cockpit and nose of the fuselage of a Bristol Beaufighter of 1941.

Besides these machines, which belong very much to our own world, stand another group that as clearly belong to a world that has almost vanished: three small narrow-gauge steam locomotives. Two are 0–4–0 saddle tanks constructed for the 2-foot gauge by Bagnall and Kerr Stuart in 1919 and 1922: neat little engines of orthodox design. The third is unique, an astonishing curiosity. It is a tank engine of the 0–6–0 type for the 2 foot 8½ inch gauge, with double frames, outside cylinders, a bell-mouthed dome, and a cowcatcher. It was built about 1874 by Belliss and Seeking, and it is the only example known to exist of a steam locomotive made in Birmingham. It worked all its life at Furzebrook, just south of Wareham in Dorset, hauling clay for Messrs Pike Bros. Fayle and Co. Ltd. Their railway was abandoned in favour of a road in 1955. Named *Secundus* (what became of *Primus?*), it was repaired, or perhaps rebuilt, at Poole in 1880 and given a new boiler by Peckett's of Bristol in 1936. When it entered the Museum it was still in working order. There is no other locomotive like it in Britain. Its nearest surviving relatives are perhaps some of the narrow-gauge engines at Stockholm (see p. 259).

These engines are mounted in a well-lighted little aisle, made gay with a series of half a dozen panels hanging transversely above them, bearing coats of arms of the old railway companies.

There are no other railway exhibits here that are as yet on public display. But when, in 1966, the original Elkington's building was demolished, the London, Midland and Scottish Railway locomotive *City of Birmingham* was moved in to occupy part of the site, standing there temporarily until a new building was erected around it. For the moment it is out in the open air. It is good to think of the engine here: not only for its association, through its name, with the city, but as the latest example of an express passenger steam locomotive to be preserved anywhere in the country. It is shown, not in its original streamlined casing—the form in which it was originally built in 1939—but with that casing removed and in the British Railways livery that it carried when it was withdrawn from service in 1964.

This is an admirable museum of applied science: lively and vigorous, making its mark on the life of Birmingham and its neighbourhood. It is always well filled, and sometimes thronged, with interested visitors, and it serves effectively a clear educational purpose. Many of the machines are explained by recorded commentaries, the attendants are numerous and helpful, and almost every exhibit bears a description, however brief. Moreover— this is an important matter, not always dealt with satisfactorily elsewhere—there is no difficulty whatever in identifying the object and attaching the right description to it: the ticketing and labelling of the bicycles, for example, is exemplary. On the other hand it must be pointed out that this is one of the few museums discussed in this book that cannot offer even the simplest printed guide. The omission may be deliberate, even understandable, but it is bound to disappoint some visitors; and especially, perhaps, those who can appreciate most fully the educational value of the Museum and the intelligence, skill, and energy that have gone into creating it.

12

NARROW-GAUGE RAILWAY MUSEUM, TOWYN AND FESTINIOG RAILWAY MUSEUM PORTMADOC

It is convenient to discuss these two museums together. They are similar in character. Both are very small, and both have been assembled in recent years as a part of the revival of the two companies with which they are associated. That revival is an interesting story, and creditable to the times we live in. The word 'revival' must, however, be used in two slightly different senses. Like the Windmill Theatre, the Talyllyn Railway can say with pride, 'We never closed'. Opened in 1866, it is one of the oldest railways in Europe that has been worked continuously in private ownership. In the inter-war years, when most similar railways fell into difficulties, it was fortunate in being controlled by Sir Henry Haydn Jones, MP, who resolutely kept it going even when it was running at a loss. None of the plant was renewed, however, or even adequately repaired, and when Sir Haydn died, at the age of eighty-six, in 1950 the railway faced what seemed almost inevitable closure. But the Talyllyn Railway Preservation Society was established, which acquired control of the railway and has gradually brought it into full and vigorous use for passenger traffic during the summer months from Towyn to Abergynolwyn. It is hoped eventually to reopen the upper section from Abergynolwyn to Nant Gwernol.

The Festiniog Railway, which is substantially older—it was opened for slate traffic in 1836—was not so lucky in the 1920s and 1930s. Its freight and tourist traffic had flourished from the introduction of steam locomotives in 1863 to the first World War;

136

but thereafter, with the decline in the slate industry and the new competition of the motor-bus, it rapidly went downhill. The passenger service was withdrawn in 1939; the slate traffic from Blaenau Festiniog to Portmadoc fell to negligible proportions and ceased altogether in 1946. The Company sought powers to abandon the railway four years later. They were not granted, however, and in 1951–54, under the inspiration of what was being achieved on the Talyllyn Railway, the Festiniog Company was taken over by a new group, with a positive faith in its future, headed by Mr Alan Pegler (to whom admirers of the steam locomotives in this country owe a substantial debt, not on this account alone). This faith was not widely shared at the time. In 1955, after a passenger service at the Portmadoc end of the line had been reinstated, the Central Electricity Generating Board was permitted to build a new reservoir, cutting the railway completely near its northern terminus, on the grounds that it could never be brought back into use. Since then the whole railway has been restored as far as Tan-y-Bwlch; the next section, to Dduallt, has been brought into use; and work has even begun on the construction of a wholly new piece of line, by a new route, to replace the one submerged by the reservoir.

These two enterprises are differently managed, and any observant visitor will find it interesting to compare and contrast them. Both, however, represent a triumph of genuine faith, emphatically vindicated by results. Both have made very substantial use of volunteers in the work of restoration and day-to-day running—and a notably courteous and cheerful staff they make, in the best tradition of the British railways of the past. And both have established museums at their terminal stations on the coast. The Talyllyn Railway's is the larger (it is at present being extended, with the assistance of a grant from the Pilgrim Trust) and the more ambitious, for it does not confine itself to one concern but embraces narrow-gauge railways in general; the scope of the Festiniog's is limited to that Company alone. But then, what a history it can boast, as the pioneer of narrow-gauge railways, mechanically operated, throughout the world!

The Towyn Museum is at present strongest in its locomotives, though some interesting rolling-stock is now in course of being arranged for display. It includes two notable eccentrics: one of the vertical-boilered engines built by the firm of De Winton in

Caernarvon for the Penrhyn Railway (1877)—a predecessor of the Sentinel type that enjoyed some success in rail-motor cars in the 1920s; and one of those designed for Guinness's Brewery in Dublin by the Chief Surveyor, Mr S. Geogehan (1895). Standing outside—temporarily, it is to be hoped—is a French six-coupled tank engine, *Cambrai*. In view of the notable want of interest in its own country in the preservation of locomotives, it is as well that this one should have found, however improbably, a good home at Towyn. But the great jewel of the collection is the little engine *Dot*, built by Beyer Peacock for use in their own works at Manchester: a tiny machine, overwhelmed with an enormous dome, glowing in rich green paint, an intimate memorial of one of the world's great firms of locomotive builders.

The other exhibits are more ordinary: nameplates and builders' plates from a long series of engines, in Ireland as well as Great Britain; a semaphore signal from the County Donegal Railways; notices and documents relating to the Talyllyn Railway itself. By the time this book is in print, no doubt the passenger and goods rolling-stock will be on display in a definitive form: a proper complement to the locomotives at the opposite side of the building.

The Portmadoc Museum contains no locomotives whatever. It is in two rooms so small that even *Dot* would be an embarrassment. In 1966 a splendid machine stood close by in the sidings— the very first Beyer-Garratt locomotive, built for the Tasmanian Railways in 1909. It is not intended for any museum, however, but for work on the railway in due course, turn and turn about with *Prince*—one of the Company's first steam locomotives, built in 1863—and the famous Fairlie double-bogie engines *Merddin Emrys* and *Earl of Merioneth*.

Two vehicles are in the Museum; and, just as it should be, one of them is normal, the other highly unusual—indeed, unique. The normal one is a slate wagon, built about 1857. The pattern had altered little since the opening of the line in 1836 and remained much the same to the end. Opposite stands a box-like vehicle, adorned with little urns at the corner of its roof and painted black. This is a hearse wagon, converted from a quarryman's carriage— with very little trouble: all that was needed was to take out the seats, block up the windows (such as those were), and fit rollers close to the floor of the vehicle, to enable coffins to slide in and out freely. The railway served remote villages and farms up in the hills, not easily accessible to any other form of wheeled transport before the motor-car established itself. Here was one of the services it performed for its society. The van remained in use until the 1920s. One of the burial-grounds to which it conveyed the dead is still to be seen, trimly kept, beside the railway at Boston Lodge.

Other relics here include a 'last vehicle' board and a working model of a locomotive of the first type used on the railway. It was made by the Works Manager at Boston Lodge in 1869 for the Spooner family, who controlled the Company, and used on a 3 foot 8 inch gauge track laid down in the garden of their home at Portmadoc.

The other exhibits are mainly documents, from the Company's full and interesting archives (which are kept up above, on the first floor of the same building): the original manuscript copy of the by-laws, sanctioned by the Board of Trade in 1865; correspondence between George England and Co. and C. E. Spooner over the construction of the first Fairlie locomotive; rules and diagrams relating to signals; archaically-phrased notices—'Dogs will not be suffered to accompany passengers in the carriages', etc. Even in the Victorian age there were hooligans, and the Company threatened them sharply: 'Any passenger cutting the linings, removing or defacing the number plates, breaking the windows or otherwise wilfully damaging or injuring any carriage' was to be fined £5 and made to pay for the damage he had caused.

These are two interesting museums, both well worth a visit. But they differ from all the others considered here in that, as museums, they are subordinate appendages to railways that are still operating. In my introductory chapter I argued that the truest railway museum of all was a working railway: not something static, but something that moved and had an economic purpose, to provide service, to make a profit. Now the Talyllyn and Festiniog Railways do just this. It is true that they have changed their function in the twentieth century. Both were built to transport slate from the quarries down to the coast: neither of them does so now. Instead, they transport visitors in the summer. But there is nothing wrong with that. Tourism has become one of the major industries of our time; and the whole economy of North Wales depends in substantial measure upon it. These two railways offer an experience that is to be had nowhere else, in Europe or further overseas, of travel by railways that are in essentials over a hundred years old and—so far from being on their last legs—are vigorous and successful. Those visitors who come to see them from all over Britain and beyond meet with a great reward. The Talyllyn runs up a beautiful pastoral and wooded country to a terminus on the edge of the wild bare mountains. The Festiniog climbs spectacularly, nosing its way into the very mountains themselves in the manner we associate with Switzerland. But it is a mountain railway built before the Swiss began theirs, a notable pioneer of mechanical traction on the 2 foot gauge, of the iron-framed bogie-coach. Here it is still cheerfully alive—the most notable of all living museums of transport.

13

PENRHYN CASTLE MUSEUM

This is a very new venture, and an interesting one: for it does things that are hardly attempted elsewhere.

Richard Pennant (?1737–1808) acquired the Penrhyn estate (near Bangor) by marriage and purchase, and it was he who began to develop the slate quarries that lie half a dozen miles inland. He was succeeded by a distant relative, George Henry Dawkins Pennant, who built the present Castle, mainly in the years 1827–37, to the designs of Thomas Hopper. Its vast scale (it is easily the biggest and the most important example of the Norman Revival in Great Britain), its massive and beautifully-worked masonry, the stone coming from only just across the sea in Anglesey, the quality of its decoration—all this proclaims its builder's almost boundless wealth. It may well survive as a monument to the slate industry when the slate itself is no longer worked.

The transport exhibits are housed in the stables.[1] They can be considered under two heads: the track and vehicles of the Penrhyn Railway and the locomotives. The Penrhyn system was built to the 2 foot gauge[2] and comprised, besides the network of tracks in the quarries themselves, a line some six miles long down to the sea at Port Penrhyn—which was constructed entirely for the slate trade, at the north-western edge of the park, where it falls to the sea. The track itself was of several different forms at different times,

---

[1] If you have come to see them and nothing else, they can be reached from the car-park. Separate entrance fees are charged for the house and the Museum. If you are coming from the house the route is a devious one, signed for part of the way, and not for the rest, with the words 'Toilets Locomotives Exit'. Unless your visit is made at the height of the summer season you will be wise to inquire beforehand of the National Trust or of the Warden at the Castle when the transport exhibits are to be seen. The hours of opening are apt to be much shorter than those for the house as a whole.

[2] Cf. C. E. Lee, *Narrow-Gauge Railways in North Wales* (1945), 9–12.

and a commendable effort has been made to display and explain them here. An extensive stretch is laid out in the open courtyard, showing a variety of turnouts and crossings, some highly unusual; and, inside, the Penrhyn vehicles are mounted on a number of different sorts of track—T-headed rails resting on chairs and iron sleepers, flat-bottomed rails spiked direct to sleepers of wood. The vehicles are a comprehensive series, including one for the carriage of slates in the normal way, others for taking the rock to be cut, for removing waste to the tips, for conveying Fullersite and coal. In addition there are three passenger vehicles. One is a well-appointed saloon for the Penrhyn family, for visitors and officials. Next to it is an open carriage with wooden benches for the slate workers, which was provided not by the management but by a subscription among the men themselves, to take them up from Bangor. This began in the seventies, long before the days of the motor-bus; but such vehicles still continued at work until 1951. The third passenger vehicle is a curiosity: a 'velocipede' from the 4 foot gauge Padarn Railway, which ran up to the Dinorwic quarries, to be worked by four men with handles connected to the axles by chains. It subsequently conveyed gangs repairing the track, but it proved unsafe in service—particularly, one imagines, in running down the gradient to the sea—and was laid aside for many years, out of use.

One locomotive from the Penrhyn Railway is also here, resplendently painted in black, red, and blue: an 0–4–0T with double frames and outside cylinders, built by the Hunslet Company of Leeds in 1882. This engine, *Charles*, has two sisters, *Linda* and *Blanche*, which are both now working on the Festiniog Railway. Another Penrhyn locomotive, *Jubilee*, is to be seen at Towyn.

With one exception, all the other railway engines here were in industrial service. The oldest of them comes from the works of the North Thames Gas Board at Beckton: a neat little machine, spruce in its bright green livery, manufactured by Neilson's of Glasgow in 1870. Many visitors from the East Midlands will remember the Kettering iron furnaces, recently closed and demolished. Here is one of their engines, built by Black Hawthorn and Co. of Gateshead in 1885. Next to its stands another stalwart, *Hawarden* (Hudswell Clarke, Leeds, 1899, rebuilt 1948), which worked for sixty-four years for Messrs John Summers and Sons Ltd of Stalybridge, who presented her to the Museum. All these are four-coupled engines. The remaining industrial machine is a little larger, and later: an inside-cylinder 0–6–0T, *Vesta*, which was built at the same works in 1916 for the Hawarden Bridge steelworks and may be said to represent this type of steam locomotive at its fullest development.

The last steam engine here comes not from an industrial firm but from the greatest of British railway companies. It is one of F. W. Webb's 4 foot 3 inch 0–6–2 tank engines, built at Crewe in 1888. Its presence here is very much to be welcomed. Far too few standard-gauge goods engines have been selected for preservation in the country as a whole, and this one forms a most suitable counterpart to the narrow-gauge industrial locomotives in its company. It is a pity that it cannot be seen at all well in its present position under the arched entrance to the stable court, and the purist will certainly criticize its livery; but these are defects that could be remedied. The great thing is that the engine has been brought in and given a suitable home.

'A suitable home.' Can the stables of a country house really be regarded as a proper place for keeping locomotives? If these were the stables of Warwick or Syon one could certainly say 'no'. But Penrhyn Castle is a country house of a different kind: a palace built 140 years ago from the profits of the chief industry of the country in which it stands. In the changed social circumstances of our own time, where could it be more appropriate to commemorate that industry itself, and the techniques of transport on which it and its fellows were dependent for their very existence?

14

MARITIME AND TRANSPORT MUSEUMS, HULL

The museums of Hull have an interesting tradition behind them. As in many English provincial towns, they developed out of private collections, brought together by a Literary and Philosophical Society. The Corporation of Hull did not make itself responsible for museums until 1900. It then appointed as Curator Mr T. Sheppard, who had spent his earlier life with the North Eastern Railway. Mr Sheppard's services to Hull were outstanding. By 1939 the number of museums in the city had grown to seven; and no less than three of them were wholly or largely concerned with transport.

The oldest of them had come by private benefaction from Mr Christopher Pickering, a Hull shipowner. To his instructions a chapel-like building was erected in the Pickering Park, which he had presented to the city, and it was opened as a Museum of Fisheries and Shipping in 1912. Thirteen years later the Hull Corporation decided to establish a Museum of Commerce and Transport, to be placed in the Corn Exchange. Finally, in 1933 a small Railway Museum was set up at Paragon station. This last was unhappily destroyed, with its contents, in an air raid. The other two, however, survive.

To take the older one first. The collection at the Museum of Fisheries and Shipping (now called the Maritime Museum) provides, within a very modest compass, a useful introduction to the subject. It is strongest on the history of whaling, a business in which Hull was heavily involved from the beginning of the seventeenth century to the later part of the nineteenth. There are some interesting paintings here of whalers at work in the Arctic—though none is as fine a picture as that in the city's Ferens Art

144

25a Shuttleworth Collection: Cottin et Desgouttes racing car (1911)

b Beaulieu: Vauxhall 'Prince Henry' (1914). As the photograph demonstrates, the car is still capable of fine performance on the road

26a Science Museum: Hildebrand prototype steam motor-cycle (1889)

b Science Museum: White steam car (1903)

Gallery, showing Samuel Standidge's four ships in 1788. Perhaps the most instructive group of exhibits here is that showing the uses to which the carcass of the whale was put; all this activity is treated, quite rightly, not as an object in itself but as serving a large economic purpose. So here are displayed many of the things that are, or were, done with whalebone and with whale oils and fats. Hull whaling died in 1868, when the ship *Truelove* completed her seventy-second and last voyage to the Arctic. She was then a centenarian; American by origin, built at Philadelphia in 1764, captured during the War of Independence and engaged in whaling from Hull since 1794. Her career did not end when she ceased to be a whaler. In 1873 she crossed the Atlantic and met with a generous reception in the town of her birth. Its citizens presented her captain with a huge flag to commemorate her visit, which is now stretched across the breadth of one of the end walls of the Museum.

The ships' models include a superb one, over 10 feet long, of the Cunarder *Persia*, built in 1856—the first iron mail-steamer owned by the Company and almost its last paddle-ship; a number of the elegant ships of the Wilson Line, of Hull; and several of trawlers built by Cook, Wilton and Gemmell of Beverley. That is a reminder that many ancient towns we no longer think of as ports have a tradition of shipbuilding, sometimes—as in this instance—coming right down to the present day. Similarly, Hessle is no longer a centre of shipbuilding. Yet there was intense activity in that business all along the shores of the Humber, even in its small creeks, throughout the eighteenth century; and here is a fine oil-painting of the 40-gun H M S *Hector* after her launch from the yard of Hugh Blaydes of Hessle in 1743.

The Transport Museum is in the High Street of the old town. The Corn Exchange, in which it is housed, is a handsome building dating from 1855, in the classical style that lingered on late in Hull. The collection occupies about two-thirds of the space available. The remainder, beyond a screen, contains the archaeological museum, and no visitor—however little interested he may be in antiquities—should fail to see the Roman pavements displayed there, removed with brilliant technical skill from Rudston in the East Riding.

Within this confined area—about 4,000 square feet in all—a surprisingly large collection is shown: some thirty large vehicles and twenty smaller ones, with accessories in cases round the walls. The very best use has been made of the limited accommodation available. The arrangement cannot be ideal, yet it is possible to examine most of the vehicles in the round and there is adequate space for movement between them.

The outstanding exhibits are the trams and the horse-drawn road carriages. The tramway vehicles number only two. The earlier was built in 1867 by Starbuck of Birkenhead for the Ryde Pier Company: the oldest tramcar now surviving in Great Britain, and the second oldest in Europe. It runs on four wheels, and in its design there is a distinct flavour of the baroque: with its bowed platforms, double curved roof, and corner-posts carved with grapes, the tram would seem to belong to Vienna rather than Ryde. Close to it stands a steam engine from the Portstewart Tramway in Northern Ireland, built by Kitson's of Leeds in 1882—a rare survival when one considers that in the nineties more than 500 such units were at work in the British Isles. It complies with the rigid restrictions imposed by the Act of 1879: its motion is completely enclosed, it is governed down to a maximum speed of 10 m.p.h., and it is fitted with a condenser to prevent it from giving out visible steam or smoke.

These are the only vehicles here that ran on rails. Of the horse-drawn carriages, the oldest is a barouche dating from the early years of the nineteenth century. It belonged to Sir Christopher Sykes of Sledmere, high on the Wolds between Malton and Driffield; and the carriage is fitted with a hinged wooden apron covering the legs and thighs of the occupants in the fierce cold of winter.

There are four other vehicles here dating from the great age of horse travel: a cabriolet and a post-chaise, and two stage-coaches. One of these plied between London and York; the other was the *Quicksilver*, running to Devonport, a mail-coach of the last type dating from 1835. The Devonport coach has been re-painted; its doors are defaced with lettering that is a coarse travesty of the elegant original—as the drawings and prints hung elsewhere in the Museum will show.

Apart from the public coaches, the most interesting carriages here are the Victorian ones. The state coach belonging to Lord Yarborough (at Brocklesby, across the Humber) is London work of the best kind, worthily continuing the fine tradition of the eighteenth century; and it is matched by a Paris-built landau of 1868. There is a good hansom cab, which plied on the streets of Hull, and another, running on three wheels, said to have been used by Edward VII. Finally, by way of startling contrast to these grave and stately carriages, we come on a Sicilian lemon-cart, plastered with the most riotous decoration, including paintings of scenes from *La Traviata* and *La Bohème*. Not a square inch of the outside is left without ornamentation; even the spokes of the wheels carry raised figures. An adjoining case contains the harness and trappings that go with the cart. Nothing could demonstrate better than this simple juxtaposition the different worlds of thinking of the Mediterranean and the North.

Excluding the motor-bicycles, the mechanically-propelled road vehicles number nine, and they all date from the years 1897–1901. The earliest is a Panhard motor-car; there is a Cleveland electric car and two steam cars (a White and a Gardner-Serpollet); among lighter vehicles, a Sturmey cycle-car, with wicker body-work, and a Marshall-Benz dog-cart.

Some twenty bicycles, tricycles, and quadricycles demonstrate well the essential steps in the evolution of these machines, from the hobby-horse that became a brief craze about 1818 through the boneshaker, the penny-farthing, and the safety bicycle of the eighties to the motor-cycle and the motor-scooter of the twentieth century. The tricycles include two whose steering was performed by the rider's abdomen, working in a curved iron frame; one of them was used by a North Lincolnshire postman about 1885.

Finally, the Museum contains two sedan chairs, one formerly belonging to the Corporation of Huntingdon, and two rare local handbills of 1809–10 giving particulars of the Sculcoates Subscription Sedan Chairs, with the rates and rules for hiring them.

The smaller exhibits ranged round the walls include some interesting documents, such as the last monthly account of the London, Lincoln and Hull Royal Mail Coach, which ceased to run in 1846, and the first Registers of Driving Licences and Motor Vehicles (letter AT) kept by the Corporation of Hull from 1904 onwards. Among the railway items are several of local interest: a preposterous ceremonial wheelbarrow, each side in the form of a rhinoceros, used at the cutting of the first sod of the Hull and Hornsea Railway in 1862, a number connected with the Hull and Barnsley, and an armorial panel from a coach of the Hull and

Holderness Railway, which maintained an independent life from 1854 to 1862.

A long series of these panels was assembled by Mr Sheppard and placed in his Railway Museum. All were, alas, destroyed. What remains in Hull is an instructive collection of the older forms of transport; and since York is only forty miles away, it seems right now to concentrate attention on them. Mr Sheppard left his mark on his town and his profession. The present collections owe much to him; but his monument is the remarkable series of 'Hull Museum Publications', which begun in 1901 and ran through to No. 213 in 1940. These were pamphlets, uniform in page-size but in nothing else, many of them offprints from newspapers or professional journals. Some were accessions lists, quarterly or annual, others were guides to the collections. Many embodied research, like Mr Sheppard's *Early Means of Transport in the East Riding* (No. 154, 1928) and his *Early Tramcars* (No. 210, 1940). They were cheap—often issued at a penny. To run through the complete series gives one a powerful impression of the work of a lively provincial museum: undertaken on a shoe-string budget but making the most of every opportunity, adding visibly year by year to the cultural resources of its town and neighbourhood. It is indeed a pleasure to see that the series is now being continued by the present Director, Mr Bartlett. May we hope that it will soon include, once more, brief guides to the Maritime and Transport Museums?

15

RAILWAY MUSEUM, YORK

The Railway Museum at York is a child of the North Eastern
Railway, and its history stretches back well over forty years, to
the time when that Company was nearing its dissolution under the
terms of the Railways Act of 1921. The Company had always
commanded an intense loyalty among its servants, accentuated by
its geographical situation, occupying almost exclusively the whole
of Northumberland and Durham, and by its history, which entitled
it to an unquestionable seniority among the railway companies
of the world. For it not only incorporated the Stockton and Darlington, the oldest of all mechanically-operated public railways;
it was the heir to the whole railway tradition of Tyneside, of
George Stephenson and his predecessors reaching back far into
the seventeenth century. When, therefore, the Company was about
to lose its independence, to be merged with a group of others whose
interests sprawled across Great Britain from Lossiemouth to
London and from Wrexham to Lowestoft, it was natural that some
North Eastern men should turn to think of the preservation of at
least a few memorials of their Company's long and most honourable
history. They were led by J. B. Harper, Assistant Superintendent
at York, and their activity resulted in the making of a collection
that was at first accommodated in the basement of the North
Eastern offices in that city—the basement that in more recent
years has provided a repository for one division of the British
Transport historical records and a students' room for consulting
them. This collection remained private—like the similar one that
was growing up at Paddington; but the celebrations of the
centenary of the Stockton and Darlington Railway in 1925 stimulated the establishment of a public museum, which was opened
in the present premises at York in 1928. These comprise the

locomotive erecting and repair shops of the York and North Midland Railway, dating from 1842 onwards.

It is best to follow the advice of Mr L. T. C. Rolt, in his delightful little handbook to the Museum,[1] and start with the small exhibits, especially the notable display of prints and drawings, which supply an excellent framework within which the full-sized rolling-stock and equipment can be placed. It is a pity that the name of the artist or the engraver is not given; Bourne and Tait deserve credit for their beautiful lithographs. Some of the original paintings are delicate and well executed: water-colours of Richmond station, for instance, and of Kingston Street goods station in Hull, a carefully accurate picture in oils of a *Jenny Lind* locomotive, its maker's plate dated clearly 1852.

The Newcastle and Carlisle Railway is well represented in the Museum at York: with a series of J. W. Carmichael's prints, with posters concerning the injunction secured by Mr Bacon Grey in 1835 to prevent the railway from employing locomotives, which stopped the traffic altogether for six weeks, and another detailing the arrangements for the official opening of the line throughout in 1838, the unparalleled 'procession of trains' (there were thirteen of them, consisting altogether of 130 carriages) from Redheugh, the Company's terminus opposite Newcastle, to Carlisle. 'No Person can be allowed to go on the engines or tender', we read. If obedience was paid to that instruction, it was paid to no other. The disorderly throng of passengers climbed in through the windows of locked carriages, usurping the places reserved for august civic guests. The trains started back from Carlisle in a thunderstorm, two of them collided, and the last did not arrive at Redheugh till six o'clock on the following morning.

The Newcastle and Carlisle Railway is remembered as the original employer of Thomas Edmondson, who introduced the first tickets printed on a card and dated in a press at Milton (now Brampton Junction) in 1837. Here are some of Edmondson's early tickets, and also some examples of Parker's Railway Check Patent Tickets—Parker being an associate of Edmondson, who

---

[1] Published by the British Transport Commission in 1958 (2nd ed., 1962). It is useful to refer also to the earlier *Catalogue* (first published in 1933 and revised several times down to 1956). It contains a great many mistakes, but its detailed descriptions are sometimes valuable; and it offers something like an inventory of the collection as it then was.

claimed that he invented the machine for which Edmondson secured the patent.

From the same Company comes a notice calling for tenders in horsing two coaches to run between Carlisle and Glasgow in connection with trains to and from London. It is dated June 18, 1844, the day on which the Newcastle and Darlington Junction line was opened, providing railway communication between London and Carlisle, via Rugby, York, and Gateshead. This route continued to be used until the Lancaster and Carlisle line was completed at the close of 1847. One wonders how successful it was in winning London–Glasgow passengers from the railway and steamer passage by Fleetwood and Ardrossan, which had been in operation since 1841.

Railway notice-boards adorn the walls, including examples from many companies other than the North Eastern. An unusual list of tolls comes from the West Durham Railway, which in the course of quoting the rates for the customary commodities—coal, lime, wrought iron, lead, cattle, sheep, and so on—gives the fares for passengers, 2d a mile, and the charges for making use of the company's bridge over the Wear close to Willington: 1d for pedestrians, 3d for horsemen.

But the most important items in this section are those concerned with the permanent way, with civil engineering, and with signalling. There are the materials here for a first-rate display of the evolution of the railway track. They are drawn from all over the north-east of England, with important additions from elsewhere —some items, for example, from the collection of C. E. Stretton, which were transferred from the Leicester City Museums in 1949. Alas, however, these are the materials only. They lie about in any order; scarcely any of them are labelled—even in the simplest form—to indicate where they came from.

Displayed like this, to anyone but an expert they form no more than a collection of scrap metal of diverting variety. To put it bluntly, these important exhibits might as well not be here. For they *are* important. Here are almost all the main early types of rail in use in this country, from the wooden track at the outset to iron in all its forms, resting on sleepers of stone, metal plates, and wood. One glass case contains a series of rails in section, exemplifying the different types used by the North Eastern and some of its constituent companies; but that piece of historical explanation stands alone. It is sad to see a subject of such fundamental importance to the history of railways so shabbily treated; and it must regretfully be added that what is done poorly at York is not done at Clapham or Swindon at all.

On the other hand, in strong contrast, the treatment of bridge-building here is extremely good. Indeed, no other museum described in this book can show original exhibits in this field that are comparable in historical importance to those at York. The earliest is an iron girder, and part of the stone abutment, of the bridge erected to carry the Great North Road over Milby Cut by Boroughbridge in Yorkshire. This dates from 1769. The famous Iron Bridge in Coalbrookdale was brought into use ten years later; and though it is a structure on an altogether different scale of magnitude from this one, we should not forget the earlier Milby Cut bridge when we call it the earliest in the world.

In the centre of this hall stand all four bays of what is unquestionably the first railway bridge to be built wholly of iron. The excellent engineer's drawing that hangs on a wall near by shows the parapet and the abutment, which are now missing. It was constructed in 1823–25 by John and Isaac Burrell of Newcastle to George Stephenson's specification for the Brusselton section of the Stockton and Darlington Railway. The weight of the track rests on iron piers, held together by bow-shaped struts. A tentative experiment, no doubt, and not repeated: yet the bridge stood for three-quarters of a century, carrying its traffic and resisting the floods and storms of that wild mountain country. The bridge was dismantled in 1900 and, with a true sense of its historic importance, it was then preserved.

Close by stand sections of two other early railway bridges: another iron one, much more elegant, from Ridley Hall near Haydon Bridge on the Newcastle and Carlisle line, put up in 1838 and replaced by a steel successor ninety-four years later; and a half-span of one of the laminated timber bridges provided by John and Benjamin Green for the Newcastle and North Shields Railway. This had an even longer life, being replaced only in 1937. The series of remarkable North-country bridges is appropriately rounded off with a model of one span of the Belah viaduct designed by Thomas Bouch for the railway over Stainmore; and those who remember that wonderful line will be glad to see, on the opposite wall, the big iron sign erected by the

London and North Eastern Company to mark its summit—the highest point reached by any standard-gauge railway in England.

The collection of signalling apparatus at York is the best in the country, though unhappily it is not very well displayed, and the description of it is lamentably inadequate. Almost all the exhibits are bunched together at the far end of this hall, beyond the Gaunless bridge. The overcrowding is easily explained—there is simply no room to show these tall and awkward objects satisfactorily. It is none the less unfortunate: for this is a vitally important branch of railway working that receives insufficient attention elsewhere.

The series of signals begins with a very early one from the Stockton and Darlington Railway's Croft branch, comprising no more than a lamp with a movable shutter. The same Company also furnishes a route-indicator, shaped like a fan, for use at a junction. There is an interesting series of signals to be installed at level crossings, showing various types of red banner, from the North Eastern and the Jedburgh Railways. The later North Eastern signals include one of the type that fell at the vertical or 'off' position into a slot in its post—a type that is still be be seen fairly widely on that Company's system, where it was retained long after it had fallen into disuse elsewhere; and a pair of the gas-operated Hall automatic signals installed between Darlington and York in 1904 (cf. p. 161). There are signals from other parts of the country too: one of the somersault pattern from the Great Northern, a 'gate' signal from the Great Eastern at Huntingdon, a Stevens signal from the Bishop's Castle Railway mounted on a lattice post, the semaphore arm at the top, the spectacles a third of the way down, the lamp being raised and lowered, when required for lighting, by a windlass and chain inside the post itself.

The earliest of the signalling frames here is one from the Manchester, Sheffield and Lincolnshire Railway dating from about 1845, operated by the feet in stirrups attached to chains hung over pulleys in a vertical iron frame. There is an early interlocking frame by Stevens and a large one of thirty-two levers from Seamer Junction outside Scarborough, the purpose served by each lever indicated on an elaborate brass plate fitted horizontally along the front. The smaller exhibits include a series of telegraph and telephone instruments, diagrams of signals and points from a number of North Eastern stations, a slate panel for indicating the passage of trains on the Great Northern main line at Newark, and a series of mile-posts, notably of the pattern peculiar to the North Eastern, placed at right angles to the line.

But how much more could be made of this fascinating section of the Museum! As long as it remains in the premises it occupies at present, no doubt it would be hard to improve the display very much. It would be possible, however, to label the exhibits better. Many of them bear no description at all, or one so brief as to be almost useless. And it would be neither difficult nor expensive to produce a little handbook to this signalling section, even if it ran to no more than a dozen pages. Without these things, this collection, assembled with so much labour and foresight, remains little more than a quaint display of assorted curiosities; with the aid of them it would at once take its place as the best grammar we have of the evolution of railway signalling.

There are also a few vehicles in this hall: notably a coach from the City and South London Railway, the first tube of the modern type in the world; important early carriages from the Bodmin and Wadebridge and Stockton and Darlington Companies, the body of a four-compartment carriage from the North Eastern Railway; a replica of a dandy-cart, in which the horse could ride when the journey was being made by gravity, and a chaldron wagon of 1826 from Cramlington Colliery in Northumberland, a pair of braziers hung from hooks on its back cross-beam as a primitive kind of tail-lamp.

Twelve original locomotives are preserved here. Five come from the North Eastern, three from its partner the Great Northern, and one from a colliery in County Durham; the rest are 'foreigners' from Brighton, Crewe, and Staffordshire.

The earliest is George Stephenson's locomotive for the Hetton Colliery, which was built in 1822 and lasted in service—albeit with much modification—for ninety years. In 1925 it took the head of the procession at the Centenary celebration at Darlington, running under its own steam. Of the North Eastern engines, the oldest is a curiosity: the little tank engine with single driving wheels, *Aerolite*. Nominally it dates from 1851, but it has been so considerably altered by subsequent rebuilding that nothing of the original machine remains. It reached its present form in 1902. For many years before it was withdrawn from service in 1933 its duty had been to haul the Chief Mechanical Engineer's saloon.

It is the only two-cylinder compound locomotive to survive in the British Isles.

Railway practice of the 1870s is well illustrated by two of the North Eastern engines here: a six-coupled goods locomotive (No. 1275) and a four-coupled express passenger (No. 910). These were built within a year of each other, but they are notably different in design. The goods engine is a late example (for this country: but cf. p. 191) of the 'long-boiler' type introduced by Robert Stephenson in 1841. The North Eastern still maintained two sets of locomotive works—one at Darlington, inherited from the Stockton and Darlington Company, with which it had been amalgamated in 1863, the other at Gateshead; and their practices remained in many ways dissimilar. This is a Darlington-type engine, built by Dübs of Glasgow to the designs of William Bouch. No. 910 is one of Edward Fletcher's, built at Gateshead, belonging to the 901 class, which monopolized the express work on the Northe Eastern main line for a dozen years and more. These engines enjoyed a great reputation, and deserved it: not for speed—they were seldom called on for any outstanding feats in that line—but for their reliability and low consumption of coal. No. 1463, which stands close by, is really a variant of the same basic design, built in unusual circumstances after Fletcher's retirement.[1]

The last of the North Eastern engines, No. 1621, is a 4–4–0 with very large driving wheels, 7 feet 1¼ inches in diameter, designed by T. W. Worsdell and built in 1893. This was one of the engines engaged in the Race to Aberdeen in 1895—a rival of *Hardwicke*, now in the Museum at Clapham—and it was responsible for a thrilling and dangerous performance on August 19th, on the last lap from Newcastle to Edinburgh, when it took its train on to the S-curves at Portobello at 80 m.p.h. and shot out of the Calton Tunnel into Waverley station still at a rate of more than a mile a minute.[2]

On that night, as on most during the Races both of 1888 and of 1895, the East Coast express was worked from London to York by the 8 foot single driving engines of the Great Northern Railway, designed by Patrick Stirling. The first of the class, No. 1 of

---

[1] For the circumstances see E. L. Ahrons, *Locomotive and Train Working in the Latter Part of the Nineteenth Century*, i [1951], 76–9.

[2] Cf. O. S. Nock, *The Railway Race to the North* (paperback ed., n.d.), 104–5.

1870, is here, and for many visitors it will be the most memorable thing in the Museum. These are among the most famous of all locomotives, for grace and performance. Together with Stirling's 7 foot 6 inch singles, they carried the burden of what was, throughout the seventies and eighties, the fastest train service in the world, into and out of King's Cross. They were able to take the racing of 1895 as a thing of course, calmly and in their stride. They had an exceptionally long and glorious innings as express engines, and as the later survivors came to be withdrawn from service, about the time of the first World War, there was general agreement that one of them should be preserved. Which one more fitting than the first of them all?

No. 1621 was a large locomotive for her day. Her boiler had a heating surface almost as large as that of the celebrated Caledonian engine *Dunalastair* of 1896, which is usually thought of as marking a distinct stage on the way to the emergence of the big express engine. But though a flyer, she soon proved unequal to hauling the normal express trains of her time, which were rapidly growing heavier. The kind of machine that succeeded her is to be seen in two examples here, both from the Great Northern Railway and both of the 4–4–2 or Atlantic type. One is the pioneer of the type, No. 990, named after the company's General Manager *Henry Oakley*—the pioneer not only on the Great Northern but in Britain as a whole. The other, No. 251, is the first of the enlarged version that proved itself, from 1902 onwards, as splendidly successful in different conditions as the Stirling singles had been in the previous generation. For these engines too had a life in first-class express service of some thirty years; and whereas the Stirling engines in the later nineteenth century had always been kept in the pink of condition and worked the trains they were designed for, these had to stand up to the totally unexpected strains and demands of the first World War, when they found themselves hauling expresses of over 500 tons out of King's Cross.

The three intruders all present points of great interest. The most surprising of them—from the remote south of England— is the London, Brighton and South Coast Company's *Gladstone*, conspicuous at once in its yellow ochre paint. It ran from 1882 to 1926. After it had been withdrawn the Stephenson Locomotive Society acquired and restored it; and since the only railway museum in the country at that time was this one at York, it found a home here, on loan from the Society. Like the North Eastern 2–4–0s and the Stirling single, it represents the mid-Victorian express engine—but to William Stroudley's most unorthodox design, with its driving wheels placed in front. The class enjoyed a remarkably long life; the last of them was not withdrawn from service until 1933. They too performed great feats of haulage, for their size. This very engine for years worked the 8.45 a.m. express from Brighton to London—for first-class passengers only, most of them season-ticket holders—with loads sometimes exceeding 300 tons behind the tender. Notice the meticulous care of the locomotive's finish, in every respect; and the name of the driver, William Love, painted inside his cab. Under Stroudley each engine was committed to the personal charge of one man, which ensured that he cared for it like a piece of his own property, or a member of his family.

The second of these 'foreigners' is *Columbine*, a little 2–2–2 of 1845. This was the very first engine to be constructed at Crewe Works. Though Francis Trevithick (the great Richard's son) was nominally responsible for the design, in reality it was largely the work of Alexander Allan, who carried some of the leading features of the type over into Scotland with him, where they survived on the Highland Railway until the closing years of the nineteenth century.

And finally *Agenoria*, whose chimney shoots up skyward to an unexampled height. Here is the oldest locomotive in the world that still keeps more or less its original form—though it is not entirely unaltered, the wheels, for example, being a replacement of those that were originally fitted. It was built in 1829 (the same year as the *Rocket*) by Foster and Rastrick of Stourbridge for the Shutt End Colliery at Kingswinford, Staffs. The line was a short one, and the engine never worked anywhere else throughout the thirty-five years of its active life. There were three other machines like it, one of which, *Stourbridge Lion*, was the first locomotive to work in the United States.[1]

The York Railway Museum is housed and equipped less handsomely than many of the others described in this book. It was started in a very modest way, as the pioneer venture of the kind in this country; and modesty clings to it still. Its premises are something less

[1] *Agenoria* is on loan to York from the Science Museum.

than convenient for their purpose, and it is unique among all the musems we are considering in that *it has recently been reduced in size*. The small exhibits were formerly housed in part of the original station building of 1841. The Museum has now been deprived of that accommodation, and obliged to concentrate itself into one building, with the inevitable result that some of what was formerly shown to the public is now no longer on display. This is thoroughly deplorable, a grave disservice to one of the major educational museums in the North of England.

One thing is done supremely well at York. This museum alone can lead the visitor back continuously, stage by stage, over the whole history of railways in Britain—beyond the passenger-carrying train and the steam locomotive to the colliery lines and wooden wagonways of Northumberland and Durham, out of which, in the eighteenth century, the modern railway began to emerge.

16

MUSEUM OF SCIENCE
AND ENGINEERING
NEWCASTLE UPON TYNE

This Museum was inaugurated in 1934. It stands on the Town
Moor—the vast and noble space opening out above Barras
Bridge, bounded on the east by the Great North Road. The building
that houses it (a legacy of an exhibition) is a rather shoddy concrete
structure surmounted by a low red dome. If anyone doubts the
real progress that has been made in the design of cheap buildings,
he should compare the main building of this Museum with the
addition made to it to accommodate *Turbinia* in 1962.

Let us look at this annex first, for it houses the most remarkable
thing in the Museum: one that would by itself justify a special
visit, from no matter how great a distance. Charles Parsons (the
son of an Irish peer) began to develop the notion of the turbine
in 1884, while working as a junior partner in an engineering firm
at Gateshead. In that year he took out his first patents and built
a turbo-generator: the prototype of some three hundred more
that were produced by his Company during the next five years.
About 1888 he began to consider the possibilities of applying
the principle to marine propulsion. This development had to be
postponed owing to the dissolution of his partnership and his
consequent difficulties over patent rights. He took it up again,
however, in 1893, beginning his experiments on the design of the
hull with a pair of models—2 feet and 6 feet long—which he
tested with a fishing-rod on a pond at Ryton. These models are
displayed here, under the prow of the completed ship: wonderful
memorials of the evolution of a great idea.

Turbinia was built in 1894, wholly on Tyneside: the hull at
Wallsend, the turbine itself in Parsons's works at Heaton. When

tested in November of that year she was a failure. It was not until her propellers had been re-designed and new turbines built that she fulfilled the hopes that had been set on her. The Admiralty was kept informed of the successive stages of this progress, but it showed so little interest that Parsons made up his mind to blaze the achievement in an audacious way that the Navy would never forget. The occasion he chose for the purpose was the Diamond Jubilee naval review at Portsmouth; and there he took *Turbinia* along the rows of warships, with their guests from all over the world, weaving his way in and out at over 30 knots, effortlessly eluding the fast picket boat sent out to teach him manners. The demonstration was conclusive. Next year the Admiralty ordered turbines from Parsons's Company for the new destroyers *Viper* and *Cobra*. Within ten years of that dazzling show the world's largest liner *Mauretania* emerged from Tyneside, driven by turbines. They helped her to gain the Blue Riband of the Atlantic, and to hold it for more than twenty years.

Here, then, is the original *Turbinia*: an historic ship, worthily displayed. Windows have been pierced in her side to show some of the mechanism and internal arrangements, though her original engines are not here. (One of her turbines is in the City Museum at Glasgow.) This new exhibition shows that Tyneside is justifiably and rightly proud of one of the great gifts it has made to the modern world.

If *Turbinia* is the outstanding object in the Newcastle museum, she is by no means the only thing worth seeing. Among the other exhibits in marine engineering one must mention the relics of famous ships associated with the Tyne—*Calliope, Carmania, Mauretania*—and the long series of models of others constructed on the river: a train-ferry and an ice-breaker for Russia, cruisers for Japan, a steam yacht built for the Sultan of Turkey in 1905, egregiously sumptuous and ornate. The full-sized original exhibits range from an engine from the paddle tug *Lingdale*, built in 1882 and in service at Dover and Middlesbrough for seventy-two years, to an early eighteenth-century anchor dredged up by a trawler off the north-east coast in 1931. Behind and beside this last is displayed a set of French prints a little later in date, showing very clearly the process of making anchors of this kind.

The majority of the most interesting exhibits in land transport

27a Birmingham: Dennis fire-engine of the Birmingham Fire Brigade (1913)

b Beaulieu: the 2nd Lord Montagu's design for a London–Birmingham trunk road in 1921. Most of the essential elements of the modern motorway are here: the road is entirely reserved to motor traffic, it has dual carriageways and flyovers. More than forty years passed before Lord Montagu's vision was realised in the M1

28*a* Beaulieu: an example of the ordinary man's car of the 1920s—a 7 h.p. Jowett selling at £120

b Brighton: Daimler 50 h.p. 12-cyl. car (1935). This car belonged to Queen Mary It is photographed here outside Buckingham Palace after it had passed out c royal service

are also of a strongly local character. The chief exception is perhaps the colliery wagon built for the Fordell Railway in Fife, to the 4 foot 4 inch gauge, about 1833 and used down to the closing of the line in 1946. It stands close to a locomotive, one of six turned out for the Killingworth Colliery in 1830 by the works of Robert Stephenson and Co. in Newcastle.[1] Around these two, in Room 4, stand pictures, models, and relics in close array. The signalling exhibits are of special interest, including an early disc signal from the Forth goods yard, Newcastle, one of the first to be operated by a lever, and one of Hall's automatic signals, in use on the main line between Alne and Thirsk from 1903 to 1933. It was worked by carbonic dioxide gas and controlled by electric track circuit. How curious to find, on the close inspection that is possible here, that though the semaphores are mounted on a tubular steel post they are themselves still made of wood!

This room also contains two important automobile exhibits: the engine and boiler of a White steam car, dating from about 1910, and a complete 15 h.p. motor-car built by Armstrong Whitworth and Co. in 1911. The body of this car (made by Angus Sanderson and Co. of Newcastle) is of interest as it provides an early example of the use of side doors.

It is, I hope, no injustice to the other great Tyneside engineering firms—to Robert Stephenson and Hawthorn Leslie, to Swan, Hunter and Wigham Richardson and Palmer's of Jarrow—to say that Armstrong's dominate the mind here, as their enormous Elswick Works must stamp themselves on the memory of anyone who has ever seen them. For they spanned, as few other firms could lay any claim to do, almost the whole range of engineering from the middle of the nineteenth century to the first World War. This car is an example of one of their minor byproducts. Their ships are to be seen again and again here, in model and picture. In the front hall of the Museum, facing the arriving visitor, is the first rifled breech-loading field-gun, made

---

[1] The accompanying description claims this locomotive as the fourth oldest in the world. This is a mistake. Seven that are certainly older survive in this country: *Puffing Billy*, *Rocket*, and *Sans Pareil* in the Science Museum (see p. 37), the Hetton engine and *Agenoria* at York (pp. 154, 157), *Wylam Dilly* in the Royal Scottish Museum at Edinburgh (p. 164), and *Locomotion*, which stands on Darlington station. As we do not know in which month of 1830 the Newcastle engine was completed, it is impossible to say whether it preceded or followed *Invicta*, which is still to be seen in the Dane John Gardens at Canterbury.

in 1855 to the designs of Armstrong himself: a weapon much in advance of its time, taken up after protracted argument by the British government (one thinks again of Parsons and his turbines) and then dropped, with inconceivable stupidity, in 1863 in favour of a return to the antiquated method of loading by the muzzle. And yet, even in the face of such rebuffs as this, Armstrong retained his massive Victorian public spirit to the very end of his life.

This is the very model of a local museum: based firmly on Tyneside, displaying its brains and skill and tenacity, yet not without reference to the rest of Great Britain and the world beyond. Good use has been made here of a very limited space. But indeed it is far too limited. Apart from *Turbinia*, the exhibits are sadly overcrowded, and it is difficult to see one in isolation from its neighbours. Much has been achieved, valiantly, with limited means.[1] Cannot the City, the University, and Tyneside find more?

---

[1] A word of praise should be given to the *Catalogue*, issued at the very cheap price of 1s 6d. It attempts to provide a description of every object in the Museum, in the order in which the visitor comes upon it. Few other museums described in this book offer anything so detailed. The *Catalogue* could be much improved by a little keen-eyed editing.

17

ROYAL SCOTTISH MUSEUM
EDINBURGH

The Royal Scottish Museum contains the Scottish counterpart of the Science Museum at South Kensington. It is housed in one of the handsomest public buildings of the mid-Victorian age, designed by an interesting engineer-architect, Francis Fowke. It was originally known as the Museum of Science and Art, and was opened in 1866. Influenced, no doubt, by the proximity of Robert Adam's University building, Fowke chose a strongly Italian style for the façade, carried through very systematically, even to the curved pantiles on the roof. Inside, the structure is of glass and iron, three stories high, with galleries all round much in the manner of the Crystal Palace: a great central hall with wings at right angles to it, one at each end. It is airy, well lighted, spacious, and flexible: a combination of merits that is very important in a museum.

Its transport exhibits include two of outstanding importance, one from the air and the other from the railway. The glider *Hawk*, designed, made, and flown by Percy Pilcher in 1896, is stated by the Museum to be 'the oldest British aircraft to sustain its pilot in successful flight'; and that carefully-worded claim is justified. Pilcher was one of the most remarkable aeronauts of the nineteenth century. When he was killed in 1899, on an experimental flight in this machine at Stanford-on-Avon in Leicestershire, he was close to attaining powered flight. His work was not lost with his death; through Octave Chanute it was known to the Wright brothers, who acknowledged their indebtedness to him.

Those great Americans find a place here too, with the engine of one of their Type B aeroplanes, made in 1910 and presented to the Museum by Orville Wright in 1927. Beside it is another historic aero engine, the Anzani 28 h.p. Blériot had used a slightly smaller version of this in the No. XI machine with which he crossed the Channel the year before. One of exactly this type powered the Deperdussin monoplane in which W. H. Ewen made the first flight across the Firth of Forth, from Portobello to Kinghorn and back, in 1911, and later flew from Lanark to Edinburgh, for part of the way at a height of 1,000 feet.[1]

It is worth noting how active the Museum was in acquiring at once important relics of flight in this period. It secured a model of the Wrights' Type A of 1908–9 in 1909, and later in the same year bought one of Blériot's No. XI.

The other outstanding machine here is one of the two oldest of all surviving locomotives: William Hedley's *Wylam Dilly*, built in 1813, the same year as *Puffing Billy*, now at South Kensington. It was designed to run on a plate-way, was rebuilt to run on eight wheels in 1815 and back into its present form, with four flanged wheels, in 1830. Meanwhile in 1822 it had taken to the water; mounted on a boat it had served as a tug during a strike of the Newcastle keelmen. It remained at work until 1866, by which time it must have been the oldest railway engine in service anywhere. For much of its life it had one driver, John Bell. His initials and his fireman's appear on the back of the boiler, cut by themselves with a chisel. A recorded description of the machine is to be obtained by pressing a button, and its mode of working is demonstrated by a model close to it.

There are some other locomotive models too: of a Bury 2–2–0 for the London and Birmingham Railway, of one of Benjamin Conner's 8 foot 2 inch singles for the Caledonian, of a Drummond 4–4–0 for the difficult Waverley route of the North British, of a North British Atlantic. The earliest of them all has interesting associations. It is a 2–2–2, beautifully made to 1 : 8 scale in 1840 at the Bedlington Ironworks, Morpeth, as a present for Professor Forbes of Edinburgh. It was given to him by four members of the Longridge family who had been his pupils. The drawings were supplied by Robert Stephenson's—the firm that Michael Longridge had left in 1837. The machine is almost identical with the 'Mail' engines built by a number of firms to Stephenson designs.[2]

It may be added that the interest of all these railway models

---

[1] There is a complete Deperdussin machine in the Shuttleworth Collection: p. 110.
[2] See E. L. Ahrons, *The British Steam Railway Locomotive, 1825–1925* (1927), 35.

is very much enhanced by the admirable way in which they are mounted, with mirrors beneath that show the working of the mechanism inside the frames and under the boilers.

There is a good series of models showing the different techniques of bridge-building, and they are accompanied by a superb set of photographs by Mr Eric de Maré—works of art in their own right and deserving the attention of anyone who knows good photography when he sees it.

Among the maritime exhibits there is an important group relating to lighthouses, many of them presented to the Museum by members of the Stevenson family, whose relation Robert Louis wrote so delightfully about them in *Memoirs of a Family of Engineers.*

The ship models are a notable collection, especially in illustrating the development of small sailing craft. A number of distinctive regional types from England are included, like the Hastings lugger, and a fine series of Scottish fishing vessels: the 'Zulu', for example, so called because it appeared in 1878 at the time of the Zulu War, the 'Fifie' fishing-boat *Newhaven,* of a year or two later. There is a splendid model of a Peterhead whaler of 1867, *Eclipse.*

The very first ship model that the Museum acquired was one of the iron paddle-steamer *Pacific,* which was built by John Elder of Glasgow in 1865 and was the pioneer of the regular steamship service between Britain and Chile, through the Strait of Magellan. She and her three sisters also had the distinction of being the only compound-engined paddle-steamers ever used in oceanic work.

Where transport is concerned, this is a small collection, but—as befits a national museum—the exhibits are of high quality throughout, and they are admirably described and displayed.

18

TRANSPORT MUSEUM, EDINBURGH

This little museum, though it is hardly publicized at all and is not very easy to find, is well worth seeing. It is run by the Edinburgh Corporation Transport Department and should be visited in conjunction with the Royal Scottish Museum, to which it is really complementary. The older museum hardly touches urban transport; this one confines itself to that branch alone.

The Museum lies within a five-minute bus ride of the General Post Office, down Leith Walk on the left, immediately opposite Leith West Goods Station. There is nothing in the street to enable you to locate the Museum, but you will see the Corporation Transport Department's works. Walk in and ask your way to the Museum. You will be shown it readily and kindly.

The Museum occupies part of a new building in the Shrubhill Works. This was originally the power-station for the cable tramway system; it then became a depot and repair shop for electric trams; now it houses the Parcels Department of the Corporation transport undertaking. The Museum comprises a single gallery, comfortably large enough to accommodate four full-sized exhibits and some smaller ones, with photographs and other such things ranged round the walls.

The oldest of the vehicles is a horse bus of the Edinburgh and District Tramways Company, rescued after lying about for years on a farm. It is a double-decker, to be drawn by a pair of horses, taking fourteen passengers on pairs of garden seats on the roof, with the usual longitudinal wooden seating inside. It is not known exactly when it was built, but it seems to date from about 1880.

Next comes a stranger in these parts—horse tram No. 1 from Aberdeen, of about 1889: a small vehicle, also pulled by two horses, with knifeboard seats on the roof. It is a far cry from this to the Edinburgh electric tram—a late one, of the four-wheeled type, dating from 1948. You are allowed to go inside. One of the first things that is bound to strike the ever-growing number of visitors who have never used a tram is the cramped quarters provided for the passengers. The seats are upholstered, and comfortable enough; but how little room there is, compared with a modern bus! The tram has many sterling merits, but in this respect we certainly do better on the bus that has supplanted it.

To the transport historian, however, none of these things represents what Edinburgh pre-eminently stands for. It was famous for its system of cable tramways, which was much the most extensive in Britain and enjoyed a long life, from 1888 to 1923.[1] It is sad that no original car has survived, but the system is explained here to some extent by models: of an Edinburgh double-decker, of an English Electric cable-car, of the cable mechanism itself, which is based on that used for the Glasgow Subway but is generally applicable also to the Edinburgh tramway system. The cable cars are shown at work in a frame of photographs from the first car setting out to work to the big scrapheap on to which the cable equipment was thrown when the system was electrified in 1922–23.

This is part of a long sequence of photographs that show most of the different types of public service vehicles that have worked in Edinburgh over the past hundred years and more, together with a little of the social life to which they have contributed: the moving of holiday-makers and football crowds, university students swarming all over one of the first electric trams as if they were passengers in Cairo, tourists starting out from the Mound and driving round Arthur's Seat in open motor-charabancs.

Some of the publicity, as shown here, has been good: notably the series of alphabetical posters naming creatures to be seen in the Edinburgh Zoo, which must have impelled many children to insist on being taken for a tram-ride to see them. The administrative side of the various Edinburgh transport undertakings is well represented, with displays of tickets, fare-tables, notices of special services, rule-books, reports, Acts of Parliament. An excellent series of maps is ranged round the walls, indicating not only the growth of the public transport system and changes in its operation but also, in explanatory captions, the wages paid

[1] See D. L. G. Hunter, 'The Edinburgh Cable Tramways', in *Journal of Transport History*, i (1953–54), 170–84.

to the staff and the hours they worked. Only one thing mars them. The routes indicated on the maps have been coloured, for clarity; but the colour has faded away altogether under the strong light to which they are exposed. The older photographs seem to be suffering from the same cause. The natural lighting here is too good. In bright sunshine it ought to be mitigated by the use of blinds.

What has been achieved in this modest museum might well be noted and emulated by other municipalities. It helps to show the citizens of Edinburgh itself, in intimate local terms that they can easily understand, something of the part that public road transport has played in the life of their community. But Edinburgh draws visitors from all over the world. It is to be hoped that an increasing number of them will find their way to this attractive exhibition of material relating to an important aspect of the city's modern history.

19

MUSEUM OF TRANSPORT
GLASGOW

The Glasgow Art Gallery and Museum have been housed together since 1901 in Kelvingrove Park. From the ouset the Museum numbered shipbuilding and engineering among its interests. It could hardly have ignored them, indeed, in view of the pre-eminent position the Clyde then held in shipbuilding and the importance of engineering in the economy of the city; the North British Locomotive Company, for example, boasted the largest works in Europe, employing 8,000 men and turning out 700 engines a year.[1] The Museum, however, had no thought of illustrating these branches of technology except by means of models and small exhibits. When it began, from time to time, to be offered original machines, it was confronted with a new problem. Not only was the floor-space that could be allocated to technology strictly limited; the design of the vestibule and entrances made it impossible to bring in any object that was more than about 6 feet wide.[2] Some storage could be provided in the basement, and a few horse-drawn vehicles and motor-cars were kept there; but the number had to be strictly limited, and they could not be publicly displayed.

What precipitated a change was the announcement in 1958 that the city's trams were to be entirely replaced by buses in the course of the following five years. The Glasgow tramway system was one of the most extensive and famous in Britain. If trams were now to be superseded there, to go the same way as those in every

[1] *Murray's Handbook for Travellers in Scotland* (8th ed., 1903), 148.
[2] A. S. E. Browning, 'The Museum of Transport, Glasgow', in *Journal of Industrial Archaeology*, ii (1965), 7–12. Mr Browning (who is the Curator of the Museum) is also the author of *Glasgow's Trams*, published by the Museum in 1964. I am indebted to both these publications for some of the material used in this chapter.

other British town except Blackpool, it would mean the end of an epoch. Much to the credit of the city, it accepted a proposal to establish a Transport Museum on a large scale, to commemorate this great change. The nucleus of it was naturally intended to be a group of Glasgow trams, but it was thought of from the outset as a museum of transport in all its branches.[1]

At this stage there was no certainty where the Museum would be accommodated. This problem resolved itself in 1962–63, when part of the Coplawhill tram depot was assigned for the purpose. It was an excellent solution. The premises lay within very easy reach of the centre of the city. By definition they were well adapted to the housing of tramcars—vehicles as tall and bulky as any that are likely to be included in the Museum. The work of adapting them to serve their new function was relatively simple, and the Museum of Transport was opened by the Queen Mother on April 14, 1964.

This summary account makes the whole process sound much easier and more straightforward than it really was. The allocation of the premises was not carried through without a struggle—for they were valuable, and other departments of the city's administration had eyes on them too. If they were acceptable in design and, on the whole, structurally sound, much careful detailed work was required, in collaboration between the Museum authorities and the City Architect's Department, in planning their conversion. The work has been admirably done. The background colour of the walls is a rich cream; where metal-work is painted, it is in a clear medium blue, enlivened by a series of red tram-stop signs on alternate piers of the central arcades. The building is well lighted and adequately (if rather noisily) warmed. Much careful thought has gone into the various floor-coverings used. Part of the original concrete has been covered with black bituminous paint: granite chippings have been placed, with good effect, under the motor-cars and trams. The main public walking-space has been laid with quarry tiles. They have outstanding virtues for this purpose, but one serious drawback: they are harsh to walk on, and very cold. 'Museum feet' is a complaint as recognizable as housemaid's knee or clergyman's sore throat;

---

[1] For the present, however, and for some time to come it is intended that the shipping exhibits shall remain at Kelvingrove.

no floor-covering that I have encountered has induced this discomfort so readily as the quarry-tiles here.

The tramway undertaking in Glasgow, like most of its fellows in other British towns, was not at first a municipal enterprise. The work was begun by the Glasgow Tramway and Omnibus Company, which started operations in 1872. The Corporation took over the privately-owned system in 1894. It did so after much acrimonious argument with the Company, which declined to afford any help whatever in the establishment of the new service. The Corporation's first trams were four-wheeled double-deck vehicles, to be drawn by two horses, and they were designed by the Falcon (later the Brush) Company of Loughborough. One (No. 543) is to be seen in the Transport Museum. A total of 384 of them were built in 1894–98, at a cost of £143 each. They accommodated forty-four passengers, twenty-six downstairs and eighteen on the upper deck; and like all Glasgow Corporation trams, they were built to a gauge of 4 feet 7¾ inches.

An experiment was made with electric traction in Glasgow on one route in 1898. It proved successful, and the system was quickly extended, with an eye to the International Exhibition due to be held in the city in 1901. By that time electric trams were running on all routes, though the horse-tram did not disappear immediately. The first new electric trams were built in these very works at Coplawhill. They showed a good deal of American influence, not least in being single-deckers. They could seat fifty people, accommodated in two saloons divided by a centrally-placed entrance platform, protected by sliding gates. One of these saloons, for smokers, had unglazed windows, with roller-blinds for keeping out the rain; the other was enclosed in the orthodox way. They were nicknamed 'Room-and-Kitchen' or 'But-and-Ben' cars, from the resemblance they presented to the usual type of two-roomed dwelling occupied by the Glasgow working class. One of these trams, No. 672, is now in the Museum.

The third and fourth, in order of time, of the trams shown here (Nos. 779 and 1088) are perhaps the most important to the student of transport history: they are examples of the standard design of four-wheeled, double-deck car evolved in Glasgow and used, with relatively minor modifications and improvements, until almost the end of tramway operation in the city. More than a thousand vehicles of this type were built in all. For the best part

171

of half a century they were the mainstay of the public transport provided for the second largest city in the United Kingdom.

The development of the design can be seen clearly by comparing the two examples in the Museum. It went through four stages between 1899 and 1927.[1] The first two cars, built at Coplawhill, ran on different patterns of truck, for comparison; and one of these, the Brill 21E, was adopted, after experiment, for the first long series of these cars, which numbered over 500. They had open tops; in the second design, of 1904, the upper deck was roofed over. No. 779, displayed here, is one of the first series, built in 1900, but modified to this second pattern.

The third stage began in 1910 and represented a marked enlargement, with a slightly wider roof and a wheelbase lengthened from 6 feet to 7 feet. Much further experiment ensued, until the final stage was reached in 1917 with an 8 foot wheelbase and the roof entirely enclosed. A total of 547 trams were converted to this new form at Coplawhill in the years 1927–35; and 455 more were rebuilt with new bodies (at the other Corporation works at Elderslie), whilst retaining their earlier trucks. No. 1088 is a car built to the third design in 1924 and subsequently reconstructed with the long wheelbase, to the final pattern.

The fifth tram to be seen here (No. 1089 of 1926) represents another flirtation with American ideas: a single-decker mounted on two four-wheel bogies, intended for high speeds and modelled on the inter-urban cars of the United States. It was designed by an engineer who was a member of the Tramways Committee, Bailie Peter Burt, and nicknamed after him. No. 1089 represents the first answer of the Corporation Tramways to the competition of the pirate motor-buses, which was by this time becoming formidable. It was not wholly successful, largely because, owing to the short radius of some of the system's curves, the vehicle had to be restricted in length; and the type was not multiplied. But if offered a demonstration, new to Britain, of the potentialities of straight-sided steel bodywork, which allowed four passengers to be seated abreast.

With No. 1173 of 1938, the sixth tram in the Museum, we reach the last phase in the whole development. The prototype of this class appeared at the end of 1936, and it went into large-scale production in 1937—whence it was generally known as the

[1] Clearly indicated and explained by Mr Browning in *Glasgow's Trams*, 9–12.

'Coronation' type: a four-motor bogie design, entirely enclosed, with folding doors to the platforms and seating sixty-five passengers. It aimed at a high degree of comfort, with leather upholstered seats, good lighting, even—at first—air-conditioning and a loud-speaker system. These cars cost well over £3,000 apiece. Before the war stopped construction of them, 152 had been built, out of a projected 850. No more were turned out when the war was over. Instead, a hundred of a slightly larger version, to seat seventy, appeared in 1948–52. They became known as 'Cunarders'. The final car of the series is in the Museum of British Transport at Clapham (p. 64).

Side by side with these original trams two trucks are shown. They are interesting to those who know what they are looking at, but their working is not explained. Perhaps, in due time, it might be possible to section one of them and mount it for demonstration?

Several series of photographs are displayed as a background to these original machines. All the main types of car are illustrated, and there is a valuable set of maps showing the development of the system. The pictures of the specialized vehicles used in construction and maintenance are interesting. Here, for example, are water cars, a rail planer, a sett car used in the paving of the tram track, a cable-layer, a crane and welding vehicle. By contrast, the decorated cars provide a touch of fantasy. Here is one tram disguised as a Viking ship, another as Henry Bell's *Comet* (for the centenary of that steamship's appearance, in 1912), a third as the *Queen Mary* in 1936; and one in the following year designed to publicize a housing exhibition, clad in a crudely-handled combination of 'brick' and 'concrete'—redolent of its time. As these pictures show, the tram could make a splendid advertising medium; the bus has seldom been used for this purpose with the same ingenuity or enthusiasm.

Trams are, very fairly, accorded pride of place here; they dominate the whole large hall. But they are surrounded by other road vehicles, some to which are quite as remarkable. The tram's great rival, its assassin, was the motor-bus: represented here by an Albion Venturer of 1949. Albion Motors Ltd are now the only manufacturers of motor-vehicle chassis left in Scotland. The chassis of the very first vehicle they built, of 1900, is here; and the third, turned out in 1901, complete with its dog-cart body.

The Albion Company interested itself greatly, as far back as 1903, in the building of commercial vehicles, and in 1913 it ceased to make motor-cars altogether. One of these early vehicles is here in the Museum: a baker's van of 1910.

Among the Scottish motor-cars are two Argylls of 1900, with single-cylinder engines; an Arrol-Johnston dog-cart, built in 1901, very grandly restored in the Museum's workshops, with others of the same make dating from 1912 and 1920; an Argyll of 1913—the year before that large and enterprising firm went bankrupt; a very neat little two-seater Galloway of 1924, and a Beardmore tourer of the following year. The series ends with a Hillman Imp of 1963, lent by Rootes (Scotland) Ltd—the first motor-car to be built in Scotland for over thirty years.

The Continental and English cars include a Benz of 1897, a superb Schneider French army staff car of the first World War, with walnut body-work, and two Rolls-Royces. One of these, lent by Mr A. McG. Dick, is of special interest: the only known survivor of a group of six built in 1905 with three cylinders. It is in perfect working order, and from time to time it is to be seen on the road.

The history of mechanical road transport in the early nineteenth century is illuminated by two exhibits of outstanding importance. One is the bicycle made by Gavin Dalzell of Lesmahagow about 1842 in imitation of that invented by Kirkpatrick Macmillan.[1] The other is the chassis of one of the steam-carriages operated by John Scott Russell between Glasgow and Paisley for several months in 1834. The service offered was an hourly one, taking forty minutes for the seven miles, and it might well have established itself but for the vehement opposition it aroused, which led to attempts to wreck it by blocking the road with heaps of stones. In trying to force its way over an obstacle of this kind, one of the carriages broke a wheel and upset; the boiler burst, and five of the passengers were killed. Thereafter these vehicles disappeared from Scotland. Though Walter Hancock's steam-carriages continued to ply sporadically in and around London until 1840, the Glasgow–Paisley service had been one of the most successful and reliable, and its withdrawal was a grave blow to the first serious effort to use mechanized road transport on a commercial scale. Though there are a number of pictures of these early steam

[1] Cf. p. 31.

vehicles, very few relics of them survive. This was found in a barn near the Paisley road and may well be from the carriage that met with disaster. It is certainly one of the greatest treasures of the Museum.

The horse-drawn vehicles are varied, well chosen, and well displayed. Here too there are some interesting commercial vehicles: a station bus, for example, which plied between Glasgow and Kirkintilloch, belonging to Messrs Lawson, who still operate buses on this route. There was then a station at Kirkintilloch. Here is a useful reminder that even in the Railway Age, before the emergence of the petrol-driven vehicle, the horse-drawn bus could and did run side by side with the railway. There is a fine horse charabanc, *Ardrishaig Belle*, seating twenty-four passengers; a hearse, decked out with wooden trimmings, painted black to resemble the loops and tassels of silk; a baker's van and a Black and White Whisky flat cart; several fire-engines, among them a manual one used in the Burgh of Gorbals in the 1820s and 1830s.

The passenger carriages include waggonettes and a jaunting car; a governess cart, a gig and a brougham; several light, graceful phaetons. There is a large coach built by Holland and Holland about 1835 for the Walker-Morrison family; it is in fact a stage-coach, with seats, inside and outside, for seventeen people. But the finest of these vehicles is unquestionably the family travelling coach built in 1817 by Rankin of London for William Innes of Kincardineshire. It is a splendid example of English coach-building at its very best. The suspension is the lightest possible, the body susceptible to even the smallest pressure of the hand. The coach has required no substantial 'restoration'; it is in beautiful condition. The upholstery and fittings are intact, including a neatly-concealed commode arrangement in the rear seat. Here is a demonstration of road travel in the age of Telford, at the height if its elegance and comfort.

When the Museum was first opened the railway exhibits were the least important. They included a few interesting models. Among them was one of a monorail designed by George Bennie in 1922 for a projected service along the Clyde. A trial section, full size, was built near Milngavie. The cars seated fifty passengers each and were intended to run at a maximum speed of 120 m.p.h. The idea was not pursued further in Scotland, but the equipment was bought by a German firm and used in a fair at Hamburg.

Another model here is of the first locomotive made in Scotland— by the Glasgow firm of Murdoch and Aitken, for the Monkland and Kirkintilloch Railway in 1831. Three years later Sharp, Roberts built *Hibernia* (also represented here) for the Dublin and Kingstown Railway. This was one of the firms ultimately absorbed into the North British Locomotive Company, a number of whose more modern engines, mostly built for foreign customers, also appear in the Museum: a Pacific for the French Etat Railway (1915), a big 'modified Fairlie' engine (2–6–2—2–6–2) for the South African Railways (1924), a 4–8–2 of 1946 also for South Africa; the series ending with the first of the 1A1–1A1 diesel-hydraulic express engines built for the Western Region of British Railways, D600 *Active*. These are models with a sad association: for some of them were presented to the Museum by the liquidators of the North British Locomotive Company after it had closed down.

When the British Transport Commission decided to underwrite three museums, at Clapham, York and Swindon, for the display of its railway relics, there were many people—not all of them Scots—who were sorry that one of them was not north of the Border. Scottish locomotives were in due course selected for preservation. Where were they to be housed and displayed?

The answer has been found here at Coplawhill—as at Swindon— through collaboration between British Railways and a local authority, though on a different basis. There was a good case for preserving most of the locomotives that had been chosen in Glasgow, for they had been built in Glasgow. Taken together they could form a noble and handsome memorial to one of the city's chief industries, now almost defunct. The machines were in store at Govan. They were brought across to Coplawhill by road in 1966 and the extension of the Museum in which they are housed was opened to the public on March 8, 1967.

There are six original locomotives, built between 1886 and 1920. The most famous of them is the oldest, the Caledonian 4–2–2 No. 123. She was built by Neilson's of Glasgow for the Edinburgh Exhibition of 1886 and purchased by the Caledonian Railway. In the Race to Edinburgh in 1888 she played a distinguished part, hauling the West Coast express from Carlisle to Edinburgh: more distinguished indeed than that of any other individual locomotive, for she alone ran on every one of the twenty-three days of racing. It was a matter of technical interest that a locomotive with single driving wheels should have been so successful in the formidable climbing required up Beattock Bank; it is largely to be attributed to her steam sanding apparatus—she was one of the first locomotives to be fitted with it—which greatly improved the grip of her wheels on the rails. She was withdrawn from service in 1935, but not scrapped. In the 1950s she was exhibited in various parts of Britain, overhauled and put to work on a number of trains, often with a pair of beautifully refurbished Caledonian Railway coaches. Can we hope that one day they will join her in this Museum?

The other two passenger locomotives here are of the 4–4–0 type and date from the twentieth century. *Glen Douglas* was one of the first of her class, built by the North British Company at its Cowlairs Works in 1913. She may be regarded as the Scottish counterpart of the Great Central engine *Butler Henderson* at Clapham, representing the final development of the classic British express locomotive of her type, with smaller driving wheels (6 feet in diameter as against 6 feet 9 inches) suited to the arduous climbing required over much of the North British system and especially on the West Highland line, where the "Glen" class were much employed.

Gordon Highlander, the other 4–4–0, is something of an oddity. The Great North of Scotland Company was unique in Britain in using 4–4–0 engines for all kinds of traffic. Apart from small tank engines, the whole of its locomotive stock was of this type. The engine preserved here belongs to Class F and was built in 1920, but it is nothing more than a superheated version of a design dating back to 1899 (Class V)—and indeed, in essentials, to the S class of 1895. This was not due simply to unenterprising conservatism. A different Locomotive Engineer was responsible for each of these three classes. All were agreed that they provided a motive power adequate for the traffic they had to handle. That traffic did not grow—from 1899 onwards the express service was even a little reduced. These were years of consolidation, after the energetic effort that had been made in the eighties and nineties to turn the Great North of Scotland from a quite abominable railway into one of the most efficiently managed in the country.

The most important of the other three engines is that of the Highland Railway: the first of the so-called "Jones Goods" class, built in 1894. It was a pioneer of the 4–6–0 type in this country. Scotland played a great part in the change to the really large locomotive that began in Britain in the nineties, and this machine represents a critical stage in the process, carried forward by the "Dunalastairs" of the Caledonian Company, with their large boilers, two years later.

It is right that the Museum should include an 0–6–0 of the standard British type. The example is a Caledonian engine of 1899. It was built at the Company's works at St Rollox and spent much of its life working in the neighbourhood of Aberdeen. It is in the Museum on indefinite loan from the Scottish Locomotive Preservation Fund.

Finally, in the furthest corner stands a small six-coupled tank engine from the Glasgow and South Western Railway (No. 9), acquired from the National Coal Board after it had worked for many years in North Wales. This was a real feat of preservation, for the Glasgow and South Western stock was ruthlessly slaughtered by the London, Midland and Scottish Company after 1923. By 1939 only fourteen of the Company's engines were left in service, and of them not one survived to nationalization—compared with 700 Caledonian engines taken over by British Railways, over 500 from the North British, some 40 from the Great North of Scotland and 25 from the Highland. This is a neat example of a shunting locomotive, with a very short wheelbase for negotiating the sharp curves that abound in dockyards. Under its original owners No. 9 spent much of its life at Greenock.

Some other miscellaneous vehicles are also shown in this gallery, including a Shand Mason fire-engine of about 1900 that belonged to the Great North of Scotland Railway and was used in its works at Inverurie. The walls carry a most interesting display of documents and photographs. An outstanding document is a policeman's report from the Glasgow, Paisley and Greenock Railway dating from 1842, including his certificate of inspecting his stretch of track. Some of the photographs show very ancient railway premises—an engine-shed of the Glasgow and Garnkirk Railway, early stations at Newtyle and Ayr, the original train-shed at Edinburgh Haymarket station, the first terminus of the line from Glasgow. More modern building is well represented by a good picture of Kirklee Station on the Lanarkshire and Dunbartonshire Railway, a handsome piece of stone and timber architecture of the 1890s, resting on a high base canted outwards —very recognizably Scottish in character.

There is also a series of photographs here of locomotives and other rolling-stock that are in the possession of the Scottish Railway Preservation Society or are to be acquired by it if possible. Among them are some outstanding pieces: a well-tank engine built by Hawthorn of Leith in 1861—a marvellous antique; a six-wheeled Caledonian brake van, a wagon of Carron Company. It is to be hoped that the Society will secure the preservation and display of all these objects, which have been chosen with discernment and are most desirable museum pieces.

The 1960s have been a difficult period in the history of Glasgow. It is greatly to the honour of the city that it should, in these very years, have established and developed a new museum so fine as this one, which takes a worthy place among the national transport museums of Europe. Scotland ought to be proud of it.

20

TRANSPORT MUSEUM, BELFAST

This is a museum of vehicles used in land transport in Ireland. Though its collection is drawn mainly from Northern Ireland, it includes also some interesting items from the Republic. There is little here, however, to illustrate Belfast shipbuilding—the absence of Messrs Harland and Wolff is conspicuous and puzzling; and neither the important aircraft industry of the Province nor its air services find any representation here.

Within these clearly defined limits, the collection is a comprehensive one. It is at present housed in a depot near the Newtownards Road in East Belfast. These quarters are very cramped, with the result that some of the larger exhibits, locomotives and tramcars, cannot be properly seen. But it is hoped before long to move the whole museum out to a new site adjoining the Folk Museum at Cultra, north of the city. If this is done, it will open up the possibility of creating, for the first time in Britain, a museum of transport that will be partly in the open air, will enjoy ample space to display its vehicles and, wherever possible, will show them in use. It is a chance to give us something like the delectable Norwegian museum at Hamar, in close association with a museum of rural life and work. The prospect is exciting, and we must wish it success and speedy fulfilment.

As you enter the Museum you mount the ramp of what is, in effect, the wooden platform of a station, at which are drawn up two railway carriages and three locomotives. The carriages are of outstanding interest. The first is a third-class four-wheeler for the Dublin and Kingstown Railway: not one of the very earliest—the railway was opened in 1834, the first in Ireland—but dating from about 1840. It illustrates, more perfectly perhaps than any other museum exhibit in Britain, the discomforts of early railway travel. It has four compartments (one a coupé) divided by low partitions, wooden seats, open sides without windows, and a single oil lamp in the middle of the roof to illuminate the whole vehicle. All the same, it *has* a roof, it *has* lighting (however feeble), it *has* seats. A good many English railway companies were carrying passengers at the same time in vehicles that boasted none of these simple amenities. Hence Gladstone's Act of 1844, which compelled the companies to provide some of them—a startling and much-resented piece of interference by government in the conduct of private business.

The other carriage is a first and second-class composite from the Dundalk, Newry and Greenore Railway: that odd Irish outpost of the London and North Western Company in England. Two of the compartments, one first and one second, are hospitably left open so that the visitor can enter them and sit down inside. To do so is indeed to make a journey back into the past. Disregard the carpeting and the hideous modern materials with which the seats are covered. All that remains is London and North Western, of the early years of this century: with the once-familiar lincrusta ceiling, the tiny narrow luggage-racks, the pale grey photographs of Dovedale and North Wales and the English Lake District, the notices on metal plates instructing you how to open the windows, and underneath the seats some of the original handsome linoleum patterned in black and gold. To sit in the hard, button-backed first-class seats, ample in size, divided from one another by broad oval arm-rests, helps one to recapture something of the spaciousness of life for the well-to-do in the Anglo-Irish world of Edward VII. It is strange to think of this vehicle continuing to work, in its opulent London and North Western livery, to the end of the service on the railway, as recently as 1951.

Two tank-engines stand next, both used for short-distance passenger work: a Great Northern of Ireland 2–4–2 (displaying all the similarities of detail to the locomotives of the Great Northern of England that have often been remarked and are perhaps to be ascribed to J. C. Park, who moved from the service of the English company to the Irish in 1880) and a very neat 4–4–2 of the Belfast and County Down Railway. Beyond these two is *Dunluce Castle*, virtually a Midland 4–4–0 of class 2, adapted to the 5 foot 3 inch gauge and built in 1924 for the Northern Counties Committee, which had passed under the control of the Midland in 1903.

On the platform itself are some interesting small exhibits: models of ships used on the Anglo-Irish services, a pair of signals and a signal-frame—though this comprises no more than a set of levers mounted in a cabin and cannot, unfortunately, be demonstrated in action. A poster on the wall brings back memories of the Troubles. It contains a warning from the Manager of the County Donegal Railways that, boulders having been placed on the track and rails torn up between Stranorlar and Glenties on September 26, 1921, and these outrages being thought to be the work of local people, the Company will close the railway altogether if they are repeated. This was a severe threat still, at a time when the motor-bus had not yet arrived. In a glass case close by is a printed circular letter, dated July 9, 1870, from the Manager of the Ulster Railway to all the Company's stationmasters requiring each of them to call his staff together and warn them to attend no meetings or demonstrations on Orange Day (July 12th). The instructions are very precise. The Company's servants are not to 'come into any unpleasant contact with the public, and to avoid making use of party expressions . . . and if any of the public make use of party expressions to them, they are to make no reply. And they are particularly to avoid drink, or anything that is likely to get them into trouble, but to do their duty peaceably on that day, and keep themselves orderly and quiet.' No doubt this was all a counsel of perfection; similar wise advice must often have been given to railwaymen in the north of Ireland during the subsequent century, though it can rarely have been spelt out with quite such minute care.

The other two railway engines of the Irish standard gauge here are as widely diverse as could be: a dock shunter from Londonderry, dating from 1891, and one of the largest locomotives that ever ran in Ireland—the Great Southern Railway's No. 800, *Maeve*, the first of a class of three designed for the Dublin–Cork expresses and built at Inchicore Works in 1939. The height of this monster as you stand below it gives you a good sense of the generous Irish loading-gauge. The type was generally similar to the rebuilt 'Royal Scot' class in Great Britain. It enjoyed no long life, for diesel ousted steam from the railways of the Republic in the 1950s.

Behind the tender of *Maeve* is another passenger coach, of exceptional interest: a six-wheeled vehicle built by Dawson of

Dublin in 1844 for the use of William Dargan. Dargan was the greatest of Irish railway contractors, and one of the most important figures in the economic life of his country in the nineteenth century. He built the Ulster Canal and a series of the chief railways, from the Dublin and Kingstown to the Midland Great Western; towards the close of his life he became Chairman of the Dublin, Wicklow and Wexford Company, and in connection with that railway he founded Bray as a watering-place. He still has a statue in Dublin; this saloon carriage, in which he lived and worked while superintending the construction of his railways, is another, and very fitting, memorial to him. He presented it to the Midland Great Western Company in 1851 and there it enjoyed a long, if never very strenuous, life. In the seventies and eighties it was the favourite carriage of the Express Elizabeth of Austria, who found relaxation from the court life of Vienna by hunting in Co. Meath.[1] Apart from the raising of its roof and the fitting of a new window-frame, the vehicle remains much as it was when Dargan used it.

The narrow-gauge railways of Ireland formed a famous system, developed in large measure under government auspices, particularly to open up the western part of the country. The majority enjoyed a life of about sixty years. The last of them, the Strabane and Letterkenny Railway in Donegal, was opened in 1909; they had almost all gone by 1960. Few of them paid at any time, most were very unprofitable. Yet they have their place in the economic history of modern Ireland, and if they had not been overtaken so quickly by the motor-bus that place might have been greater. Some of them made gallant efforts to defeat this formidable competitor by the simple expedient of using internal-combustion engines on the railway. Several examples of that practice are to be seen here, and they are among the most interesting things the Museum has to show. In 1906, for instance, the County Donegal Railways purchased from Allday and Onions of Birmingham an inspection car, with a petrol engine. Subsequently they converted it into a tiny rail-bus, with a Ford engine installed in 1920. In this form it continued in service until about 1947. Here it is: one of the oldest and smallest of such vehicles to be seen anywhere. The collection also includes two of the earliest diesel vehicles to work on railways in the British Isles. Both, again, belonged to the same company, though it inherited them from the Clogher Valley

[1] J. Taplow, *Fifty Years of Railway Life* (1920), 125.

Railway. One is an eight-wheeled diesel railcar, dating from 1932; the other, *Phoenix*, a four-wheeled locomotive originally built as a steam engine at Wigan in 1928 and converted to diesel traction four years later. There is also a County Donegal trailer coach that was constructed as a Drewry petrol railcar for the Dublin and Blessington Steam Tramway about 1926, and when that line closed in 1932 was altered from the 5 foot 3 inch to the 3 foot gauge, served for a time as a railcar and then, with its motion power removed, became a trailer. Such vehicles were almost infinitely adaptable to the changing requirements of those who managed the railways on which they ran.

There are two narrow-gauge steam locomotives, used in general service, in the collection. *Kathleen*, a 4-4-0 tank engine built by Stephenson's in 1887, worked on the Cavan and Leitrim Railway until it was closed in 1959. *Blanche*, of the County Donegal Railways, exemplifies the ultimate development of this kind of machine: a 2-6-4 tank fitted with a superheater and built by Nasmyth Wilson in 1912. She too was in service until 1959. The industrial locomotives include one of those designed for Guinness's Brewery by Mr. Geogehan, like that at Towyn, but dating from ten years later.

The passenger rolling-stock from these railways preserved here includes the framework of a balcony-ended bogie coach from the Cavan and Leitrim line, built by the Metropolitan Carriage and Wagon Company in 1887. It awaits full restoration and will amply repay it.

Ireland was an early and important pioneer in the use of electric traction on tramways and railways. The first line in the world to be operated by hydro-electric power was that of the Giant's Causeway, Portrush and Bush Valley Company in 1883. Here is a trailer car with toast-rack seating from that pioneer enterprise, which did not close down until 1949. The Giant's Causeway line was soon imitated by the Bessbrook and Newry Tramway, three miles long, which maintained a placid life from 1885 to 1948. One of its electric cars is here: a hybrid, for the body is that of a Dublin and Lucan car of 1900, into which has been fitted a set of the original Mather and Platt motors from a Bessbrook car of 1885.

Among the other tramcars in the Museum, one is widely renowned: that from the Fintona branch of the Great Northern Railway in Co. Tyrone, which was operated by horses throughout

29a Beaulieu: *Golden Arrow* of 1929, in which Sir Henry Segrave raised the land
speed record to 231 m.p.h.

b Birmingham: Railton Special car, in which John Cobb attained a world's speed
record of 394 m.p.h. in 1947

30a Clapham: Til
horse bus, c. 1

b Edinburgh   T
port Museum:
Edinburgh   h
bus

c Clapham: chas
of Tilling-Stev
petrol-electric
motor bus

31a Clapham: LT bus, built for the London General Company in 1929

b Clapham: early Green Line coach (1931)

32a Hull: the sec[ond]
oldest tramcar [still]
extant in Euro[pe]
built by Starb[uck]
of Birkenhead [for]
the Ryde [Pier]
Company in 186[

b Utrecht: h[orse]
tramcar with to[ast]
rack seating (18[

c Clapham: h[orse]
tramcar from
Douglas, I.O[.M.]
(1883)

33a Edinburgh Transport Museum: Aberdeen horse tramcar

b Crich: Starbuck tramcar from Oporto (1873), hauled by Wilkinson steam tram engine of 1895

34a Utrecht: Amsterdam electric tram (1903)

b Edinburgh: Transport Museum, photograph of cable car

35a Clapham: the first electric tramcar for urban operation in Britain. Blackpool had the distinction of running not only the first such cars in the country but also the last

b Clapham: this tram worked at Bournemouth from 1914 to 1936, when it was sold to the Llandudno and Colwyn Bay Electric Railway

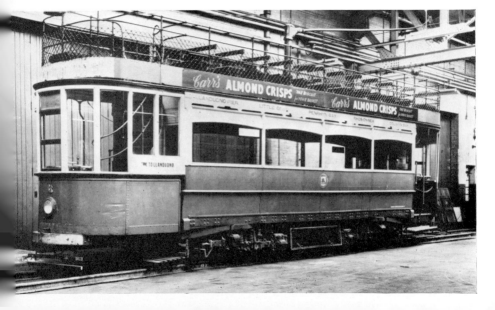

36a Crich: a general view of the track along the Cliff Side. On the left-hand track a Blackpool 'Dreadnought' car; on the right, Blackpool–Fleetwood car of 1898, with Glasgow cars 1100 and 22 behind

b Glasgow: general view of the road vehicles, with 'Coronation' tramcar in the foreground

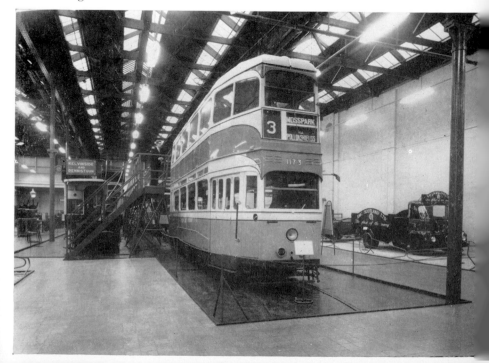

its entire life. This was unusual when the line opened in 1883, though such things had been not unknown in Victorian England—at Weston-super-Mare, for instance, and Port Carlisle. It was quite unique in the 1950s. One feels that the horse and its car would have been running still, as by the force of inertia, if the railway from Omagh to Enniskillen, with which it connected at Fintona Junction, had not been shut down in 1957.

The Museum includes three trams from the city of Belfast; they are all double-deckers, and they are the only vehicles it contains that are built to the English standard gauge of 4 feet 8½ inches. First comes a horse-tram, constructed at the Museum from a body and undercarriage that originally belonged to different vehicles; then a horse-tram converted to electric operation about 1905 and in continuous use until 1951; and finally a modern car, built by Brush of Loughborough in 1929. From the Irish Republic comes a Hill of Howth car (Brush, 1901), similar to the one displayed at Crich.

Belfast also boasts one of the few surviving examples of the steam tram-engine: one from the Portstewart line, the fellow of that at Hull.

Several of the horse-drawn road vehicles here are notable. Can one see anywhere else in Europe an American doctor's buggy? This one was in use at Gettysburg, Pennsylvania, in 1863, the very year in which Abraham Lincoln made that town immortally famous. Of the two horse-buses—rarities, again—one was built at Newport Pagnell in 1863. The trade vehicles include a smartly-painted baker's delivery van and a hand-cart loudly advertising Drummer dyes: characteristic minor elements in urban transport, which few museums have thought of noticing.

There, perhaps, lies something of the special charm of this Museum. It comes in part, very obviously, from its Irishness, its faithful reflection of a story that differs, again and again, from that of transport elsewhere in the British Isles. But it is due also to the care and intelligence that have gone into the selection and treatment of the exhibits. There is a loving eye here, quick to note not only oddities but also the common things that ought to be preserved but are seldom thought of until they have gone, and it is too late. When the collection can be rehoused at Cultra, taking its setting and its contents together, it will earn a major place among transport museums.

II. WESTERN EUROPE

21

MUSEE DES ARTS ET METIERS
PARIS

Of all the museums described here, this one has the longest history. Its origins go back to the eighteenth century: to a decree of the French Revolutionary Government, passed on October 10, 1794, setting up a Conservatoire des Arts et Métiers (literally, a Repository of Arts and Trades, or of what we should now describe as the Applied Sciences). This formed part of a policy of establishing public museums stocked with the vast collections of the royal family, together with those confiscated from private people and, in due course, those captured in war. Two things were novel in this plan: the notion of displaying these exhibits to the public, who were to be admitted to see them as a matter of right, not of grace, and that of extending the scope of the exhibition beyond works of painting and sculpture to include the applied arts. In both these ideas we can see something of the spirit of the Revolution: egalitarian, rationalist, violently and suddenly released from the conventions of the past. In this, as in so much else, we stand here on the threshold of the world we know today.

With a characteristic gesture, the Revolutionary Government assigned the Priory of St Martin-des-Champs (St Martin-in-the-Fields) in Paris to house the new Conservatoire. On the face of it, a more inappropriate building could hardly have been chosen; but the Government had a great deal of confiscated religious property on its hands, and uses had to be found for it. This curious arrangement has lasted to the present day. It works rather better in practice than might have been expected.

From the beginning it was intended that the Conservatoire should be a scientific institute, for instruction and research. It comprised a library and a school of technical education. The

189

museum, for the display of instruments and processes of the past, developed more slowly. The buildings of the priory comprised two eighteenth-century wings, enclosing an uncompleted court-yard, and these were assigned to the Conservatoire for its teaching; the refectory—dating from the thirteenth century, one of the earliest Gothic buildings in Paris—became, and remains to this day, the library; the priory church was used as a store for the objects deposited with the Conservatoire and eventually became the Museum.

Some of the greatest treasures of the Museum today were made over to it by the Government at a very early date: Cugnot's steam carriage, for example. And once it had begun, the flow of these objects was uninterrupted. They came from the state under every régime, and from innumerable private citizens. The whole story is full of fascinating ironies. Not the least of them confronts the visitor in the very first room he sees in the Museum. In the entrance hall are assembled all the most important relics of Lavoisier the chemist that are known to exist—furniture and personal belongings as well as scientific instruments and papers. Now Lavoisier, after a distinguished career of public service under the Revolutionary Government, found himself on the wrong side in a political *coup* in 1794 and was sent to the guillotine, in the same year as this great institution, which commemorates his so well today, was founded.

Like our Science Museum in South Kensington, the Conser-vatoire des Arts et Métiers embraces the whole of the applied sciences. Its transport collections fall into two parts, in different quarters of the buildings. The railway exhibits are all shown in a room immediately to the left of the entrance hall. There is no original material here at all; but among the models are some that are of exceptional interest. The earliest is a contemporary one of Marc Seguin's locomotive of 1829 for the Lyon–St Etienne Railway, the first to be equipped with a multi-tubular boiler. Another almost as old—made in 1833 and given to the Museum before 1849—is of a Stephenson 0–4–0 engine, similar to *Samson* and *Goliath* on the Liverpool and Manchester Railway.[1] It was the first railway engine of English type to be built in France under licence: 'robust, practical . . . [it] constitutes the prototype of

[1] For these engines see E. L. Ahrons, *The British Steam Railway Locomotive 1825–1925* (1927), 20–1.

all the European and American locomotives of that time'.[1] Another early 'foreigner' here is a 4–2–0 by Norris of Philadelphia: one of the type chosen by the Birmingham and Gloucester Railway for use on the Lickey incline.[2] This model was one of several presented by the Norris firm to potential purchasers—in this case Louis Philippe. It was demonstrated in steam on a short track in the Tuileries. The king gave it to the Louvre in 1846, whence it came to its present home in 1904.

It is fascinating to observe the interplay of French and British ideas and practices in locomotive design: especially, perhaps, in the second half of the nineteenth century, the reception of certain British practices in France, to become domesticated there and to continue long after they had been abandoned in their country of origin. The long-boilered 0–6–0 engine, with its wheels in front of the firebox (a type pioneered by Robert Stephenson in 1841) is a case in point. Here is a fine example of the type, built for the PLM Railway from 1857 to 1882. A more famous instance is that of the Crampton locomotives, represented by a magnificent model, to a scale of 1 : 5, of *Turenne*, a 4–2–0 built in 1849 by Derosne and Cail for the Chemin de Fer du Nord. In the succeeding fifteen years nearly three hundred of them were turned out, and they continued to be employed on express work down to 1890. One of them, belonging to the Chemin de Fer de l'Est, was tested in that year on a stretch of the Paris–Lyon main line and attained a speed of almost 90 m.p.h. Crampton's design provided for a boiler with a low centre of gravity—which was thought to be an aid to stability at high speed—and at the same time driving wheels of very large diameter, such as an express engine required, their axle being placed at the rear behind the firebox. Their drawback was the low adhesive weight borne by the driving wheels, but this mattered relatively little when trains were light and the track was weak. They certainly enjoyed a successful career in France and Germany[3]—though the Arts et Métiers catalogue is mistaken in saying, as an unqualified generalization, that they made possible the establishment of express trains.[4] The first express trains in the world were unquestionably those put into service

---

[1] *Conservatoire National des Arts et Métiers: Catalogue du Musée, Section DB, Transports sur rails* (1952), 46.

[2] Cf. Ahrons, 42.

[3] Cf. p. 252.

[4] *Catalogue, Section DB, Transports sur rails*, 42.

between Paddington and Exeter in 1845, on which Daniel Gooch's engines, very different from Crampton's, were employed.

Among the more recent machines shown here, some are of types that one is apt to consider distinctively French: the Paris–Orléans 2–4–2 express engine of the eighties, for example, attached to two interesting four-wheeled first-class coaches—one, very plain, of 1855, the other a *voiture de luxe*, internally vestibuled, with sleeping-berths and lavatories; a Mallet 0–6–6–0 of about 1900—a model made for Anatole Mallet himself; a De Glehn compound Atlantic of the Nord Company (something larger than this very tiny model would have been welcome); an Est 2–8–2 tank engine of 1910, one of the prototypes of the big engines that still puff in and out of the Gare du Nord and the Gare St Lazare on suburban trains. It is natural to look here for an early Pacific, and disappointing not to find one. One hopes that the Museum will acquire at least a model of one of the splendid machines that remain in service today, in the twilight of steam.

Among the electric locomotives, an early example is of special interest: the first of a series built to the designs of J. J. Heilmann. His principle was that steam should be used to generate power in electric motors; the engine has therefore a boiler at the rear, complete with chimney and water tanks. It is mounted on sixteen driving wheels, disposed in four bogies. This locomotive (hopefully called *La Fusée*, 'The Rocket') was tried out between Paris and Le Havre in 1894, but it turned out to be too heavy for the track. The same defect appeared in those that Heilman designed subsequently, and the experiment proved a dead end.

Two models represent what may be called the Middle Ages of the electric locomotive—the period between the wars. Both were designed originally for the Midi Company, though the earlier one, of 1922, is shown here as it was used on the Moroccan Railways. The second engine, of two years later, is a very large machine, mounted on eight driving wheels and two four-wheeled bogies. The modern electric locomotive—carried wholly on driving wheels, smaller, lighter, but more powerful—is represented by a splendid Bo-Bo machine (No. 12105) with its motion entirely covered in transparent plastic, its working well demonstrated at the push of buttons. It is surprising, however, to find no reference here to the type that set up the world's speed record of 205 m.p.h. in 1955.

The railway exhibits are virtually confined to locomotives and rolling stock; they do not illustrate track or signalling or fixed equipment of any kind.

The rest of the transport collection is housed in the old priory church. Marine and aero engines are disposed on the floor of the beautiful twelfth-century ambulatory and eastern chapels. The place of the high altar is, approximately, occupied by a big model of the Atlantic liner *France* of 1912. The aeroplanes are suspended in flight, high in the nave of the church. It all symbolizes the very spirit of the French Revolution.

It is an odd arrangement, but it has merits. The nave makes a splendid large hall, with ample cubic feet of air space and good lighting from the clerestory windows. If only the authorities could persuade themselves to redecorate the building, to substitute a light and fresh colour for the present hideous brown and maroon, which has, only too plainly, been on the walls for a great many years! After all, the church has become a museum gallery for good. Why not recognize that and treat it in the same spirit as the other galleries in the building?

There are only four aeroplanes here, but they are all original machines and of great interest. This limitation is very sensible, since a much bigger collection has been assembled in the Musée de l'Air at Meudon, in the south-eastern outer suburbs of Paris. The earliest is shaped like a large bat, with a wooden frame and powered by steam. In it Clément Ader stated that he flew 300 metres in 1897 and then crashed. His claim is not now accepted;[1] but the machine is, nevertheless, a rare and valuable survival from the prehistoric age of flight. Next in time comes the metal monoplane in which Robert Esnault-Pelterie made a number of flights in 1907, followed by the most celebrated of all these aeroplanes: that which carried Louis Blériot across the Channel on July 25, 1909—beyond question one of the historic machines of the twentieth century. This aeroplane was not something unique specially built for that famous test. The design had been evolved in 1908 and shown at the *Salon de l'Aéronautique* in Paris that winter. It became Blériot's standard aeroplane, and the type was multiplied over the next five years. It could be purchased, if one was so minded, for £480.[2] The series concludes with a Bréguet biplane of 1911, which flew in that year from Casablanca to Fez;

[1] Cf. C. H. Gibbs-Smith, *The Aeroplane* (1960), 204–6.   [2] *Ibid.*, 241, 246.

and what is perhaps the oldest helicopter to survive anywhere in the world, made by the brothers Dufaux in 1905.

Below these flying machines, on the floor of the church, stand the mechanical road vehicles, which are the pride of this transport collection. They begin with a machine quite as famous as Blériot's, though important for what it foreshadowed rather than for what it actually achieved: Cugnot's steam carriage of 1770. How many models of it have been made! You can see them at Munich, for instance, and South Kensington. But no model can begin to convey the impression made by the original, of its huge, unwieldy bulk.

This historic vehicle is well described in a brief pamphlet published by the Museum for one franc. Cugnot was a military engineer whose early studies were chiefly of the art of fortification. In 1769 the French Government agreed to bear the cost of building a model of a steam carriage he had devised. It was tried out in the following year in the presence of the Minister Choiseul, and though it was not a success, the potentialities of the idea were seen to be so important that a second, full-sized vehicle was put in hand. This was built at the Arsenal in Paris and finished in June 1771. Here is the machine we are concerned with.

It was intended, almost certainly, for the haulage of heavy artillery, which could be conveyed on the flat timber-strutted carriage, mounted on two massive wheels, at the rear. In front is the pail-shaped copper boiler, with the two cylinders directly behind it, driving on to a single wheel. We know almost nothing of the vehicle's history. One tradition is that it proved impossible to steer—which seems likely enough—and that on trial it broke down a wall; another, that it never made even a single trip. What is certain is that it remained in the Arsenal, that early in 1801 it was again proposed to try it out, and that later in that year it was made over, as a museum piece, to the Conservatoire des Arts et Métiers. It was one of the earliest machines of first-class importance to find its way into the Museum.

As in Britain, so in France, a good many experiments were made with steam road vehicles in the second quarter of the nineteenth century. Among the most successful were those of Charles Dietz. His father built the first road train, tried out between Brussels and Antwerp in 1832; Charles's ran out from Paris to St Germain and Versailles in 1835–37, but they were soon put out of business by the opening of the railways, which offered a smoother and faster journey. The work of the Dietz family is represented here by good models made at the end of the nineteenth century.

Close by, in a series of revolving frames, is an interesting collection of prints, chiefly concerned with steam road vehicles. The majority of them are English, and some are very rare. They do not date exclusively from the 1830s. One of them shows the steam carriage *Albert* of 1843, another a vehicle intended for service in the neighbourhood of Windsor in 1860.

The truth is—though we often forget it—that the steam car had a continuous history, tenuous but distinct, from the famous early experiments of the 1830s until the internal combustion engine began to emerge in the eighties. Even then, steam was not wholly defeated by petrol. The relative merits of the two were still in dispute when the twentieth century opened, and the steam car continued to be built in America down to the second World War.[1]

One of the most important of all surviving steam cars is here: the first vehicle built by Amédée Bollée at Le Mans in 1873. It ran on four wheels. He named it *L'Obéissante,* on account of its tractable behaviour on the road: one sign that Cugnot's problem of steering a heavy steam machine was moving nearer solution. Again, one's first impression, on seeing the original machine, is of enormous size. Its weight on the road in working order with the twelve passengers it was designed to carry was 4,800 kilograms, or 4·72 tons. It was not only ponderous; it was handicapped by the necessity of stopping every 10 kilometres on the road to replenish the boiler with water. Yet Bollée succeeded in driving *L'Obéissante* from Le Mans to Paris, a distance of 230 kilometres (143 miles) in eighteen hours, attaining 20 kilometres an hour on the level road. Some of his later vehicles did better. *La Mancelle* of 1878 (one of two Bollée carriages that are now in the Museum at Compiègne) was capable of twice that speed: *La Nouvelle* (1880) achieved distinction as the sole steam car to complete the course in the race from Paris to Bordeaux and back in 1895.

Another notable French pioneer of steam road propulsion, Léon Serpollet, is represented here by a steam tricycle of 1888, with a single wheel in front and a pair of driving wheels behind, and a steam car of 1903, which once attained a speed of 83 m.p.h. Another steam tricycle here, built by the firm of De Dion, Bouton

[1] Cf. p. 96.

195

et Trépardoux in 1885, could make 30 m.p.h. on the level and climb gradients as steep as 1 in 10. It is also claimed to be the first vehicle ever to work on superheated steam.

The collection is rich in cars of the 1890s, by the French pioneer firms Panhard-Levassor, De Dion-Bouton, and Peugeot. Among those of the early twentieth century one may perhaps single out a very stately Peugeot of 1909. It is aptly described as a *voiture de grand tourisme*. The two principal grand tourists are accommodated in the saloon body, where provision is made for two more passengers, on tip-up seats facing them; one more can take his place beside the driver in the open, protected at the sides only by curtains. A rack of the ample proportions required for grand tourists' luggage is provided on the roof.

Among the more modern cars are one of Marcel Leyat's driven by an airscrew at the rear; two Citroens of 1927 and 1931 (the latter sectioned); and the experimental Dynavia, a Panhard design worked out during the German occupation of France in 1944–45 and subsequently developed as the Dyna-Panhard—overblown, curvaceous, a singularly repulsive object.

The bicycles form an interesting series, well displayed in chronological order and clearly described. They include two early pedal cycles by Michaux; Meyer's bicycle of 1869, the first to be driven on the rear wheel by means of a chain; an Otto safety bicycle, built by the B S A Company in 1879, with two large wheels side by side, the cyclist sitting between them; the machine on which Jiel Laval won the race from Paris to Brest in 1891, fitted with a pair of the earliest removable pneumatic tyres by Michelin; and a Magnan cycle of 1894 with two-speed gear. Of the motor-bicycles, the most striking is that by Félix Millet of 1893, with its prototype, his motor-tricycle of 1887. Both incorporate his 'sun wheel', enclosing five cylinders that revolve with the wheel itself; the motor-cycle took part in the run from Paris to Bordeaux in 1893. The only motor-cycle here of what we regard as the normal modern type is a Triumph side-car combination of 1913. The motor-scooter is represented by a Bernardet of 1953, literally bedaubed with metal plaques, indicating membership of societies and towns visited.

Finally, three English machines of other sorts must be mentioned. Two of them are fire-engines: one operated by hand and inscribed 'Bramah fecit Piccadilly', the other a steam engine by Shand,

Mason and Co. These were acquired by the Museum in 1814 and 1870 respectively, as examples of types currently in service. The third is an agricultural steam engine built by Tuxford and Sons at the Skirbeck Iron Works, Boston, and bearing the maker's number 106. This also, when it was added to the collection in 1852, was the latest thing, not in any sense a 'museum piece'.

And that makes a fitting close to a visit to this great collection. It is housed in venerable buildings and has a history as a museum that reaches back more than 170 years; but now, as always, it is designed to illuminate the present as well as the past—the one in terms of the other. What it does in transport it does, perhaps with even more notable success, in other fields of technology. Here is evolution continuously displayed.

22

BELGIAN RAILWAY MUSEUM
BRUSSELS

It is a special distinction of Brussels that it can claim a more completely rational main-line railway system than any other capital in Europe. As elsewhere, when the railway arrived in the nineteenth century it was kept at a respectful distance from the centre. Of the city's three chief stations, two were placed just outside the line of the old ramparts (already, in the French manner, occupied by boulevards), one on the north side, the other on the south; the third, for the Luxembourg line, lay well away to the east. In due course all these were connected by a circuitous loop line (again on a French model, set in Paris), but that was never a very satisfactory arrangement. Under King Leopold II a grandiose replanning of the city was undertaken, one element in which was the building of a line, mainly in tunnel, to link the Nord and Midi stations. Work was started on it in 1903. Interrupted by two World Wars, it took almost exactly fifty years to complete. It is a splendid piece of engineering, and it has given Brussels a railway system that is ideal for a city of its size. Its two biggest stations are linked, so that most long-distance trains serve both; a new Central station and two halts have been constructed between them, affording some of the facilities of an Underground. Both the old termini have been re-sited and rebuilt, and in the Gare du Nord a railway museum has been opened, on two floors, leading off a flight of steps from the main booking-hall.

The Museum is not a large one, and unfortunately at present only one of its two floors is open to the public. The whole collection is to be removed to other quarters in the Parc du Cinquantenaire, near the Museum of Carriages described in the next chapter. Nevertheless, even as it stands, the Museum deserves a brief description here.

It is the only one of all the railway museums discussed in this book to attempt to display and explain systematically the successive stages of evolution of the track itself. Since the track was, from the outset, the distinguishing mark of the railway, it deserves much more attention than it generally gets. The Brussels Museum shows something of the means by which its evolution can be effectively demonstrated.

The display begins with the fish-bellied iron rails employed on the first Belgian railway of 1835. It then passes to the 'reversible' rail, a bright idea of the Stephensons in the 1830s for achieving economy by allowing the rail to be turned upside down when its first surface was worn; but a bright idea that did not work out well in practice. It is odd to find that it was introduced into Belgium only in 1848, by which time it was already seen to be a failure in England. Next we come to the steel rail, adopted in Belgium in 1864 but still in conjunction with a very light ballast, usually of cinders, which did not provide the track with the support it needed to withstand the pressure of increasingly heavy trains. The modern rail may be said to appear in 1886, laid on a ballast of broken stone and weighing more than a third as much again. The steel sleeper arrives, joined to the rail by a variety of devices, in 1929–33, followed by the first experiments with concrete in 1934. After 1940, when the country's whole output of steel and concrete was diverted into the German war-effort, the railways returned to timber, going back to concrete again from 1947 onwards, though still very slowly—so that even today one sees timber sleepers used almost everywhere in Belgium. Finally, in 1950 the welding of rails begins—a process that has now advanced quite a long way on some of the main lines.

Here, then, are the successive stages, each clearly marked and explained. The display is a model, neither costly nor demanding much space. It cries out to be imitated, and extended, in England.

The central position in the Museum is occupied by the one original locomotive it possesses: a 2–2–2 tank engine, bearing the name *Pays de Waes*. The first locomotives in Belgium were supplied—like the first locomotives in nearly all European countries—from England; a model of one of them, built in Robert Stephenson's works, is here, with the train it hauled between Brussels and Malines in 1835. *Pays de Waes* was built in Brussels in 1842, one of a series of nine engines made by Portula and Co., at the 'Ateliers du Renard'—a firm that enjoyed no long life, for it had disappeared before 1860—for the railway from Antwerp to Ghent. This is the line that still leaves from the Linkeroever station in Antwerp and crossed the rich tract of country known as the Pays de Waes by way of St Niklaas and Lokeren. It was built (for what reason?) to an odd gauge (3 feet 9 inches). The engine shows little affinity with English practice, as that had developed by the time of its construction. Its cylinders are placed at the rear, under the footplate; the valve-gear is that of De Ridder; the brakes, operated by the usual hand-turned screw, are applied not to the wheels but flat on to the rails.

The other locomotives displayed here are models, nearly all of them constructed by apprentices in the workshops of the Belgian National Railways. Between them, they exemplify most of the features that, to an Englishman, seem to characterize Belgian railways: the enormous chimneys, often square at the base, making the engine appear top-heavy at the front end; double frames, retained faithfully till very late in the nineteenth century; the Belpaire firebox—a Belgian invention, adopted much earlier in its native country than in Britain; and then, from the nineties onwards, a tendency to follow British models, often with inside cylinders, manifested above all in the State Railways' well-known purchase of 'Breadalbane' 4–4–0s designed by McIntosh of the Caledonian Company and Peter Jones's 'Castles' of the Highland. (But those famous purchases do not stand alone. You can still see in Belgium inside-cylinder 0–6–0s, which apart from details like the shape of their chimneys and cabs are entirely British.) Among the freaks one cannot pass over a double-framed Atlantic of 1889. The interesting ideas of M. Flamme are well demonstrated here in machines of 1908 and 1909.

The finest workmanship is to be seen in the remarkable model of a 2–2–2 engine made by a railwayman of Malines, G. P. de Stobbeleere, in 1854. It is absurdly over-decorated; but the craftsmanship in metal is superb. Every one of the engine's tools is here, and even the minuscule lettering on the regulators, *ouvert* and *fermé*. Its maker called it *La Patience*. He must have had good cause to choose that name for it.

The coaches and wagons include a *diligence* of 1864, with second-class coupés at the end and two first-class full compartments, sharing one entrance, in the middle; a six-wheeled third-class carriage of 1889, seating eighty and heated by foot-warmers; a three-coach diesel railcar unit of 1936; a railbus of 1939; and some very advanced long flat trucks mounted on bogies from 1860 onwards.

The signalling equipment includes sets of the old disc-type apparatus, of the upper-quadrant semaphores that replaced that and are still largely in use, and an example of the latest colour-light installation.

The windows of one wall of the Museum give on to the station itself. On that wall there is a working model of the locomotive valve-gear invented by E. Walschaerts when he was barely of age in 1841. It is right we should remember that two of the improvements in the locomotive most widely adopted throughout the world in the past hundred years have emanated from Belgium, from MM. Walschaerts and Belpaire. Perhaps this neat and modest Museum may be regarded as, in part, their memorial.

23

CARRIAGE MUSEUM, BRUSSELS

This Carriage Museum (Le Musée de la Voiture) is not very easy for a stranger to find; nor, having arrived there, can he be certain of gaining access to it. It is situated on the ground floor of the Musée d'Art et d'Histoire in the Parc du Cinquantenaire and can be reached quite easily (at present: Brussels is changing fast, and the transport system with it) by a 23 bus from the Opera in the centre of the city. The Belgian national museums are in course of rearrangement—this wing of the building was severely damaged by fire in 1946; and the carriages are visible only on the uneven days of the month (Fridays excepted, when the museums are closed altogether). Even on those days you may have to plead with the attendant in the entrance hall for admission. You will probably be successful, and the effort is worth making, for this is a fine and representative collection of horse-drawn vehicles, the closest counterpart perhaps on the Continent to our own museum at Maidstone.

Several of the vehicles, and much of the best of the equipment that goes with them, come to the Museum from a single family, of the Dukes of Arenberg. The coachmen's uniforms and horse-cloths are superb, in perfect condition and well shown in illuminated glass cases. Nowhere has more trouble been taken to display these appurtenances of the aristocratic world. How fine it would be if a set of them could be mounted on lay figures on the driving seat and box of a coach; how magnificent if the coach could be taken out with real riders on occasion, in the grounds of the Museum or, best of all, in the streets and squares of the eighteenth-century quarter of Brussels!

For the coach is an integral, a vital part of the world of the late eighteenth and early nineteenth centuries that we now admire so much—the world of Fragonard and Mozart, of Napoleon and

202

Stendhal. We tend too often to think of it in the wrong way, just as part of the comic apparatus of *A Sentimental Journey* and *The Antiquary* and *Pickwick Papers*. But it was in truth much more than that: a means of regular and comparatively easy travel, if not for the poor—it was the railway that gave them their freedom to move—then at least for the middle classes and the rich. Here in Brussels you can see exemplified not only the aristocratic private carriage but the public vehicle too: the stage-coach and the horse-bus, much as know them in England, together with that peculiarly Continental vehicle the *diligence*. This was long, heavy and clumsy, never able to attain the speeds of the much lighter and more manœuvrable stage and mail coaches. All the passengers sat inside; the luggage was piled high on the roof. This one plied from Ghent: acceptably enough, no doubt, on the easy roads of Flanders and Brabant, but very slowly indeed when it had to negotiate hills.

A few yards away is a great curiosity: an eighteenth-century charabanc. It is most literally a 'carriage with benches', for twelve passengers; but how elegantly curved are their shallow backs, how far we are from the jolly vulgar 'sharrabang' of the early motor age!

Of the royal and aristocratic vehicles, four belonged to Leopold I of the Belgians (one of them presented to him by Queen Victoria) and two to Napoleon III. The grander of these two is the state coach used at his wedding to the Empress Eugénie in 1853. But perhaps the most perfectly beautiful of them all is a somewhat earlier carriage, made for an unknown prelate. It is hard to conceive how any vehicle could ever be more graceful than this. It is a classic achievement of the carriage-maker's art, admirably restored by the old, famous, and still flourishing Belgian firm of coachbuilders, Van den Plas.

There are twenty-eight of these coaches in all, together with a few miscellaneous wheeled vehicles, such as a *brouette* (cf. p. 87) and a hand fire-engine; an impressive collection of sledges, some of them delightfully decorated in the Louis XV style; and—a prize piece, tucked away in a far corner at the end of the gallery—a Brussels horse tram. This takes us back almost to the origins of the tramway in Europe. It is one of the cars built by George Starbuck at Birkenhead (an associate of G. F. Train, who played a conspicuous part in the introduction of the tram into England from across the Atlantic). It dates from 1869 and reveals its origin at once in the Gothic framing of its windows, closely resembling the pattern used in Train's vehicles that ran in London experimentally in 1860-62. This Brussels tram was drawn by two horses and accommodated forty people, sixteen inside on longitudinal seats, upholstered in red plush, twenty-four on a knifeboard seat on the roof. It is to be hoped that it was used only on the flat streets of the Old Town; if it had to be hauled up the steep hill to the Upper Town, the poor horses must have had a hard time of it.

Among the bicycles, it is worth noticing that the Museum has no less than four original *draisiennes* (see p. 31), a tricycle that belonged to Leopold II before he succeeded to the throne, and a very early motor-bicycle of 1892—hardly more than a safety bicycle with a small motor attached to the front wheel.

There are three motor-cars here, quite unrestored and presenting, to tell the truth, a rather forlorn appearance. But the student of the motor-car will find something remarkable on the walls behind them: a series of original water-colour drawings signed by H. van den Plas and dated 1903-6, to show different types of bodywork designed for cars. They belonged to the Duke of Arenberg, and they are a precious survival of the early motoring age. Drawn and coloured with delicacy, some of the designs—especially those for open cars—still show very plainly how the older traditions of coachbuilding were carried on and adapted to the motor-car.

It will, I hope, be clear that though this collection cannot at present be said to be very satisfactorily shown, it is intrinsically an important one. Anyone who comes to Belgium to see the museum at Schepdaal, described in the next chapter, should try to see this one while he is in the country.

24

TRAMWAY MUSEUM, SCHEPDAAL

This delightful Museum is within easy reach of Brussels. It lies seven miles to the west of the road to Ninove and Oudenarde. The most agreeable and appropriate way of getting there is by the Ninove tram. This runs every half-hour from the Porte de Ninove —which can itself be reached by tram either from the Nord or from the Midi station in Brussels on the circular route 15. In Britain the country tram was never a common thing. On the Continent, however, it was widely used, and nowhere more than in the Low Countries. There too it is now in retreat; it has virtually disappeared in Holland. Its last stronghold is in Belgium—thousands of English visitors must still use every year the system that stretches out for twenty miles on either side of Ostend. It is entirely proper that Belgium should offer us in this Museum the most complete presentation of the country tram (*le vicinal*) that is to be found anywhere.

The tram route was opened from Brussels to Schepdaal, with steam traction, in 1887. The Museum's premises comprise the Schepdaal station and depot, built (with the exception of one shed) when the line was new in 1888. The buildings are of brick and include the station itself, three substantial car-sheds, a water-tower and a sand-store. All are fully occupied. Already, indeed, some vehicles have to stand out in the open air, with the usual unfortunate consequences.

The contents of the Museum are admirably described in a small guide-book (available in French) by Dr P. van Campenhoudt; and many of the vehicles have summary accounts on boards placed near them, with texts in Flemish, French, German, and English.

The Museum is the property of the Société Nationale des Chemins de Fer Vicinaux (s n c v), but it is managed by the Tramway Museum Association (a m u t r a), established in Brussels in

1961. It was opened on May 26, 1962, as Dr van Campenhoudt puts it, 'in the most Belgian manner possible: with a local fanfare, with banners and distinguished persons and speeches, in teeming rain and with local beer'.

The Museum's great strength lies in its remarkable collection of rolling-stock. This includes four steam locomotives, some three dozen passenger tramcars, and more than another dozen freight and baggage vehicles: a thoroughly representative selection, of which the earliest examples date from 1888 and the latest from after the second World War.

Shed I stands immediately opposite the station building. It contains two complete trains, with their steam engines. The train on the left (as you enter) is the older of the two. It comes from the Groenendael–Overijse line south-east of Brussels, which continued in service until 1949. The engine was built in 1906 at the St Léonard workshops; the two carriages come, one from Malines, the other from Monceau-sur-Sambre, and they worked on the line from its opening in 1894 to the end of the service. The other train comprises a locomotive and three coaches. It shows something of the way in which the country tramways resumed their work after the first World War. The engine (No. 1066) belongs to one of the most numerous types used on the system; 126 were built from 1910 onwards, more than half of them after 1918. This particular machine came from Haine St Pierre in 1920. Of the coaches attached to it, the first two are of the same date; the third is earlier (1912) and it retains its first livery of plain varnished teak, as distinct from the later vehicles, which are painted in the standard green livery of the Vicinal system. No wonder teak was in such demand by railway coachbuilders. This vehicle required nothing more than cleaning and a coat of varnish to put it into its present excellent condition, some forty-five years after it was built.

To reach Sheds II and III you walk past the water-tower and move to the other end of the site. The two sheds are virtually one, since they are adjacent and there is internal communication between them, and their contents are moved about from time to time.

The Belgian local tramway system played an important part in the war of 1914–18, and the British Railway Operating Division ordered fifty tram engines for work in the Ypres and Armentières sectors. Nearly all were subsequently purchased by the Belgians.

Here is one (No. 974). Built by Hawthorn's of Newcastle in 1917, it went into civilian service in the Brussels district when the war was over. A fourth steam tram engine has recently been acquired by the Museum: No. 303, very much older than any of the others, for it was built at Tubize (between Brussels and Mons) in 1888.

Two of the passenger vehicles here, a second-class carriage (A 596) and a baggage car (A 2249), are the oldest in the Museum dating from the same time. Another one standing near by (A 1625), readily distinguishable by its striking blue livery, has an interesting history. It was built some ten years later, and when it was still new it was fitted up as a saloon for the use of Leopold II and his family on their frequent visits to Ostend. Though it is not quite the only surviving narrow-gauge royal saloon (there is a Norwegian one at Hamar), as a royal tramcar it is probably unique. Its fittings are handsome, but—surprisingly, one may feel —they are not ostentatious: red upholstery and curtains, folding steps that can be lowered almost to the ground (the King was lame), the decoration limited to the royal arms and monograms and six little crowns on the roof. It is a wonder indeed that the carriage survived. It passed into ordinary service in more democratic times and continued at work until 1956. It has been admirably restored by the SNCV.

There is one horse-tram here, an open toast-rack car from Liège. Strictly speaking it is an intruder, for it worked on a municipal system, and this museum is devoted to the country tram; but one ought not to grudge such an antiquity a good home.

Electric traction began well before the end of the nineteenth century on some of these lines. The first of all was that from the Place Rouppe in Brussels to La Petite Espinette (to the south, on the edge of the Forest of Soignes), inaugurated in 1894. One of the first cars to work on it is at Schepdaal (No. 9004), together with another (No. 19) of 1896 and a trailer car (A 1590). No. 9004 was somewhat modernized—for example, by enclosing the platforms —in 1909; its fellow was most carefully restored by the SNCV to its original condition some years ago. As far as their bodywork is concerned, both follow closely the pattern set by the steam-hauled cars of the time, though the undercarriage, with its pair of motors, is of course entirely different.

The remaining electric trams provide a representative series down to the second World War. Among them should be mentioned particularly the car of 1910 (No. 9314) with its trailer A 8497, from the Brussels section of the s n c v. Dr van Campenhoudt draws attention to the advertisements in the motor-car, redolent of the 1920s. The trailer is of the toast-rack pattern, open at the sides; to an Englishman it is surprising to find that it was built as late as 1916. All these cars, motor-vehicles and trailers alike, run on four wheels. Four-wheeled cars are still to be seen in substantial numbers in and around Brussels, but they have given place in large measure to larger units mounted on two bogies. Examples of these are already to be found in the Museum, and no doubt more will be added as they pass out of service in the future.

The Museum has attracted a number of gifts from outside the s n c v, among them a car and trailer from the city of Luxembourg and one car from Fribourg in Switzerland.

It is an excellent feature of the Museum that it is, at every point, alive, demonstrating the continuity between present and past. The diesel cars that have in some sections, especially in the Ardennes, supplanted their steam and electric predecessors are also represented here; one of them, which worked from Marloie, between Namur and Luxembourg, was constructed as recently as 1949.

The s n c v was not responsible for passenger services alone. In Britain we are not accustomed to thinking of the tram as a carrier of freight—though some undertakings, such as that of Huddersfield, did perform this service, and more might have done so but for the opposition of the railways. In Belgium, however, the local tramways did much work of this kind; and here at Schepdaal are a number of the wagons they used, both covered and open. The earliest are small 5-ton vehicles, but from 1888 onwards 10-ton wagons were built, and the latest type had a capacity of 20 tons.

Between the station-house and the water-tower is a low building of brick, which served originally as a store but now contains, among other things, a small exhibition room. Here is displayed a representative selection of photographs and some small relics of the earlier days of the s n c v. The exhibition picks up some useful points—illustrating, for example, some of the country lines that crossed international frontiers, like those from Chimay to Rocroi and from Antwerp to Bergen-op-Zoom—and it introduces us to some oddities, such as the pair of Garratt locomotives built for the Liège lines in 1929-30. One such 'sport' seems never to have been used in regular service: the steam tramcar designed by W. R.

37a One of the 'living museums' of transport in N. Wales: Talyllyn Railway, train in service at Towyn Wharf station. Locomotive No.2, *Dolgoch*, built in 1865

b Portmadoc: hearse wagon, Festiniog Railway

c Towyn: narrow-gauge locomotives. *Left*, De Winton vertical-boilered locomotive (Penrhyn Railway) *right*, Beyer Peacock works engine *Dot*

38a Swindon: the Churchward Gallery. Locomotives (*left to right*): *North Star*, 'Dean Goods' No. 2516, *City of Truro*, *Lode Star*

b Munich: the locomotive hall. On the track, *left to right*: Bavarian Railways 2–4–0 (1874), replicas of Norris 2–2–2 *Beuth* (1844) and *Puffing Billy* (1813). On the right the rear end of a Bavarian 4–6–2 and, in front of it, the oldest electric locomotive in the world, built to the designs of Werner von Siemens in 1879

Rowan that was put through its paces experimentally on this very Schepdaal line in 1888. Similar cars, to Rowan's designs, were at work elsewhere, in Denmark and Russia for example. The International Tramways Union held its annual conference in Brussels that year, and an inspection of this machine figured in its programme, shown here. It is interesting to think of these tramway experts pondering over it, debating among themselves if it marked the way forward—just when the potentialities of electric traction were beginning to come into sight.

Tramways call forth everywhere a fervid loyalty from those who admire and love them. It is particularly strong in Belgium today, when the system is gradually being pared down but so much of it still remains; and where, to a greater extent than anywhere else, the tramway still serves both urban, suburban, and rural society. The Museum at Schepdaal is staffed by volunteers—each of the vehicles is assigned to one individual, and he makes himself responsible for its cleanliness and good order. Perhaps one may feel that the venture is happiest of all in the partnership on which it is based between the amateurs and the SNCV. Your very ticket of admission is a good symbol of that: an ordinary tram ticket, overprinted with the initials AMUTRA. Riding back to Brussels on the tram (which is well patronized—as many as three trailers are apt to be required in the rush hours) there is a great deal to think about: the sensibly-directed loyalty and enthusiasm that have built up the Museum, the stout social service that the local tram has rendered to the country for the best part of a hundred years.

25

NETHERLANDS RAILWAY MUSEUM, UTRECHT

Utrecht is unquestionably the right place for a Dutch railway museum. It is the headquarters of the State Railways, the centre of the whole system. The Dutch Museum enjoys, moreover, one outstanding advantage. It is housed in a railway building that is a work of architectural distinction in its own right: the Maliebaan station, opened in 1874 to serve the line to Amsterdam via Hilversum. Damaged in the second World War, it fell into disuse as all traffic came to be concentrated in the big Central station, a mile away. It was a happy decision to restore it for housing the homeless collections of the Netherlands Railway Museum.

Their origin stretches back some way into the past. The earliest efforts to establish a museum of the kind in the Netherlands were made before the first World War. The originating spirit was Mr G. W. van Vloten, himself a railway official and an enthusiastic collector. In 1927 the Netherlands State Railways decided in principle to support a museum and placed Mr van Vloten in charge of it. Unluckily he died only six months later. He was succeeded by Mr Henry Asselberghs; and it is to him and to his daughter Miss Marie-Anne Asselberghs (the Director in charge today) that the Museum owes its present admirable form. It had many tribulations still to pass through, including the dispersal of the collections on account of the second World War, before the Maliebaan station was assigned to it by the State Railways administration in 1951. That decision owed much to its great President, Dr F. Q. van Hollander, who took a personal interest in the whole project and helped to make available the funds that were needed for realizing it.

At this point it was determined to make the Museum something more than an historical display, by adding to it a section dealing with current practice, which could be used to demonstrate technical matters to railwaymen themselves.

The building is approached across an open courtyard, and any visitor must be struck by its elegance. It is not common to find an architect still working, so easily and naturally, in the classical tradition as late as the 1870s. It comprises a two-storey block, flanked by long, low wings. The material is the reddish-brown brick, characteristic of so much of the building, ancient and modern, in Utrecht, liberally relieved with stone dressings. A *porte-cochère* projects in front, and the arms of the Dutch royal family appear serrated against the skyline.

The plan of the Museum is simple. You enter by the central block, which is a very handsome hall, open to the roof and crowned by a low rectangular dome. To the right is a series of small rooms (I–VIII) containing the small objects of historical interest; to the left Room IX, with the working models of the modern railways. In front is the station platform, at which eight of the original locomotives are drawn up. Beyond it are other railway tracks, which continue in use for freight traffic; at the right-hand end of the platform is a bay, and a small group of other platforms in the open air, where the tramway rolling-stock is displayed.

Since we are offered here a view of the present as well as of the past, let us begin by considering the present, turning first into Room IX. Two large model installations are mounted here. One illustrates the techniques of electric traction; the other, an elaborate piece of work, is designed to demonstrate the signalling system now used in the Netherlands. Its centre-piece is the new Leiden station, and among the 'hazards' to be negotiated by the trains on the line are a level-crossing and a lifting bridge, based on that over the Koningshaven in Rotterdam. Down the middle of the room, on a series of stands, are models of rolling-stock now in use on the State Railways. A visitor from Britain will be interested to note among them a six-wheeled diesel shunting locomotive manufactured by the English Electric Company, of a type much used on British railways.

The entrance hall contains a series of models of locomotives; a large beam engine made for railway use in Amsterdam in 1843 and still in working order; portraits of eminent Dutch railway

officials; and banners belonging to trade-union organiza-
tions.

The right-hand wing is divided up by light partition walls, some
eight feet high, into a sequence of eight rooms for the display
of the smaller historical objects. Though each room is usually
concerned with one main theme—stations in Room II, signalling
in Room V, and so on—there is so much cross-reference that it is
perhaps best to consider the material collected here as a whole
and choose illustrations from all sections at once, indicating the
location of exhibits by their room number.

The early history of the railway is displayed by examples not
only from the Netherlands but from other countries too. Inevitably, such prints as Ackermann's of the Liverpool and Manchester
line are much in evidence (I, VIII); much less well known is a
set of pictures of the first railway in Belgium—that from Brussels
to Malines, opened in 1835 (I). After their political divorce from
the Dutch in 1830, the Belgians turned their minds quickly to the
development of railways, hoping thereby to attract international
commerce to their country through the ports of Antwerp and
Ostend. They went ahead more vigorously than the Dutch, and
to a coherent plan imposed by the government in Brussels. The
Dutch got their first railway, from Amsterdam to Haarlem, in
1839, but their system developed slowly and piecemeal in the
forties and fifties and they lost ground to the Belgians for a time
in consequence.

That is not to be explained solely by sluggishness and short
sight. The physical difficulties presented by the country itself were
far greater than those that had to be overcome in Belgium. Indeed,
if we except Switzerland—whose railway system also developed
late—we can say that no country in Western Europe presented,
relative to its size, so many formidable problems to be solved
by the railway engineer: in laying a secure foundation for the
track and its heavy loads to rest on; in spanning the innumerable
rivers, most of which were busy highways of traffic, carried still
in sailing-boats with tall masts; in guarding against the recurrent
danger of flood. Over a century ago the notice of the ordinary
English traveller was drawn to these wonders: 'The line from
Rotterdam to Amsterdam deserves the attention of the engineer,
from the number of canals which it has to cross, which presented
considerable difficulty, overcome by ingenious expedients, such

as rolling and swing bridges. A large part of the line is founded on piles, often under water, and the roadway is laid on faggots bound together by stakes and wattles.'[1]

As any new building site or road works that are in progress today will reveal, the soil consists almost wholly of sand; and the difficulties this presents are displayed with clarity in a series of photographs (IV) of the building of the nine miles of light railway from Gouda to the little silver-working town of Schoonhoven. This was not undertaken in the early days, when the techniques for dealing with such problems were still being worked out, but only about sixty years ago. The first attempt was made in 1901 and abandoned in the following year when the sandy foundations of the railway embankment had fallen in. The works then stood derelict until 1910, when the project was resumed, with State help, and the line was at last opened in 1914. After all this labour, it enjoyed a life of only a few years, before it was closed down, owing to bus competition.

The same room contains a splendid series of working models of lifting and opening bridges, beautifully constructed in wood and metal, as well as some fine pictures of them: for example, an architect's water-colour drawing, some 16 feet long, of the Westerpoort bridge over the IJssel (1895–1901). The most important of all the earlier works of this kind was the Moerdijk bridge south of Dordrecht: for until the mile-wide Hollands Diep has been spanned, all railway traffic from the Netherlands to Belgium and France had to be transhipped and suffered serious delay. The bridge was built in 1869–71. Its construction is well demonstrated here in a set of excellent photographs, showing every stage in the process from the driving of the piles to the completed work, as well as in a delicately-executed series of engravings illustrating the techniques employed.

The station architecture of the Netherlands shows a lively variety, well displayed here in pictures and models. It tended at first to follow classical patterns, as in the extremely handsome Westerpoort station at Amsterdam (II), though Gothic patterns also appear at Rotterdam (Delftsche Poort). As the nineteenth century advanced, it was touched strongly by the romantic spirit, which appears at its most powerful in the Central station at Amsterdam by P. J. H. Cuijpers, completed in 1885. (A reminder

[1] Murray's *Handbook for Travellers on the Continent* (11th ed., 1856), 4.

of the difficulties encountered here too with the foundation work is to be seen in the cartoon of the station sinking into the water, exhibited in Room VI.) When the entrance hall of that impressive building came to be reconstructed twenty years ago the architect responsible was Mr H. G. J. Schelling. His new version of the hall is shown in a coloured drawing (II): as sensitively handled as his work of restoration at the Maliebaan station, which is all about us here.

The social impact of the railway is displayed in a long series of prints in hinged frames in Room VIII, among them some striking ones from Japan; in a sequence of Daumier's satires (VI); and in some more conventional, 'straight' renderings of scenes of railway travel. Among these are two pretty oil paintings by C. Cap of Antwerp, both dated 1885 (VI): 'The Proposal' (in a railway-carriage) and 'The Honeymoon', more interesting than the familiar Solomon paintings in the same *genre*. There is a long series of medals, commemorating railway activities in many parts of the world, in Room VIII; and the frames of prints in the same room contain a remarkable display of children's dice-games based on transport of all kinds.

The landscape paintings deserve special mention. Though the Dutch genius in that art declined in the eighteenth century, it never wholly died. It exemplifies itself here occasionally, taking account of the picturesque addition of the moving train to the scene: as in H. W. Mesdag's 'View of Scheveningen', with the steam tram on the left, painted in 1895 (VIII). The same thing appears in F. Carlebur's sharply-lighted picture of the river at Dordrecht in 1861 (VIII), showing two of the railway steamers that plied between Rotterdam and Moerdijk before the Hollands Diep was spanned by a bridge. The background is still the same as in Cuyp's paintings of the town two centuries earlier, with the windmills and the huge stump of the church-tower; but the shipping has altered beyond recognition.

Moving out now on to the station platform, eight locomotives confront us, drawn up in approximately chronological order from left to right. Since all of them present points of interest, they may be enumerated. First stands 2–4–0 No. 13, built for the Netherlands State Railways by Beyer Peacock of Manchester in 1864 (a model of their No. 1, a 2–2–2 also from Beyer Peacock, stands in the entrance hall). It has all the firm's customary elegance of finish, and it remained at work until 1932. The third of these engines is a somewhat larger version of a similar type, with double frames, which was in service from 1881 to 1936. In between stands a German machine, *Nestor*, built by Borsig of Berlin for the Holland Iron Railway Company in 1880 and running till 1936: also very highly finished, and as unmistakably German in character as the Beyer Peacock engines are English.

The fourth engine is a 4–4–0, the earliest bogie locomotive to work in the Netherlands, built for the Dutch Rhenish Company by Sharp Stewart of Glasgow in 1889 and withdrawn from service only in 1940. It is plain, even severe, with its stove-pipe chimney, but most graceful in its lines: the ideal kind of locomotive, one would suppose, for hauling fast light trains over a level country. The type did indeed prove popular; for next in the series here is a big version of it (Holland Iron Railway, No. 504), built by Schwartzkopff, of Berlin in 1914, to the specification of Dr W. Hupkes. Was Berlin turning out any other locomotives with inside cylinders by that time?

The fifth of these engines is the only one built in Holland: State Railways No. 3737 (originally 731), a handsome 4-cylinder 4–6–0 from the N.V. Werkspoor at Amsterdam, dating from 1911. This was the last steam locomotive to run in the Netherlands; it was handed over to the Museum in 1958.

Next to it stands a huge 4–8–4 tank engine (State Railways No. 6317), again built by Schwartzkopff, in 1931: designed primarily for use on heavy coal trains in the south, in the Province of Limburg. And finally we come to a British War Department 2–10–0, built by the North British Locomotive Company in Glasgow in 1945: the 1,000th British freight locomotive to be shipped to the Continent after D-day and named *Longmoor*, from the headquarters of the Royal Engineers Transportation Corps.

In the bay at the end of the platform is a replica of the first train to run in the country, comprising a 2–2–2 engine *De Arend* ('The Eagle'), built by Longridge of Bedlington, Northumberland, in 1839, and three four-wheeled carriages. They are not distinguished by differently-numbered classes. The first, painted green, is a *diligence* and has glass windows; the second, a yellow *char-à-banc*, affords protection to the occupants by means of canvas flaps; the third, a brown *waggon*, is open at the sides—though it has a covered top. This train was built in the State Railways workshops at Zwolle in 1938 for the celebration of the centenary of railways in the Netherlands in the following year.

Beyond, in the open air, stands the tramway rolling-stock. This comprises a couple of light toast-rack cars; a complete train of the Rotterdam Tramways, with two goods vehicles and a steam locomotive built by Orenstein and Koppel of Berlin as late as 1920; an enclosed steam tram engine, *Vrijland,* built by Henschel of Cassel for the Zutphen–Emmerich line in 1904; and an Amsterdam electric tramcar of 1903. Some other pieces of railway equipment have also been mounted out here; among them some semaphore signals and a cumbrous level-crossing gate, running on wheels with its own track across the road.

No Continental country has been so heavily influenced by Britain in its railway practice as the Netherlands. Of the nine railway locomotives chosen for preservation in the Museum (including *De Arend*), five were built in Britain. Beyer Peacock supplied the first locomotives to the State Railways in the 1860s; they were still building for the Netherlands forty years later—see the model of the 4–6–0 for the North Brabant Company of 1908, resplendent in its royal blue and scarlet livery in the entrance hall. There too you will see, among a collection of destination plates affixed to the sides of carriages, one marked *SLIPRIJTUIG VOOR HILVERSUM*—'slip carriage for Hilversum'—coming from the Holland Iron Railway about 1900. The slip carriage was a favourite device of several British railways; but it was to be met with on the Continent very rarely. Coming down to our own day, we not only find *Longmoor,* a standing memento of the Liberation. The London and North Eastern Company lent the State Railways the prototype electric locomotive built in 1941 for the Manchester–Sheffield line, the electrification of which was delayed by the war. The Dutch christened the engine *Tommy*; it returned to England in due course, and it still bears the name as it climbs the Pennines today.

There are particular reasons for this close connection, other than those of propinquity. Much British capital was put into railway building in the Netherlands: one of the country's chief companies, the Dutch Rhenish, was in its origins almost wholly a British concern. The Dutch never developed locomotive works of their own on a large scale, and for political reasons they were not at first eager to do business with the neighbouring firm of

Cockerill at Séraing in Belgium. They bought at first almost wholly from Britain. When, later, they looked for other suppliers, it was generally to Germany, as the display here shows. English patterns of design tended to prevail in Holland: inside cylinders, brightly-coloured paint, copper caps to the chimneys and much polished brass-work, a care for neatness of design that is seldom to be met with in so refined a form elsewhere on the mainland of Europe.

Anybody in Britain who is interested in railways will find a trip to Utrecht rewarding. The Museum is admirably set out, and quite intelligible to those who read no Dutch; though if you have even a slight acquaintance with the language and a pocket dictionary at hand, Mr Asselberghs's excellent guide-book *Vurig Spoor* ('The Fiery Track') will add greatly to your enjoyment. The strong British associations—and, at times, also the sharp contrasts in practice—are always interesting. And when the Museum is shut, there is much else to see in Utrecht. There is a vast, mutilated cathedral. The canals have a trick of disappearing into little tunnels; away from the centre of the city they run between green banks bright with daffodils in spring. And the Nieuwe Gracht may well be considered one of the most entirely beautiful streets in Northern Europe.

26

SWISS MUSEUM OF TRANSPORT
LUCERNE

A modest Railway Museum was set up in Zürich before the war, and in Berne (which is the headquarters of the International Postal Union) there is a well-established Postal Museum. But it was not until 1959 that a comprehensive Transport Museum was opened in Switzerland. In this, as in a good many other fields of enterprise, the Swiss were not first in the field. They have, however, turned out to be what is often quite as good as pioneers, and sometimes better; for they have perfected the techniques and ideas of others, profiting from their mistakes. Just as they were very slow—for political and economic reasons—to develop the railway in the nineteenth century, and then drove ahead in the twentieth to forge a railway system that ranks among the highest technical achievements of Europe, so they have now produced a Transport Museum that sets an example which any other European country should envy.

It is a private venture, not governed by any national or municipal authority, though it enjoys very active aid and support from the Swiss Federal Railways, Swissair, and the Swiss Post Office, as well as from the town of Lucerne. Moreover, it is something more than a museum. This Verkehrshaus der Schweiz—for that is its proper title—is the headquarters of the Swiss Institute of Transport and Communications, a body concerned with the study of transport as a whole; and the buildings at Lucerne house the library and archives of this Institute besides providing a spacious lecture hall, serving as a meeting-place for conferences. The Museum is the chief responsibility of the Institute, and it occupies much the largest part of the buildings; but it is only one of a series of inter-

218

locking enterprises, all of which have their centre in the Verkehrshaus.[1]

It is not extravagant to say that the site of the Verkehrshaus is a perfect one. To begin with, it was a happy notion to establish it at Lucerne, which has long been the chief tourist centre of Switzerland—one of the chief tourist centres, indeed, in the whole of Europe: a pre-eminence it has deservedly retained through the excellence of its communications, its intrinsic beauty, and the thoughtful care it has taken to make visitors welcome. The Verkehrshaus lies two miles east of the town centre, readily accessible by a brisk service of trolley-buses. It has parking space for private cars, and in summer it can also be reached in a few minutes by motor-launch across the lake from the Station Quay. The Museum is not hemmed in, as it would have been on any site within a town; its buildings are deployed on a spacious plan, and there is room for expansion to the south-east. Nor is it the least among these attractions that the static calm of the Museum is frequently interrupted by the passing of trains close by on the main Gotthard railway, offering the spectacle several times a day of the huge international expresses running past in charge of some of the most powerful (and perhaps the most handsome) electric locomotives in Europe.

The plan of the buildings is simple, based on two rectangular courtyards. The units are of irregular heights. They were designed by four different architects; yet they achieve harmony through the use of common materials—concrete, aluminium, a little red brick checkered occasionally with yellow, and much glass. (Too much glass perhaps for comfort and economy when the weather is cold or hot.) The entrance hall extends straight through the building. Above it is the accommodation provided for the library and archives. In front it gives straight onto a large courtyard, and this has been delightfully treated. The left-hand half of it is a plain lawn; to the right, in contrast, is a small formal flower garden, and lying diagonally across it, in dry dock, the paddle-steamer *Rigi*. She was one of the many that were constructed in Britain for service overseas. Her builders were Ditchburn and Mare of Blackwall. She made her way

---

[1] The text of most of this chapter first appeared in an article in the *Journal of Transport History*. For permission to reproduce it I am indebted to the publishers, Leicester University Press.

out by water from London, up the Rhine to Strasbourg; thence she went to Basle by rail, and by road from Basle to Lucerne. Her maiden voyage down the lake to Flüelen was performed at a speed of 12 knots on April 1, 1848. She remained in service for 104 years. She received new engines in 1893, and before being placed on exhibition her superstructure had to be rebuilt as the timber was worn out. Otherwise she remains essentially unchanged. The preservation of old steamships is a matter presenting so much difficulty that very few indeed have survived anywhere in the world. But the problems have been solved here with skill. *Rigi* has been allowed, as it were, to preside over the whole Museum, the most graceful thing in the place. And though she can no longer sail, she still earns her keep; for in summer-time she affords a restaurant for fifty people.

The normal tour of the Museum moves in a clockwise direction, and it begins with the section devoted to railways. At the entrance to this section stands the oldest of the exhibits: a *Grubenhund* or wooden trolley dating from about 1780, used in the coal-mine of Schwarzenmatt in the Simmental. One of the engravings from Agricola's *De re metallica*, thoughtfully reproduced beside it, shows how little the pattern of these things had changed since the Middle Ages. Opposite stands a tank engine built for the diminutive 2 foot 6 inch gauge. The great popular attraction comes next: a model (scale 1:89) of the northern section of the Gotthard railway, from Erstfeld up to the Naxberg Tunnel, just short of Göschenen. Its popularity is merited; for the model is a fine achievement (it took members of the Lucerne Model Railway Club 30,000 hours of their spare time to build it), a true microcosm of the railway itself, which will long remain an outstanding monument of the skill and resolution of man. Meanwhile, the visitor is being offered a rapid view of the evolution of the Swiss railways. It seems a pity, however, that there should be only half a dozen photographs of the Gotthard railway, and those in another room. Would it not have been right to offer an extended series here, showing the construction and working of the line in the past, to give depth to the model's demonstration of the practice of the present?

Room 3 is devoted largely to the current work of the Swiss Federal Railways, and it is here that one of the chief themes of the Museum first makes itself felt. Presumably all good museums have, in the main, two purposes, to instruct and to give pleasure. The best will certainly do both, as this one does in Lucerne. But the instruction may be 'pure' or 'applied': educational, that is, in the broadest sense of the term, or with a practical end in view. This Museum leans heavily towards applied instruction. Each of the main branches of transport is so presented as to display its functions in the economy and society of Switzerland; and, pretty evidently, with an eye to recruiting intelligent staff to run it.

The next room (4) is the most spectacular in the Museum, showing the original railway and tramway rolling-stock, together with a fine series of models, beautifully displayed (some of them upstairs in a side gallery). Of the steam locomotives the most interesting are perhaps the 0–4–6 *Genf*, built for the Swiss Central Railway in Germany in 1858, and two of those for mountain railways: the first to be used in Europe, on the Vitznau–Rigi line (1873), and a more modern rack-and-adhesion engine of the Brünig Railway, which has been partly sectioned and is demonstrated in operation. There is also a steam tram (with separate locomotive) built for Berne in 1894, and a car of the first electric tramway in Switzerland, which had started to run between Vevey, Montreux, and Chillon six years earlier.

The most notable things here, however, are the electric locomotives. Here is one of the first standard-gauge electric locomotives to work in Europe, which went into service on the Burgdorf–Thun Railway in 1899 (its fellow is in the Deutsches Museum at Munich). It was constructed in partnership between the Winterthur Works and Brown Boveri of Baden, two of the firms that, with Oerlikon of Zürich and Sécheron of Geneva, have remained suppliers of electric locomotives to the railways of Switzerland, and of many other countries, throughout the past sixty years. A little farther on is one of the 2,500 h.p. engines that opened the Lötschberg line in 1913. It is good to see it here: for these are surely to be counted among the most majestic machines ever built for a railway.

In summer-time the doors at the end of this room are opened, enabling some of the exhibits to stand outside in the yard beyond, next to the Swiss restaurant car of 1914 (built by Ringhoffer of Smichow, near Prague), which has been used for the service of coffee.

Room 5 is given over to road transport. The largest division, on the ground floor, is that of mechanical traction. First comes an elegant model of the carriage patented by Isaac de Rivaz in 1804: one of a series that may claim to be the earliest vehicles driven by internal combustion engines. The motion arose from the explosion of a mixture of hydrogen and air. The remainder of the gallery contains full-sized vehicles, beginning with two of 1898 (an Oldsmobile and a Lorenz-Popp car with hydrocarbon propulsion) and continuing with a fine selection down to a Maserati of 1961. A special emphasis is naturally given to the Swiss contribution to automobile engineering: to the work of the Saurers, father and son, and the brothers von Martini; to Marc Birkigt of Geneva, founder of Hispano-Suiza, and to the man with the most famous name of them all, Louis Chevrolet, who was born at La Chaux-de-Fonds in 1878 and emigrated to the United States in 1911. Among individual vehicles here one may perhaps single out as particularly interesting the stately crimson Renault of 1908, the Berna post-bus of 1921, and the Hispano-Suiza—one of the last of its distinguished line, built in 1937. An English visitor will note with pleasure the Austin Seven and the Rolls-Royce of 1926, unmistakable of course yet given a slightly strange character through the styling of its body, made in Switzerland.

Like everything else in this Museum, these vehicles are excellently displayed. Each has plenty of space to itself and can be closely examined with ease. Several have been sectioned, so that engine and bodywork can both be seen. One thing, however, seems to be at fault here. The vehicles are mounted haphazardly. One section is devoted to the Swiss pioneers; otherwise the order of the exhibits is neither that of date nor typological. No general introduction is available, to help the visitor to trace the continuous evolution of the motor-car. If he wishes to understand it properly, indeed, in terms of the carriage of passengers, he must reach farther back, beyond the internal combustion engine. For that he must go upstairs.

The eight horse-carriages on the first floor make what, to my way of thinking, is the finest piece of display in the whole Museum. As you ascend the light staircase through this airy glass-walled building you see them standing, almost as it were on a raft, floating in mid-air. Any sense of bareness that might arise from the generous proportions of their spacing-out is brilliantly counteracted by the device of filling the whole of a central panel from floor to ceiling with a uniform series of drawings of carriages, stencilled in outline. In front of this great screen, in the place of honour, is a hansom cab of 1890. Round the walls, in between the carriages, are cases containing small displays. Here is an enlarged photograph of the blue-prints for the construction of a past carriage of 1911; there a group of passports and customs documents—particularly important in a country where each canton levied its own customs dues until 1848.

The top floor brings us to roads and road construction, from the Roman road system of the country down to Maillart's concrete bridges and the problems of road traffic in our own time. This is potentially one of the most important sections in the whole Museum; but it gives the impression that it is not yet fully developed. Here, and below, the labelling is often inadequate. The splendid series of drawings of carriages, for example, is not described. The admirably clear illuminated map of the Roman roads loses much of its meaning from the failure to give modern equivalents of the Roman names: one is left to infer that Octodurum is represented today by Martigny and Vindonissa by Brugg. Is there not an opportunity here, moreover, to extend the range of colour in the illumination so as to indicate at a glance which modern roads represent a Roman original?

Aviation, shipping, and the tourist industry at present share a single gallery (6), though it is intended later to give a separate one to each. They are certainly a little crowded at the moment. Aviation, in particular, will gain when greater space is available for it. Among the objects displayed are the carriage of one of the balloons of the Swiss pioneer, Eduard Spelterini; the biplane made by the brothers Dufaux in 1910, in which Armand Dufaux flew the length of the Lake of Geneva—41 miles—in 56 minutes; a Blériot monoplane of 1913; the engine of the aircraft in which Walter Mittelholzer crashed in the Glarus Alps—miraculously escaping death—in 1922. Mittelholzer is indeed one of the key men in the development of Swiss aviation out of the experimental period into its commercial fulfilment. That fulfilment is well illustrated by a series of exhibits devoted to the history and the present operations of the national aviation company, Swiss-air.

At the back of the Aeronautical Gallery is the section concerned with shipping. This has its surprises. One would expect attention to be paid to lake and river navigation, to the one major Swiss port of Basle, to hydro-electric schemes and their effect on the rivers' flow. This is done mainly by means of pictures, which convey something of the difficulties and achievements of inland navigation and of the part played during the past hundred years and more by the lake steamers—like *Rigi* outside—in the economic and social life of Switzerland.

But the rest of this section takes us far away, out into the open seas. The Museum is fortunate in being able to show, on loan, some of the fine models of sailing ships from the collection of Mr Philipp Keller of St Niklausen. These are set off to great advantage by their display in cases in front of enlarged prints of ports like those that would have been familiar to these ships in the eighteenth and early nineteenth centuries: a splendid idea that gives life to the models, an accurate setting that is worthy of them. On the wall facing them is a chart showing the history of the Blue Riband of the Atlantic: well conceived and drawn, with outlines of some of the ships that are mentioned, but marred once more by the failure to provide an adequate explanation of the display. How is the visitor to make out which ship is which?

The floor above is given up to the tourist business. Appropriately, since this is Switzerland, which has long been pre-eminent in the art of attracting travellers and catering for their wants; since, too, this brings the visitor face to face with something more than the means, the instruments, of transport—with one of the main purposes for which it has developed. The story starts far back with Swiss spas of the sixteenth century, the baths the visitors went to for their health and the inns at which they stayed. This first theme has by no means vanished today: there are still twenty-two spas in operation in Switzerland, besides the innumerable sanatoria of the Grisons.

The remainder of this section is devoted to the spectacular development of travelling and the tourist business in Switzerland during the past two centuries. The photographs include some evocative pictures of the Rigi-Kulm Hotel in its early days (together with a group of its visitors' books), Edwardian hotel interiors, and pioneer mountaineering parties. There is, moreover, a small selection of the usual equipment of tourists in the nineteenth century: a travelling trunk, a telescope, guide-books— though neither a Baedeker nor a Murray. Thereafter the exhibition

39a Lucerne: Room 4, showing (*left to right*) the Burgdorf–Thun electric locomotive of 1899, a replica of the first train to run in Switzerland (Zürich–Baden, 1847), and a rack-and-adhesion locomotive of the Brünig Railway

b Hamar: general view. Kloften station is on the left

40a Royal Scottish Museum: *Wylam Dilly* (1813)

b Science Museum: *Rocket* in the state in which it was received the Commissioners of Patents in 1862

changes, to become a rather glossy and conventional presentation of the tourist industry in Switzerland today, almost indistinguishable from the ordinary paraphernalia of a tourist office.

To my mind, this section of the Museum, which ought to be one of the most entertaining and instructive, is really the least successful. The presentation of the earlier history is excellent, gripping the attention with its odd vitality. The presentation of the modern part of the story seems, by contrast, rather humdrum; and one of the reasons for this is that the exhibition becomes at this point very much less precise. Many of the hotels of which photographs are shown are not named. We have moved into a world of types, not of individuals. There are exceptions to this general statement: portraits of some of the celebrated Swiss hotel-keepers, for example. But—perhaps from fear of affording advertisement, to the advantage of one hotel against another—this part of the exhibition is disappointingly generalized. Surely the objects in a museum must be identifiable and precisely described, or they are nothing?

The exhibits in Room 7 also extend the Museum directly into the field of social history; for they display the postal services and telecommunications. Here the Museum is not entirely self-contained. It is in some respects complementary to the Postal Museum in Berne. If the visitor wishes to see postage stamps, for example, he must go there. Postal uniforms, too, are displayed at Berne; only a few fragments are exhibited in this Museum. The evolution of that characteristic Swiss institution, the post-bus, is shown from the horse-drawn sleigh and coach to the motor vehicle of 1963. In front of a splendid coupé-landau that plied over the Alpine passes from 1880 to 1920 a stand has been placed, by happy inspiration, with a postman's horn and hat. At the touch of a button it gives out four of the calls the horn played, repeating them then with the jingle of the harness of the approaching horses. It is a deeply affecting sound, which transports you at once out into the pure upper air of the Alps.

The main emphasis in this section of the Museum is not historical: it is firmly placed on things of the present—on the technical equipment of the telephone system, on radio and television. No Post Office in the world could wish for a better shop-window than this. It is a full demonstration of modern services in their widest range.

In a short study it is impossible to do more than indicate some of the main features of a museum so large and varied. One or two more things must, however, be said to round off even a simple sketch.

I have ventured to criticize the descriptions of some of the objects displayed, suggesting that they might with advantage be fuller and that the relationship of one object to another might be made more clear. But several things are to be placed on the other side of the account. First of all, nearly everything *is* labelled. Secondly, the descriptions are given in four languages, German, French, Italian, and English. The German account is the standard one, and sometimes the translations are abridged; but this is an admirable practice, to be recommended also in countries that have not the multi-lingual character of Switzerland. Thirdly, the labelling is outstandingly plain. No peering here at descriptions typewritten with a faded ribbon, placed below the level of one's knees; these labels are all fixed at a reasonable height—whether for adults or for children—and they are enlarged photographically from printing in a bold black type. Lastly, the Museum has started to issue an excellent series of descriptive booklets: a general guide to the whole collection by the Director, Dr Alfred Waldis, and a number of sectional guides, including one to the motor-cars, together with a compact and expert survey of the early history of aviation in Switzerland by Dr W. Dollfus.

There can be no doubt whatever that the Museum is a resounding success. It was opened on July 1, 1959. In its first five years of life, well over a million people were admitted to it. And these were paying visitors, too: the standard charge for admission is 2 Swiss francs (3s 6d), with appropriate reductions for children and parties. It may perhaps be suggested that the Museum owes its success to three things: the intrinsic interest of its collections, its felicitous site, and the skill and imagination that have gone into its construction and display. This is not a museum of dead things, but of activities that are alive and concern everyone urgently. The sense of space that has been allowed to develop around the objects displayed enables them all to be seen and carried separately in the mind.

Here is indeed a notable addition to the museums of Europe. Everybody must wish it continuing success, and the opportunity to extend its buildings quickly on to the adjoining land that awaits them.

27

LEONARDO DA VINCI MUSEUM
MILAN

This is a national institution, similar to our own Science Museum and to the Deutsches Museum in Munich. It contains a substantial section dealing with land transport, to which another dealing with aviation is to be added before long; and it shares a building with a shipping museum, the Civico Museo Navale Didattico. There is a guide-book, in Italian, to the land transport section, published in 1964: useful, but expensive.

The Museum was inaugurated in 1952. It is housed in magnificent quarters: the former Olivetan convent of San Vittore. This was heavily damaged by bombing in the second World War and in large measure rebuilt in 1948–52; a vast series of buildings on four floors, including open-air space around two internal courtyards. It is conveniently situated not far from the centre of the city and close to the basilica of Sant' Ambrogio, which almost any visitor to Milan will wish to see.

The land transport section is in the semi-basement, reached by stairs immediately to the left of the main entrance and then through sections devoted to metal-working and the exploitation of minerals. It is designed to cover in outline the whole development of land transport, and it makes more use of models and reproductions than of original machines and instruments.

It begins with an excellent display showing the evolution of the wheel. This is in Room 2, to the right of the entrance to the section. (The rooms are numbered on the plan and in the guide-book, but nowhere on the walls or doors.) The wheels are mounted in a single sequence along one wall. They are not originals, but they are full-size replicas that have been made for this display, after a close study of the evidence available from archaeological

227

discoveries and on bas-reliefs and other sculpture. The earliest is a wheel of a type used at Ur in the fourth millennium BC. The next, dating from about 1500 BC, is among the earliest wheels known to have been used in Europe; the original was discovered near Arona, only forty miles away. The series continues with Near Eastern, Greek, Etruscan, Roman, and Scandinavian examples, followed by a group from the Renaissance that includes two illustrating the ideas of Leonardo da Vinci himself.

At this point the story is broken off abruptly, to be resumed after a gap of three centuries with a series of pneumatic-tyred wheels from 1904 onwards. This seems a pity: for considerable variations in design are to be noted in the wheels used in the golden age of horse traction, and they too need to be demonstrated.

We are next shown models of wheeled vehicles, among them two of the earliest attempts at mechanical propulsion: one by Giovanni Fontana (1420), which was moved by chains actuated by the passenger from inside the carriage; the other that of Robert Valturio, dating from 1465, which had a sail at each side, like those of a windmill.

In the sixteenth century Italy became the leading supplier of coaches to the rest of Europe, and Milan was the centre of their manufacture. One or two examples of this coach-building would have been welcome at this point.

Some original carriages of the nineteenth century are shown next door in Room 3; others are dispersed round the arcaded first floor of the front courtyard of the building (reached by a door on the right immediately inside the main entrance). They include the fire-engine of Chiaravalle, a formidably large and heavy Victoria, and a low-slung horse cab, complete with its charging meter.

This section is rounded off (Rooms 1A, 1B) by a display of horse furniture, comprehending one eighteenth-century set from Prince Pio Falcò and one of the nineteenth century from Count Gnecchi Ruscone. The setting here is splendidly contrived against a background of polished panels and rush matting, relieved by touches of a rich royal blue. It is marvellous to look at; but for most visitors it must be quite meaningless in the absence of a brief written explanation.

Bicycles and motor-cycles appear in Room 10, at the further end of the long gallery (2) in which we began. The hobby-horse caught on in Milan early in the nineteenth century: here is a printed notice issued by the city police in 1818, stating that the riding of these machines has proved dangerous to passers-by and banning them altogether from the streets at night, on pain of confiscation. A *draisienne* of 1820 is shown here, together with an early pedal-cycle by Michaud.[1] The later machines include a monocycle of 1865; a vast bicycle of 1868, over 11 feet long, with pedals connected by spindles to the back wheels; a tandem (1935), on which the two riders are mounted side by side; and a parachutist's bicycle of 1939.

The motor-cycles displayed along the other wall of Room 10 make a disappointing show. They are crammed too close together, and there is little to distinguish one from another. In particular, one would have expected this museum to give some attention to the evolution of the motor-scooter. It can be traced here, but without the help of any labelling. A graceful early French motor-scooter, the Monet-Goyon, anticipates in 1919 the essential characteristics of the Vespa of 1946 and the Lambretta of 1947. Both those famous types are represented here, but they deserve to be singled out for more honourable treatment from the crowd of rather ordinary motor-cycles surrounding them. Were not these noisy, convenient little machines the first sign given to the world after the war of the resurgence of Italian technical skill and originality?

If that is a missed chance, it is made up by the imaginative treatment of the racing motor-cycle in Room 4, the Sala dei Primati. Here half a dozen of the Italian machines that established world records for speed between 1932 and 1955 are shown in a round gallery designed to look like a racing track. Under powerful lighting from above and behind, this display contrives to give, within a very small space, a real illusion of movement.

Rooms 6 and 7 contain railway models. To avoid isolating them in separate glass boxes, they are shown as if standing in the open air, with a painted background of rural landscape and town streets. The effect is, however, very curious, for these models have been haphazardly assembled and they stand in line on track of different gauges, built to various scales. Again the barest description appears with them, or none at all. As they are at present set out, these rooms have not much to offer the visitor.

---

[1] For these machines see pp. 31-2.

The full-sized railway exhibits are in Room 9. They include some signalling apparatus, manual and electric, which would be interesting if it were more fully explained, and a steam tram engine, built in Brussels in 1912. It was the last to work on the Milan system and it continued in service until 1958.

This brings us to what must be reckoned the most instructive section here: that showing the evolution of public transport in Milan (Room 8). Models are used throughout, set in delicately-painted street scenes.

In this, as in so much else, the brief Napoleonic occupation of northern Italy served to release new ideas. *Fiacres* (the French hackney-coaches) were introduced into Milan in 1801, *diligences* twelve years later. When the Austrian Government assumed power in Lombardy in 1814, it developed the long-distance *diligence* for its own purposes. The first railway, running out to Monza, was opened in 1840. Its station was outside the walls, and through the instigation of the railway a company was established to operate horse-buses to and from the centre of the city. The horse tram makes its appearance here, in the seventies, closely followed by the steam tram. The wide flat Plain of Lombardy was the ideal terrain for the operation of that cumbrous machine; and once it had taken root, its hold was more lasting here than anywhere else in Europe. Milan got its first electric trams in 1893, its first motor-buses twelve years later. In 1906 it played with the notion of the elevated tramway, for visitors to the International Exhibition of 1906; but that proved to be a gimmick, and no more.

The huge square in front of the cathedral was the hub of the whole tramway system: the Carosello, or roundabout, it was called. By the mid-twenties this was producing intolerable congestion, and the decision was taken to break up the roundabout, dispersing the terminal points or running the services through from one side of the city to another. At the same time the population was growing fast, and the suburbs extending further and further outward. To meet these needs a new type of vehicle was introduced in 1928, doubled in length and capacity and running on eight wheels. The trolley-bus has appeared since, the use of the motor-bus has been extended, and now there is an underground railway: yet Milan remains faithful to its electric trams still. In many other large cities, where they survive it is with an apologetic air, as if they were there only on sufferance pending their suppression by the bus; the track is being allowed to run down, the vehicles themselves often need a coat of paint. Nothing of this appears in Milan, where the system is as good as ever it was.

Each of these critical changes in the development of the transport system in Milan is illustrated in this series of excellent models; and each is accompanied by a descriptive notice.[1] If the story is to be told in terms of the vehicles employed, it could scarcely be done better.

The evolution of the motor-car is dealt with in a similar way (Room 11), with models to illustrate the earlier phases of the story. Among the full-sized originals is the chassis of one of the earliest motor-vehicles wholly of Italian construction, a tricar designed by Enrico de Bernardi about 1895; and a car produced by the famous firm of cycle-manufacturers, Bianchi, in 1901. The best-known Italian names—Fiat, Alfa Romeo, Isotta Fraschini —are represented only by cars of the 1920s and 1930s.

Adjoining Room 11 is an elaborate display of the methods of extracting and refining petroleum: a gift from the Italian Shell Company. Everything is carefully and amply explained. In this respect the presentation here reaches a much higher standard than prevails at present in the rooms we have been considering.

This is a young museum, still in the early stages of its development. The transport section will benefit greatly from two additions that are to be expected before long. An aeronautical display is being prepared; and the railway museum formerly established in the commodious basement of the Termini station in Rome is to be transferred here. That was a notable display. If it can be fully absorbed into these collections and adequately housed, it will help the Leonardo da Vinci Museum to become one of the chief transport museums of the Continent.

[1] It is, however, regrettable that some egregious nonsense should be talked here about the origin of the word 'tram'. We are offered a new version of the hoary legend connecting it with the name of the engineer Benjamin Outram: it derives, we are told, from the English town of Dutram, where it was first tried out. The word has, in fact, a long Teutonic ancestry, meaning a beam of wood. Cf. C. E. Lee, *The Evolution of Railways* (ed. 2, 1943), 20–1.

28

DEUTSCHES MUSEUM, MUNICH

The Deutsches Museum starts with a number of outstanding advantages. It is a national institution, and its nation is one peculiarly well disposed to support a museum of this kind. By its very title it stands as a symbol of German unity, prized all the more while the country has been partitioned during the past twenty years. But it is a German national institution *seated in Munich*; able therefore to count on the support of Bavaria, always jealous of the encroaching power of Prussia and Berlin. It is indeed, as everyone who visits it must see at once, no mean tourist attraction in itself. That is not surprising when one considers its situation, occupying its own island in the River Isar, close to the centre of one of the most famous cities of central Europe. The Germans have come to take a special pride in their achievements in technology; and it is precisely this Museum's function to display them. It has attracted to itself the help of German industry in many ways, taking very substantial forms. The Museum is well supported from public funds, from the admission fees paid by visitors, and from private benefaction alike. With all this help, and with the pride and enthusiasm of Germany behind it, the Deutsches Museum might be expected to be a thundering success. It is.

The Museum owes its origin to the vision and energy of one man: Oskar von Miller (1855–1934). He was the son of a prominent ironmaster in Munich, born therefore to commercial position and wealth. He formed his great idea while still a comparatively young man, partly as a result of visits he paid to the Conservatoire des Arts et Métiers in Paris and to the South Kensington Museum in London. Should not Germany have similar museums? It is to be noted, however, that from the outset, though his vision was of a German museum, he rightly saw the science and technology he

41a York: part of the bridge over the River Gaunless at Brusselton, Co. Durham, designed by George Stephenson for the Stockton and Darlington Railway (1823–5)—the first iron railway bridge in the world

Clapham: original drawing (subsequently engraved) by J. C. Bourne of the retaining wall at Camden Town under construction for the London and Birmingham Railway, 1837

42a York: chaldron wag[on]
from Cramlington c[ol]-
liery, Northumberla[nd]
(1826). Fires burni[ng]
in the braziers h[ung]
from the frame ser[ve]
the purpose of t[ail]
lights

b York: 3rd-class [and]
covered 2nd-class [ve]-
hicles of the Bod[min]
and Wadebridge [Rail]-
way, c. 1840

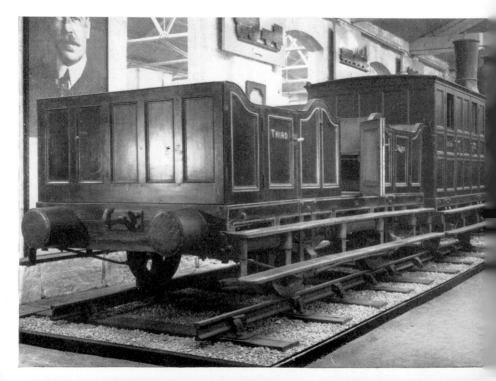

43a Penrhyn Castle: velocipede from the Padarn Railway

b Clapham: turntable for moving carriages at Euston, London and Birmingham Railway

44a Stockholm: locomotive *Fryckstad* built for the Fryckstad Railway (3 feet 7¼ inch gauge) in 1855

b Hamar: metre-gauge tank engine *Alf*, built by Beyer Peacock of Manchester in 1870

45a Copenhagen: Rendsborg station, S. Schleswig Railway. Oil painting of 1846

b Copenhagen: second Central station in Copenhagen (1864–1911), with horse tram in front

46 Utrecht: 'The Honeymoon.' Painting by C. Cap of Antwerp, 1885

47 Clapham: Painting by Robert Collinson *c*. 1865

48a Science Museum: Cook's block signalling indicator, Norfolk Railway, 1845

Swindon: gong for alarm signal in use on broad-gauge engines of the Great Western Railway

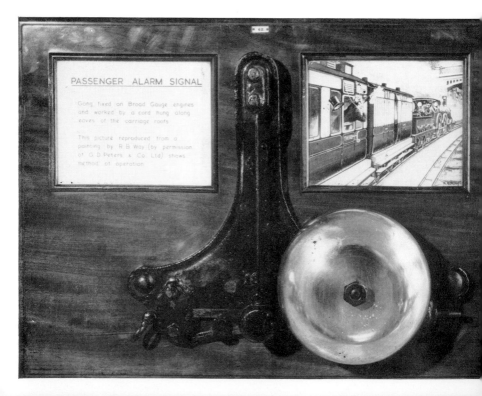

wished to display in it as international; and those responsible for the Museum have always resisted a narrowly chauvinistic policy, remaining faithful to the spirit of their founder's ideas.

Von Miller took the first steps to establish the Museum in 1903. The collections were opened to the public, in temporary quarters, in 1906; and on the same day the foundation stone of a permanent building was laid, with a great deal of ceremony, by Kaiser Wilhelm II. A large official painting of the function hangs on the first floor of the Museum. One notices among the distinguished company the names of Diesel, Siemens, and Röntgen. The building went ahead rather slowly; but it was opened at last, in the presence of the founder himself, on his seventieth birthday in 1925. Seven years later the second main block of buildings, containing the library, was brought into use. By the time he died in 1934, Miller must have had the satisfaction of seeing his creation established as one of the great museums of Europe. It continued to grow, and in 1935 it acquired a large conference hall. But in the second World War, like most things in Munich, the buildings were heavily damaged; and something like one-fifth of the collections were destroyed. Very quickly when peace came the work of reconstruction began. Now almost the whole of the building is open to visitors once more.

As the Deutsches Museum embraces technology in all its branches, it contains much that will not concern us here. (An excellent short guide-book is available, in German, French, and English editions.) It should, however, be emphasized that wherever one turns in it, one finds the same high standard of selection, description, and display; and—a matter of great importance—a large proportion of the machines are in working order. This is a museum that communicates a sense of movement and life.

Most visitors coming into the Museum for the first time will walk up the short flight of stairs that faces the entrance; an instinctive movement, which will bring them face to face at once with the most spectacular of its displays. The stairs lead into an open hall surrounded by galleries and lighted chiefly by windows high up on the first floor. In the centre is a large rectangular well, which contains an entire wooden sailing ship of about 1880, *Maria Finkenwerder*. She belongs to the type known to the Germans as the *Ewer*, the characteristic craft of the lower Elbe: river boats, but capable of voyages across the North Sea to England. She is shown with all her sails set, her mainmast reaching almost to the roof, on a level with some of the historic aeroplanes suspended there. One of her sides is cut away, to show the construction of the ship and something of her quarters below deck. The whole job is admirably done: as well as possible, indeed, without the essential element of water—and if the ship were to be kept afloat her timbers would, steadily and inevitably, deteriorate. Here she is as safe as she can be made, for good.

She is surrounded with other smaller wooden boats and with models illustrating the evolution of the ship from Ancient Egypt and Greece down to the twentieth century. (Rather oddly, no example of a Viking ship appears.) The original boats include dug-out canoes, an Eskimo kayak, a Venetian gondola, a coracle from Ireland, and the first of all motor-boats, built by Gottlieb Daimler in 1886. Among the models are some of the last and largest sailing ships, including the *Herzogin Cecilie* and *Preussen*, both dating from 1902; the *Preussen* was the largest square-rigged ship ever built. The evolution of the steamship is shown from the work of Fulton and Symington, passing on through the *Great Britain* of 1843 to the German Atlantic liners, culminating in the *Imperator* (which became the Cunarder *Berengaria*) and the *Bremen* of 1938. Very good use has been made here of photographs, displayed on the walls behind, showing the ships' internal fittings and appointments. The first-class dining-rooms of the *Auguste Victoria* of 1888 and the *Kaiser Wilhelm II* of 1902 are encrusted with unbelievably florid decoration—eating in the *Kaiser Wilhelm II* was like eating in the stalls of a theatre, surrounded by two tiers of galleries. By way of contrast you move on to the quite Spartan third-class accommodation of the *Imperator* in 1913 and then to the furnishing of the *Bremen*, wholly without fuss, clean and pleasant in all its lines.

At the far end of the hall, illuminated in a broad dark bay, there are models of fishing vessels sailing on a transparent sea, their trawling nets resting on its bed. The remaining side is devoted chiefly to the craft employed in the huge German rivers, including a noble paddle-wheeled tug built for service on the Rhine in 1906.

Beside the sailing ship's bow in the centre of the hall is a staircase descending to the basement, where the story of navigation is continued. First you are offered glimpses (in full-sized mock-up) of the living quarters on ocean-going ships: a reconstructed scene between decks on an emigrant ship about 1870 and then two cabins —one for a first-class passenger, the other for two members of the crew—on a liner of 1936. Instruments of navigation are displayed, and you can handle a full-sized steering wheel yourself, mounted in such a way as to give you a realistic idea of the difficulty of holding a ship on to a fixed course.

One of the best things in this section of the Museum is a demonstration of the use to which models are put by naval architects— in this case showing how changes in the design of the ship's hull can reduce resistance to the waves. One notes with pleasure the tribute paid to the fundamental work of William Froude from 1856 onwards, which initiated this kind of research.

Ships of war occupy a relatively modest place here, and, with one single exception, their development is shown almost wholly through models, from the *Grosser Adler von Lübeck* of 1566 down to the battleships of the last war. Special attention is given to under-sea work, in weapons and human diving; and the entire end wall of this group of rooms is occupied by one of the outstanding exhibits of the whole Museum—the original submarine U1 of 1906, the first to be commissioned for the German navy. One side of her casing has been removed, to show her engines, equipment, and living quarters.

There is a complement to this section in another, devoted to hydraulic engineering; but that lies in a different wing of the building, and it is perhaps better to move next to the first floor of the central block, to the Aeronautics Gallery, which encloses at a high level the masts and sails of *Maria Finkenwerder*. The display begins with balloons and passes on quickly to airships, where it is centred almost exclusively on the work of Ferdinand von Zeppelin. Most properly, too: for he was far more successful than anyone else has ever been in promoting the development of the airship and its use both in war and in peace. With their memories coloured by the disasters that overtook R34 and R101, English people are apt to forget that German airships operated successful commercial services in the 1930s (cf. p. 46).

You now come, by way of parachutes and kites, to winged flight, and here too there is an outstanding German pioneer to be honoured—Otto Lilienthal. Mr Gibbs-Smith has characterized him as 'the key figure in aviation during the last decade of the [nineteenth] century, and one of the greatest men in the history of flying', adding that 'he may fairly be described as the world's first true aviator; that is to say, he was the first man to build practical heavier-than-air aircraft and fly them consistently and successfully.'[1] Lilienthal's main work was confined to five years, beginning in 1891. He was well on the way to developing a powered glider when he crashed on a flight in 1896. As he lay dying in a Berlin hospital he remarked, 'Sacrifices have got to be made'. His work led directly on to that of the Wrights in America. Wilbur Wright, indeed, said: 'My own active interest in aeronautical problems dates to the death of Lilienthal.'[2] A diorama here shows some of Lilienthal's earliest attempts at gliding, and a full-size reproduction of his biplane of 1895 hangs above, not far from one of a Wright biplane of 1908, flown in the following year by Orville Wright from the Tempelhof airfield in Berlin, and another of the machine in which Blériot crossed the English Channel in 1909. From the first World War there is an original Fokker D VII of 1918. Here, as in other similar collections, we look in vain for any machine of the 1920s. But there is a Junkers 52 of 1932, complete except for the removal of one wing; you can pass through the cabin and look into the cockpit. A Messerschmitt 109 of 1935 is here—one of the most numerous of all types of aircraft. More than 33,000 were built, in Germany until the end of the second World War and then under licence in other countries: they were still being turned out in Spain and elsewhere as late as 1958. And finally we come to a Messerschmitt 262, which in 1944 became the first jet aeroplane to go into mass-production anywhere in the world.

Critical points in the construction of aircraft are illustrated by a series of exhibits, showing types of propeller, sections of wings, examples of important engines, and navigating instruments. There is also a large model of an airport, demonstrating the complicated controls required for regulating modern traffic.

The remainder of the transport collections are in a side wing of the Museum, reached by going back to the entrance hall and turning left.

The first section is concerned with hydraulic engineering. It demonstrates the manifold uses of water-power and the distribution and control of water-borne transport. Though seaports are represented here, by illuminated models of Hamburg and Bremen,

[1] C. H. Gibbs-Smith, *The Aeroplane* (1960), 28, 30.   [2] *Ibid.*, 29, 36.

and though the entire display is dominated by the flashing beams of the lantern of the lightship *Borkumriff*, which was stationed at the mouth of the Ems from 1911 to 1956, the main emphasis here is placed on inland navigation, illustrated throughout by models. The various methods of changing level on waterways— by lock, inclined plane, and lift—are shown. These models are somewhat unreal since they lack water; there is another of a lock, in which this fault is remedied, downstairs. The work of dredgers and diving-ships is shown clearly, the river-bed appearing through clear glass. There is an outstandingly good diorama of the river-port of Würzburg about 1840, with a passenger steamer and sailing barges on the Main and horse-drawn vehicles on land. On the quay in the foreground is a large wooden crane, built in 1768–73. It is housed in a solid building like the lower part of a tower-mill, crowned by a low dome, baroque and elegant. At the pressure of a button the lower part of the wall descends to expose the huge wooden wheels of the mechanism. This crane continued in service until 1910. It was not unique; other, more modest, examples of the same sort of machine are still to be found on German river-quays today. Apart from the technical interest it offers, this is a deeply satisfying model to look at, the bulk of the crane and the ships in the foreground beautifully balanced by the grand mass of the Bishops' Palace high up on the opposite shore. It is complemented by another diorama, placed next to it: of the north harbour of Duisburg-Ruhrort as it is today.

Leaving this room at the far end, by the brightly-coloured diagram of the port of Hamburg, turn right and right again into the adjoining gallery, which is devoted to road-engineering and bridge-building. This is an outstandingly imaginative and successful achievement, combining perfectly the model and the full-sized exhibit, illustrating with unfailing precision the critical stages of technical evolution from perhistoric origins to the motorway and the concrete bridge of the twentieth century. Only one thing is missing—original material; for almost everything here is a model or a mock-up. But this is, in the nature of the case, hard to avoid.

The general arrangement is chronological. Roads are dealt with, chiefly by means of models and documents, on the left-hand wall, bridges in the centre of the room and to the right. This conception is obvious enough. What gives it distinction is the framing of the whole exhibition within a sequence of five full-sized

sections of bridges, built up to the height of the ceiling, constructed of stone, brick, timber, steel, and prestressed concrete:
an unforgettable demonstration of these changing techniques
and the different masses and forms they have produced.

We begin in prehistory with a timber baulk road excavated
near Osnabrück in 1892, and a picture of a clapper bridge on Dart-
moor. These are framed within a reproduction of part of a Roman
aqueduct in Provence, built in stone. Medieval bridge-building
is represented by some fine pictures—from Pavia and Verona and
Cahors—and a model of the fifteen-arch bridge at Regensburg.
A splendidly elaborate model shows Peronnet's bridge over the
Seine at Neuilly under construction. Timber bridges are well
illustrated, from a bridge of boats built over the Rhine to the
orders of Julius Caesar in 55 BC to another, dating from 1865,
over the same river near Karlsruhe, designed to carry a railway
as well as a road. The examples chosen range widely all over the
world, including timber bridges in Japan and the roads of the
Incas, as the Spanish invaders found them.

Moving towards the end of the eighteenth century, you are
made aware of the impact of Britain on Europe. Here is a drawing
of the Iron Bridge in Coalbrookdale and a photograph of a much
more modest version of it, small and low, built over twenty years
later in Silesia—the first iron bridge on the Continent; or again
you can compare Robert Stephenson's Britannia Bridge over the
Menai Strait with another at Dirschau on the railway between
Berlin and Königsberg, completed seven years later. The display
on the opposite wall shows us something of the work of Telford
and McAdam, with a clear demonstration of their contrasted
methods of road-making. The development of the suspension
bridge is traced from its medieval origins through Telford's
Menai Bridge to Roebling's Niagara Bridge of 1855 (wrongly
described as the first built for a railway: Samuel Brown's at
Middlesbrough came twenty-five years earlier, though admittedly
it was unsuccessful) and the superbly austere Severins Bridge at
Cologne (1959). The last full-sized section, spanning the room, is
of a bridge over the Moselle at Koblenz in pre-stressed concrete,
completed in 1953.

In road construction, the later exhibits are chiefly concerned
with motorways, in the development of which Germany took a
leading part in the 1930s. The methods of construction of these

roads are well shown by means of models. Where they are leading our civilization appears, also very well, in a frightening diorama of a wide stretch of open landscape criss-crossed—garrotted, one might almost say—by the fierce, white multiple bands of the motorways.

Another aspect of transport engineering is demonstrated in the next section, at the opposite end of the hall devoted to roads and bridges. This is tunnelling, exemplified not only in models, showing the different methods employed in Germany, Austria, and Belgium, but, most impressively, in a full-sized reproduction of a piece of the Simplon Tunnel, built in 1898–1906. Peering in through the massive timber scaffolding at the men working in the depths of the mountain beyond, you get a sense of the greatness of the work, the extraordinary achievement represented by it in human and technical terms, stronger than anything that can be communicated by verbal descriptions or photographs.

And so, finally, to vehicles. At Munich they are a distinguished company; but, as the preceding pages will have shown, they are to be seen here in their proper perspective as one part, and one only, of the whole complicated apparatus of transport.

Among the horse-drawn road vehicles, which you come to first, a state coach of Ludwig II of Bavaria stands in a class by itself; it is rightly displayed in isolation from all the other carriages. It was built in 1878 and from one point of view it may be regarded as the last of a long line: such coaches, elaborately decorated for the rare ceremonial appearance of sovereigns, took a standardized form in the seventeeth century; and if this is compared with, for example, the Swedish state coach of 1699 that stands in the entrance hall of the Northern Museum in Stockholm, it is clear that the two vehicles are, in essentials, very closely similar. But the decoration of the Bavarian coach belongs to the fantasy-world in which Ludwig moved—the floweriest kind of baroque, realized in harsh nineteenth-century terms. Its quality becomes stranger still when one discovers that this weird anachronism was the first road passenger vehicle ever to be lighted by electricity.[1]

The conveyances for more normal passengers begin with a group of sleighs. The carriages are all of the nineteenth century.

[1] An earlier coach, built for Ludwig II on the occasion of his wedding in 1871, is also to be seen in Munich: at the Marstall Museum, in the stables of the Nymphenburg Palace.

They include one with an interesting association—the landaulette, built about 1825, used by the Bavarian ambassador in Rome to smuggle Pope Pius IX out of the city to the safety of Gaeta during the revolution of 1848; a Swiss postal coach; and a travelling carriage of 1895 made for the Regent Leopold of Bavaria, of the type called by the Germans a 'mylord'. Horse-transport is evoked also by a series of small exhibits in alcoves on the opposite wall.

The first moves towards mechanization came in the eighteenth century, and one is well illustrated here: a four-wheeled light car with a seat for a single passenger, put into motion by a servant behind, treading pedals connected by a rope with the back axle. It was built by Jackman of London in 1765 and used in the park of the Nymphenburg Palace.

It is a natural transition from this to the bicycle, which is shown, with its motorized successor, in the upper gallery of the big hall next door. Though the Baron von Drais, who invented the hobby-horse (often called after him the *draisina*) about 1817, was a Bavarian, there is no original hobby-horse here, only a replica of one found at Karlsruhe. The earliest pedal bicycle in the collection dates from about 1853. The 'ordinary' and the 'safety' bicycles then follow, including several made at Coventry. Among the more modern machines are a four-man tandem of about 1908 and a German army portable bicycle, dating from the early part of the first World War, made in two hinged sections and folding back compactly. It weighs 40lb.

At the foot of the stairs leading up to this gallery, not very conspicuously placed, is a replica of the first of all motor-bicycles, constructed by Daimler in 1885. Considered simply as a bicycle, it is old-fashioned for its date, made of wood and representing a return to something like the Macmillan pattern evolved more than forty years earlier.[1] The original was preserved with care in the Daimler works at Canstatt until it was destroyed in a fire there in 1903. The reproduction was made by Paul Daimler in 1921.

From this original, we can observe the motor-cycle developing here in a series of machines built between 1894 and 1960, including a Triumph and a Douglas from England. Among them is the first German motor-scooter, produced by Krupp in 1919. It is

[1] Cf. p. 31

240

49a Birmingham: *Secundus*, built in Birmingham in 1874

b Belfast: *Kathleen*, which worked on the Cavan and Leitrim Railway from 1887 to 1959

c Penrhyn Castle: 3-foot gauge industrial locomotive (1885)

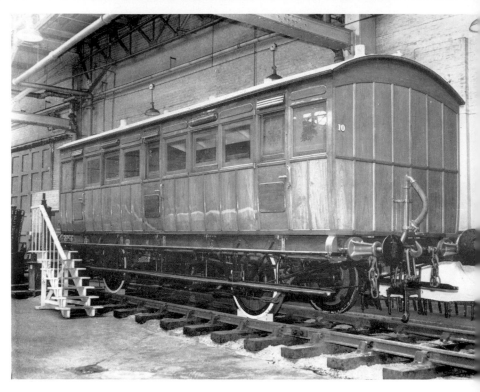

50a Clapham: Directors' saloon, North London Railway (1872)

b Lucerne: restaurant car built for the Swiss Federal Railways by Ringhoffer of Smichow, near Prague, in 1914

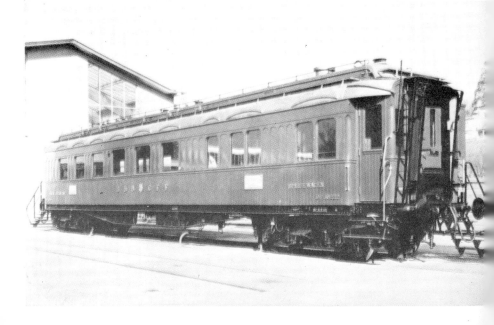

interesting to see how this idea—developed simultaneously in France (see p. 229)—languished, to be taken up and turned to success by the Italians with their Vespas and Lambrettas, produced directly after the second World War.

The story of the motor-car starts here with a bang. Its fascinating prehistory is virtually ignored; to follow that through one must go elsewhere—to Paris and Lucerne, South Kensington and Glasgow. At Munich we begin with Benz's three-wheeled vehicle of the 1885 and Daimler's quadri-cycle of 1889. The latter was a critically important machine, for it led to the foundation of the motor-car industry in France through the firm of Panhard et Levassor, which secured a licence to manufacture and sell Daimler engines. Emile Levassor quickly improved on Daimler's work, to produce what became known as *le système Panhard*, combining nearly all the essential features of the motor-car as we know it today, in 1891. Here, on a raised platform at one end of the hall, are portraits of Levassor and Benz, of Daimler and his partner Maybach, above examples of the vehicles built by them in 1886–96. Below these, and in an adjoining room, stands a wide range of other cars, made in Western Europe and America during the succeeding seventy years. They are not disposed very systematically, and—something rare in this well-ordered museum—they are not all labelled. Here are just a few examples, of vehicles that are of special interest.

First of all, two steam cars: a Serpollet of 1891 (its inventor had driven another model from Paris to Lyons, nearly three hundred miles, in the previous year) and a Stanley of 1900. These Stanleys may claim to be the first cars to be produced in large quantity in America. They had a large and interesting progeny. A Stanley held for a time the world's speed record: 121·6 m.p.h., attained in 1906. Steam cars of this make continued to be produced down to the second World War.

Three early motor-tricycles are here: one built by Léon Bollée at Le Mans in 1896, the other two both of 1899—one from Augsburg, the other from the already famous partnership of De Dion and Bouton. The ordinary man's medium-priced touring car of the years before the war is represented by a De Dion of 1909 and a German Adler of 1910. From the years between the Wars come two interesting small cars, both with their engines mounted at the rear: a Rumpler streamlined car of 1921, a real oddity; and a Hanomag two-seater of 1925, strangely crude in comparison with the English Austin Seven, which had been in production by then for two years. At the opposite pole there is a noble Hispano-Suiza of 1919 and a grandiose Mercedes-Benz sports car of 1928. The series ends impressively with a very recent Opel, its body made partly transparent to display its construction and mechanism.

It must be clear that this is by no means an exclusively German display; but the English visitor will notice only one car from his own country, the chassis of an M G, and he may fairly be surprised that no room has been found for a Rolls-Royce or for an outstanding British small car, an Austin or a Morris. The omission must emphasize to him once again how small and unimportant a part Britain seems, in the eyes of foreign observers, to have played in the development of the motor-car. In a sense she lost the race from the beginning, in the eighties and nineties, when Daimler and Benz, Levassor and Panhard and Ford got in ahead of her.

With the railway, earlier in the century, the opposite had happened; and that too is faithfully reflected in the Deutsches Museum. The early development of the railway is unquestionably, in the main, a British achievement. That appears plainly enough from the railway exhibits here, most of which are mounted in the same hall. Among the models there is one of the *Rocket* and another of the *Adler*, built in Newcastle for the first German steam railway (cf. p. 252); and the series of full-sized locomotives begins with a replica of *Puffing Billy*. This is followed by another replica—a very fine one—of *Beuth*, a 2-2-2 engine built in 1844, after the pattern of Norris of Philadelphia. It was a very early production of the firm of Borsig of Berlin. Engines of this type were widely used in northern Germany, even into the 1860s.

The other five locomotives here are originals. Next to *Beuth* stands the thousandth engine built by Maffei of Munich, a 2-4-0 for the Bavarian Railways (1874). It is sectioned on one side, and its motion can be admirably demonstrated by electric power. The modern steam locomotive is splendidly represented by a Pacific of 1912, resplendent in the Bavarian livery (like that of the Great Western Company in England, a rich dark green set off by polished brass and copper), exhibited under a canopy out of doors, close to this building and visible from it. The rear end of another of these engines, comprising the firebox and cab mounted on the trailing wheels, is shown indoors; steps lead up to it, and the visitor can see for himself something of the complexity of driving one of these big machines.

The most remarkable exhibit here is not, however, a steam locomotive but an electric one: a tiny four-wheeled thing, which stands at right angles to the Bavarian 2–4–0. This is the first of all electric locomotives, built by Werner von Siemens and shown at the Berlin Trade Exhibition of 1879. There it ran on a circular narrow-gauge track 300 metres long, hauling three vehicles, on which the passengers sat with their backs to one another. This was not a mere stunt. Siemens's little locomotive was quickly developed for use in mines. The first standard-gauge electric engines appeared in the United States, on the Baltimore and Ohio line, in 1894. The first in Europe went into service between Burgdorf and Thun, in Switzerland, five years later. One of them is here; another is preserved at Lucerne (cf. p. 221). More modern electric traction is represented by a German State Railways locomotive (Type 50 Hz), which stands outside next to the Bavarian Pacific.

The bays by the windows contain a comprehensive series of models of locomotives and rolling-stock, and there is an elaborate working model of a railway in a room near by. What is conspicuously missing—here and at Nuremberg—is any account of the evolution of the track itself. If only a room could be devoted to railway construction, comparable with the one that illustrates road-building!

Anybody interested in transport may care to end his tour of this splendid museum by looking at the series of prime movers (*Kraftmaschinen*) that are shown in two large halls not far away, nearer to the entrance. They include, for example, a turbo-jet aeroplane engine of 1943 (two years later than Whittle's at the Science Museum); a long series of diesel engines, including Diesel's first, stationary engine of 1897; the early internal combustion engines of Lenoir and Otto (1861–76); and the oldest steam engine now extant in Germany, erected by an Englishman, William Richard, at Eisleben in 1813.

One other part of it calls for mention. On the first floor, above the entrance, is a Hall of Fame, round whose curved walls are ranged busts of eminent German scientists; and, next door, a small portrait gallery. Here, as we should expect, are Helmholtz and Liebig, Humboldt and Euler. It is a German Pantheon. One foreigner is included, and only one: George Stephenson. It is a tribute than an Englishman will remember.

The main object that Oskar von Miller had in mind when he planned and founded the Deutsches Museum was to demonstrate the part played by this country in the development of modern technology. That object is completely attained. In transport, it is not too much to say that our present practice springs principally from work developed in Germany during a span of twenty-one years (1876–97): the years that begin with Otto's four-stroke engine, continue with Siemens's electric locomotive, Daimler's motor-cycle and motor-boat, Benz's motor-car, Lilienthal's glider, and conclude with the first engine of Diesel. Here at Munich these historic machines can be seen and studied in the round. They are among the most important of all the forces that, for better and for worse, have shaped the modern world.

29

TRANSPORT MUSEUM NUREMBERG

The German railway system owes its creation primarily to one force: the Prussian Government. In the movement for political unification Bismarck and his colleagues saw the railway as one of their most powerful instruments. They hurried on the building of strategic lines in the fifties and sixties; and they reaped the reward of their prescience in the wars of 1866 and 1870, which created the German Empire—under Prussian, not Austrian, leadership—and made it the strongest power in Western Europe. But Prussia was not the pioneer of railways in Germany. That honour belongs to Bavaria; and the Royal Bavarian Railways kept a quite distinct character of their own, deriving partly from the nature of the kingdom itself and partly from its engineering enterprises, like the locomotive works of Krauss and Maffei in Munich, right down to the formation of the German State Railways in 1924.

In one respect at least they led Germany, even the rest of the world. In 1882 an Exhibition of Industrial Art was held at Nuremberg. To this the Bavarian Railways contributed a series of models of rolling-stock and equipment, which excited so much interest that it was decided not to disband it but to make it the nucleus of a railway museum. It was housed for a time at Munich, where it could be seen only by railwaymen and the employees of other transport undertakings. But the collection grew, until there was no longer room for it in these quarters. Thereupon the city of Nuremberg offered to accommodate it in a disused pavilion from the Exhibition of 1882 on the Marientorgraben. The offer was accepted, and the Museum opened to the public in 1899. Its scope was originally limited to railways, but two years later it was enlarged to embrace posts and telegraphs also, and the title of the whole became the Royal Bavarian Transport Museum.

Thus though Bavaria could not boast the first public museum in this field—that distinction must be claimed by Norway (cf. p. 265)—the idea was first formed there, and the first steps taken to realize it, in the 1880s.

The Museum grew steadily, and soon it was too big for its building. The municipal authorities of Nuremberg were evidently well aware by now of the value of having the Museum in their city; for in 1914 they granted a site for a new and larger building, making also a contribution to the cost of erecting it, on the sole condition that the collections should be retained in Nuremberg. The realization of the project was interrupted by the first World War; but the building was finished in 1923 and the Museum reopened in its new quarters on April 22, 1925. If the building is somewhat grandiose for our taste today, it is spacious and well lighted. It enjoys, too, the useful advantage of direct rail access to sidings close to Nuremberg station. The Museum was again closed during the second World War, and many of the most important pieces in the collection removed. That was fortunate: for whereas the greater part of central Nuremberg was destroyed by bombing, the building was hit only twice. For this reason, however, the accommodation it could afford was especially valuable, and it was requisitioned to house part of the railway administration, whose adjacent premises had been almost entirely destroyed. It proved possible to reopen a section of the Museum in 1953, and more has followed since. It must nevertheless be understood that what is to be seen today is but a part—if a substantial one—of the entire collections. The whole building comprises a little over 100,000 square feet; only two-fifths of this area is at present available to the Museum.

In these circumstances it must be a standing temptation to overcrowd the galleries that are in use. It is much to the credit of the Director and his staff that this temptation has been effectively resisted. With one exception, to be mentioned later—and that arises from the design of the building itself—the layout is spacious, and there is ample room to examine the objects that are exhibited. Nor is the display merely spacious. It may be called beautiful: quiet and harmonious in colour, admirably lighted, the furniture

and casing simple and unobtrusive. One other word of commen-
dation at the outset—and to me it is the highest praise of all.
Almost without exception, every object is carefully, intelligently,
and legibly described. In this respect the Nuremberg Museum
sets an example to nearly all the other museums described in this
book.

Although it is called a Transport Museum, it is in practice
almost entirely confined to two branches of transport, the railway
and the postal service. But it interprets these widely, so as to
include for example a room devoted to water transport operated
in conjunction with railways.

Let us begin by taking a brief look at the postal section of the
Museum, since it carries us so far back in time. The postal service
is shown here evolving from its medieval origins through the
long monopoly of the Imperial posts held by the Counts Thurn
und Taxis to the Royal Bavarian post of the nineteenth century and
the Deutsche Bundespost of the twentieth. The Taxis post has
a unique and fascinating story stretching from the thirteenth
century, when the family first began to run posts in Italy, to the
nineteenth, when they lost their privileges with the end of the
Holy Roman Empire in 1806. It was not until 1867 that they
surrendered their rights in Prussia to the government, at a
very handsome price indeed. Here in the Museum are documents
relating to the Taxis post, badges and fragments of uniforms;
and then we begin to see the modernizing of the posts in the
hands of the Bavarian government, the transition from the
mounted postman to the postal road vehicle, exemplified both in
originals and in models. The originals include a sleigh, a horse
bus of 1898, and the first postal motor-bus of 1905, resplendent
in blue, yellow and white. The models include one of a postal
street tram.

The Museum comprises also a very large collection of postage
stamps. It is strongest, naturally, in those of Bavaria, which was
the first German state to issue them, in 1849, and continued to do
so until the unified German post was established in 1920; but it
includes also a very comprehensive collection of those of all other
countries of the world. The Museum does not confine itself to
postal services proper. It embraces also the telegraph, the telephone (with some early instruments of bizarre design), radio and
its extensions in our own day.

Though the railway section includes some splendid original machines, it is perhaps fair to say that its greatest distinction arises from its models: a truly marvellous collection, faultlessly made—almost all to the same scale—showing the evolution of the locomotive and of passenger and freight rolling stock in Bavaria from 1835 to 1914. They cannot be matched in any other museum in the world.

A series of forty-one models of locomotives are shown together in one large hall. They start with the first locomotive built for the Bavarian Railways, a 2–2–2 by Maffei of Munich. It has often been remarked that the Stephenson long-boiler engine proved more widely popular, and for a longer time, on the Continent than in Britain. Here we can see one built to this design as late as 1890—incorporating, too, another device invented in Britain and long since discarded there, Allan's link motion. The brief influence of the American Atlantic design in the opening years of the twentieth century is exemplified here, with a Vauclain compound built for Bavaria by the Baldwin Works in 1901; a highly eccentric variant, a 6–4–2, *Dr von Klemm*, incorporating a supplementary drive on to a second pair of cylinders off the small leading wheels (a primitive version of the 'booster' that came to be popular for a time in the 1920s); and a Bavarian Atlantic of a more orthodox pattern. The type went through just the same history in Germany as in England and France; it was soon eclipsed, on most railways, by larger, six-coupled designs that could cope with the trains of rapidly-increasing weight that were becoming common everywhere in these years. But not before it had shown what it could do: one of the original engines preserved here is a Bavarian Atlantic of 1906, which is credited with having reached a speed of 98 m.p.h. on the line between Augsburg and Munich. We shall look at this machine a little later.

Two examples of the six-coupled engines that displaced the Atlantics are to be seen here; and then we move on into a smaller adjoining room to follow through the remainder of the story, down to the last types of German steam locomotive. (With the exception of the mixed-traffic 2–6–2 of 1940. One of them, built in 1959, was the very last steam locomotive commissioned by the German Railways. The type is represented by a splendid model, to a larger scale than the rest, displayed in lone grandeur in the entrance hall to the Museum.) Models of electric and diesel locomotives are also shown in this room, together with an interesting series, in the wall cases, illustrating the evolution of the railcar. A double-deck steam car of 1882 is a striking curiosity —one cannot be surprised to learn that it remained in service only a short time. Then come an electric railcar of 1900, a battery car of 1901, and a steam railcar, of the type we are familiar with in Britain, of 1908; and so to the railbuses, the diesel electric and hydraulic cars of our own time.

Upstairs on the first floor is a room devoted chiefly to passenger and freight vehicles. It begins with a train on the Munich–Augsburg line of 1839 and then shows a series of twenty-four beautifully-made models of vehicles of different kinds on the Royal Bavarian Railways, stretching from the 1840s to 1905. Of particular interest, perhaps, are those of early goods vehicles (often overlooked), one of a horse-box with its door open and roof off to expose the internal arrangements, a long bogie wagon of 1894 for transporting rails, and a grand coach of 1905 for the express running between Rome and Berlin via the Brenner Pass. Among the models of more recent vehicles is one of a purple coach from the first Rheingold Express of 1928.

This room also contains a case of uniforms of railway officials (the Prussian State Railways even had a gala uniform for engine-drivers, comprising a royal blue surcoat with copper buttons); and round the walls there is a remarkable series of delicately-executed water-colour drawings of railway scenes in Bavaria, dating from 1846–53. Among them are several depicting bridges and earthworks under construction. One shows the building of an embankment near Rentershofen in 1852, with women at work pushing small trucks side by side with the men.

To return to models: in the next room is a most interesting set devoted to the servicing of locomotives, including a coaling-plant and a fixed crane for lifting engines under repair. Again the quality of the workmanship is outstanding, and the meticulous attention to detail. In the model last referred to, for example, every part removed from the engine is lying beside it, ready to be re-assembled. The same room also contains a large working model of a section of the Black Forest Railway, which runs from Offenburg to Villingen—a mountain line with thirty-six tunnels on this sixteen-mile stretch. Some demonstrations of techniques in the building of tunnels and bridges (with well-illuminated interiors) follow.

The adjoining room is devoted to navigation, chiefly as an adjunct to rail transport. There is a model of the harbour and train ferry arrangements at Grossenbrode, for the traffic to Scandinavia. But most of the space is given to the Lake of Constance (the Bodensee), including models of the ships used there, from the *Wilhelm*—built in Württemburg in 1824 with an engine supplied from Liverpool—to the *München* of 1962. The climax of elegance comes here, as it did almost always, in the opening years of the twentieth century, with the *Lindau*, built by Maffei in 1905.

One other small section here takes us away for a moment from railways altogether. It illustrates the remarkable chain haulage system, operated with steam tugs on the River Main between Mainz and Bamberg, installed in stages from 1886 to 1901 and disused in 1938. A great deal of traffic passes along the river still today, but now it is dealt with by diesel traction.

Next door is a display of signalling equipment arranged for demonstration to an audience in rows of seats; and the sequence here ends with another model railway, showing the working of many different kinds of traffic simultaneously. It is operated several times a day.

The full-sized machines now remain. They are on the ground floor. First, to the right of the entrance, is a series of sixteen stationary engines, nearly all dating from the second half of the nineteenth century. They include one for a machine designed to test the strength of materials, built at Nuremberg in 1852 for the Bavarian Railways, and a gas-motor engine used from 1878 to 1887 for the first electric light plant to be installed in Munich Central Station. All of them are admirably displayed, built up on simple brick plinths, most of them free-standing in the room so that they can be examined from all sides.

The full-sized locomotives and rolling-stock are reached through the end of the model room. It is best to follow a sign pointing to the right and to move first along a raised walk, turning to the right again; this leads into the 'Hall of Honour', which contains a replica of the Nuremberg–Fürth Railway train of 1835, made for the celebration of its centenary. Then, descending steps, we move between two rows of vehicles and machinery.

First come the moving parts of two electric locomotives; then the earliest Bavarian locomotive to survive intact, *Nordgau*, a 2–4–0 built by Maffei in 1853 and in service till 1907. Opposite *Nordgau* is a Mallet 0–4–4–0 engine of 1896, and next to it a small 0–6–0 tank engine of 1906, the first Bavarian locomotive to be fitted with the Schmidt superheater. Inconspicuously placed in the corner are the boiler, smokebox, and chimney of *Haardt*, built for the Palatinate Railway in 1847—the oldest piece of original locomotive machinery in the Museum.

You now move through a right angle into the remainder of the hall. On the left is part of a coach of the 'Flying Hamburger' of 1932, the first diesel express train in Europe, the ancestor of the Trans-Europe Expresses of today. On the other track, a little farther on, stand three very remarkable vehicles. The first, a green four-wheeled coach, is a private saloon built for Bismarck in 1872. There is a modest filigree cresting round the roof, and the door-handles are somewhat more elaborate than usual. Otherwise it is all very plain, with a day saloon well set out for business, lighted by oil-lamps in pairs round the walls, and a small single bedroom. Nothing could be more startling than the contrast with the vehicles that stand next to it: a pair built for King Ludwig II of Bavaria some ten years earlier. They are sumptuously styled outside; and their interior decoration is among the richest and most fantastic that has ever been applied to railways in Europe.

The bigger saloon comprises four sections: an end coupé for two attendants, a day saloon, a sleeping saloon, and a toilet compartment. The day saloon is decorated predominantly in the Bavarian colours of blue and gold. Its ceiling is heavily painted and gilt; in the centre is a marble-topped table of great elaboration. Indeed, apart from the marble itself, there is scarcely a plain surface to be seen anywhere. It makes all other royal saloons, like Queen Victoria's at Clapham (p. 571), look very austere.

The other vehicle is a 'terrace coach', intended for open-air travel in fine weather. Most of the sides are open, though there is a small enclosed compartment in the middle. It is fitted out with light garden furniture, painted cream and gold.

Poor Ludwig II! He lived in an inner dream of the past. The fantasy of these vehicles is touching. They can have been used so little, and within a few years of their construction such power as the King had had was closely circumscribed by the creation of the German Empire, the work of Bismarck, whose coach now stands next door. But one may observe that Ludwig had at least the advantage of comfort: for his larger saloon ran on bogies, on eight wheels, and his smaller on six, whereas Bismarck's, though built later, had only four.

Facing these vehicles, on the other track, is *Landwührden*, a plain 0–4–0 tender engine, of interest as the first to be turned out by the firm of Krauss of Munich, in 1863. It was awarded a gold medal at the Paris Exhibition of 1867. One wonders why, for it was certainly far from the vanguard of progress.

Next to it is a much more remarkable machine, which dates from the same year: *Phoenix*, a 4–2–0 to Crampton's patent, built at Karlsruhe for the Baden State Railways in 1863. These engines remained popular in France and Germany long after they had been superseded in England;[1] this one remained in service until 1903.

The last pair of engines, though technically they belong to different worlds, have one feature in common, which can be seen to perfection as they stand in the Museum. One is a Bavarian Atlantic (Maffei, 1906); the other a German State Railways 4–6–4, built by Borsig of Berlin thirty years later. Both types were intended for high-speed work, and both fulfilled their designers' purpose in this respect. The Bavarian engine was timed at 98 m.p.h. in 1907; one of the 4–6–4s reached 125 m.p.h. between Berlin and Hamburg in 1936—to be fractionally excelled by the English engine *Mallard* (p. 56) two years later. The earlier of the two locomotives shown here was given an 'air-smoothed' casing at the front end, like the contemporary 'wind-cutters' of the PLM company in France. The later one was completely streamlined. As they stand together now, the genesis of this idea can be seen very clearly. Between them they represent very well the last stage in the development of the express steam locomotive.

And finally, putting chronological order into reverse, let us look at the small room, leading off the entrance hall, that is devoted to the first steam-operated railway in Germany: the Nuremberg–Fürth line of 1835. The prospectus is here, dated 1833, the statutes and royal charter, a list of the subscribers and a share certificate. The first engine, *Adler*, was supplied by Robert Stephenson's works at Newcastle. But, as on the Stockton and Darlington Railway ten years earlier, traction on the line was,

[1] Cf. p. 191.

in the beginning, shared between the locomotive and the horse. A set of rules of 1836 makes this quite clear. The morning trains are to be hauled by horses; the trains leaving Nuremberg at one and two o'clock to be worked 'as a rule with the steam engine', and the three o'clock train also on busy days; for the remainder, up to six o'clock, horses are to be employed. At first the line was used solely for passenger transport; goods traffic did not begin until 1836. Among the small relics of this early railway preserved here are tickets, of admission to the opening ceremony and for ordinary journeys in the first year; medals commemorating its 25th, 50th, 100th, and 125th anniversaries; and a photograph of a quite elaborate portrait of William Wilson, the first engine-driver in Germany, who doubtless came over with *Adler* from Newcastle.

It should be added that the Museum also includes a large department of archives. Since 1907 it has been the place of deposit of the official records of the Bavarian Railways. Those of other transport undertakings in Bavaria have been added, making a comprehensive collection of documents stretching in time from 1806 to 1920. There is also a large assemblage of photographs, and a library of printed books running to more than 20,000 items.

Within its clearly-defined limits, therefore, this is one of the most complete museums described in this book, and its display is among the best-presented. Where railways are concerned, the most important element at present missing from the exhibition is the track itself; but this will no doubt figure in one of the additional galleries that still remain to be opened in the re-arrangement that has followed the upheaval of the war. With this considerable exception, it may be said that anyone who wishes to understand the development of the mechanically-operated railway can see it demonstrated as well in Nuremberg as anywhere.

30

RAILWAY MUSEUM
COPENHAGEN

The administrative headquarters of the Danish State Railways are established in a handsome set of buildings originally erected as barracks in 1769, facing on to the delightful King's Garden and the Rosenborg Palace. The Railway Museum at present occupies a series of rooms on the top floor; and it is open to the public on one afternoon a week in the summer months. There is a good little guide-book, in Danish.

The earliest railway to be built in the Danish dominions was the line from Altona to Kiel (in what is now part of Western Germany), which was opened in 1844 and was followed three years later by the first stage of the main east–west line across Denmark, from Copenhagen to Roskilde. This was the nucleus of the Zeeland Railway Company, which extended the line to Korsör in 1858. The westward advance of the railway was stopped there by the Great Belt, an arm of the sea more than ten miles broad dividing Zeeland from the neighbouring island of Funen. A ferry service had long been in operation across the strait, and four years later a train-ferry was designed in Britain for use here, on the model of that first eatablished across the Forth in 1850. This was not in fact built, and the earliest train-ferry in Denmark was that across the Little Belt, which went into operation in 1872. The Korsör–Nyborg train-ferry became a reality only in 1887. Today the ferries make it possible to travel without changing trains from Copenhagen to all the main Danish islands, as well as to Sweden and Norway and through Germany to the mainland of Europe. Nowhere has the railway acted as a more important unifying force than in Denmark. For it is a state comprising the peninsula of Jutland, seven large islands and about a hundred others that are inhabited; and it has to be governed from Copenhagen, a capital most inconveniently situated at the extreme eastern end of the country.

One further thing needs mention. The early Danish railways developed under English influence, and partly through the investment of English capital. In the 1870s the Danes began to turn more to Germany. Today the ubiquitous diesel locomotives that haul most of the chief passenger trains were made in Sweden. But it is worth remembering that the greatest work of railway engineering in the country, the Storstrøm Bridge, was built in 1932–37 by the English firm of Dorman, Long.

The Museum comprises six rooms, numbered in the opposite order to that in which the visitor sees them. Room VI is concerned with the train-ferries. It includes an excellent series of models, beginning with one of the abortive ferry of 1862 and including a particularly fine and large one of the *Sjaelland* of 1887. Ice-breakers —a necessary adjunct to the ferries if the service is to be maintained all the year round—also appear here: among them a sailing vessel of 1880. Besides the models, this room also contains examples of the ships' equipment, from clocks and instruments of navigation to ships' bells, life-belts, and a gigantic pair of sailor's boots.

Room V illustrates some of the processes of running a railway, with telegraph and telephone instruments, ticket-printing machines and the tickets they produced, notices to passengers. There are several pieces here connected with the first Danish railway, the South Schleswig Company. Rendsborg station is shown in a charming oil-painting, executed in 1846, not long after the line was opened. Below it is a letter written by the Manager of the Company in 1862. He was John Louth, an Englishman, who displays his countrymen's customary ineptitude at foreign languages: for he never learnt Danish, and this letter, appointing a Dane to an assistant's post in the telegraph and booking office, is written firmly in his own language. He must have remained very much of a foreigner. And yet, when the war with Prussia came in 1864, he showed no feeble neutrality. Rendsborg, right on the border as it then ran, was in the front line, and Louth himself hauled down the Danish flag that flew from his station and saved it from the Prussian invaders. The flag is here in a corner of the room: a memento of that war, which the Danes have certainly never forgotten.

Below it are a settee and a chair from a royal saloon of Frederick VII, and the next room (IV) contains the desk made for it. There are also copies of two delicate drawings made by the English artist Alfred Stevens (from originals in the Tate Gallery in London). They are alternative designs for the first Danish royal saloon. Neither was in fact adopted, but it is interesting to be reminded here of Stevens's work, for he was the only major Victorian artist, outside William Morris and his circle, to design for industrial purposes.

Room III is given up to rolling-stock. The models include one of a double-deck coach used on the Copenhagen suburban services —third-class accommodation on the top and in the two end compartments below, second class in the centre. There are also some interesting pictures here: a photograph of a Crampton locomotive at work on the Zeeland Railway in 1858—the flat, straight road should have suited those machines to perfection and some of them had a life lasting into the 1880s;[1] a number of others showing the early English-built engines, among them a Stephenson long-boiler locomotive of 1868. Like other Continental countries, Denmark retained this design long after it had been abandoned in England.

Room II is devoted to track and signalling. A good series of rails is mounted here for comparison. The Danish signalling system is clearly explained by means of models. There are some signal frames in their original state; one notices how much lighter and easier they are to work than the characteristic British manual levers.

The last room (I) is a very interesting one, containing exhibits relating to stations and bridges. A series of models shows the three successive main stations in Copenhagen; and there are photographs illustrating the construction of the 'underground' line beneath the old fortifications of the city on the western and northern sides. There is a particularly attractive painting of the second station (1864–1911), with a horse tram standing in front. The great bridges characteristic of the Danish railway system are all represented. It is interesting to compare the swing bridge over the Masnedsund at Vordingborg (1883) with the Storstrøm bridge that made it superfluous and swept it away fifty years later: the one heavy, low on the water, encrusted with Gothic decoration;

---

[1] Cf. W. Bay, *Locomotives of the Danish State Railways* (Lingfield, n.d.), chs. 3–5.

51a Clapham: an effective Underground poster, *c.* 1912. Its point is not lost today

b Clapham: wall panel in blue tiles made for the Bridge Inn, Hanley, showing a train on the Loop Line of the N. Staffs. Railway

52a Utrecht: model of N. Brabant Railway locomotive No. 31 (1908). The royal blue livery is almost identical with that of the Great Eastern Railway of England

b Utrecht: inside-cylinder 4–4–0 locomotive built for the Holland Iron Railway by Schwartzkopff of Berlin in 1915

the other sailing up on a curve high into the air, to leap across two miles of the sea. The models and photographs here are invaluable in facilitating comparisons of this kind.

There the Museum finishes at present. It is a compact and well-chosen collection, in which junk of merely sentimental interest finds no place. The Danish State Railways have, in addition, preserved sixteen locomotives, built between 1868 and 1920, and eleven passenger and goods vehicles, including two royal saloons of 1871 and 1900. These are at present stored in railway depots up and down the country. A Technical Museum is now planned at Elsinore, into which all these exhibits, large and small, will be moved. It is very much to be hoped that this project can be realized soon; for the collection thoroughly deserves more ample accommodation, in which it can be continuously displayed to the public.

31

SWEDISH STATE RAILWAYS
MUSEUM, STOCKHOLM

The museums of Stockholm offer, between them all, a more complete view of transport than those of any other city in Europe, except London. The Technical Museum, in a fine open situation on the east side of the city, embraces all forms of power, road transport, and aeronautics—including a Swedish traction engine of 1861, a helicopter of 1932, and a flying-boat. Next to it lies the Swedish National Maritime Museum: a distinguished building by Ragnar Östberg, the architect of Stockholm Town Hall, housing a comprehensive collection, spaciously displayed. Among the superb contents of the Northern Museum are some notable horse-drawn vehicles—Oxenstierna's sleigh and a carriage belonging to the Swedish general Torstensson from the seventeenth century, a group of gorgeous state coaches from the eighteenth. Municipal transport is catered for in a delightful little museum built into the Odenplan station on the new Stockholm underground railway. There is a Postal Museum, not far from the Riddarholm church. And if you cross the bridge to Skeppsholm, the small island in the Baltic occupied by Stockholm's naval station, you can go on board a barque of 1862, moored permanently there and serving as a youth hostel; it is named *Af Chapman*, from the Yorkshireman who became Sweden's chief naval architect in the eighteenth century.

With so much attention paid to transport, where is the railway material? The answer to that question is curious. The Swedish Railways have assembled a magnificent collection of original locomotives and rolling-stock; but they have, as yet, found no adequate means of putting it on show. For some years now, parts of it have been opened to the public in vacated railway premises at Tomteboda, a northern suburb of Stockholm. But they are difficult to get to. It seems somehow characteristic that on the official maps of the municipal transport system this should be listed among the city's museums, but not marked; and if you do make your way there, with pertinacity, you find that the Museum is open no more than four hours a week, in the summer months only. Its other branch, near the Central station, containing small-scale exhibits, gets no mention in maps or guide-books at all.

The premises at Tomteboda are really only a temporary store. They lie on the edge of a goods yard, and the site is now needed for other purposes by the railway administration. It has been decided, in principle, to move the whole collection out to Gävle, a port on the Baltic rather more than a hundred miles north of Stockholm. There it should have room to spread itself and grow, rather as the Norwegian museum has done at Hamar, which also lies a couple of hours' journey away from the capital. But this project moves forward slowly. Meanwhile the Museum can show its treasures only in this modest and limited way.[1]

The locomotives form a splendid collection. There are twenty-two in all. Eighteen of them are what we may perhaps be allowed to call 'Victorian', built between 1855 and 1892; the other four 'Edwardian', of the years 1904–10. Six were designed for various narrow gauges. Let us look at some of those first.

The earliest is a little 0–6–0 well-tank engine, *Fryckstad*. It was built in 1855 by Munktell of Eskilstuna for the Frykstad Railway in Värmland, which had previously been worked by horses. The gauge of the line was 3 feet 7¼ inches. The engine worked on the Frykstad Railway only until 1872. Thereafter it was used for a time in the naval base of Karlskrona. A little 2–4–0T, *Trollhättan*, comes next (4 foot gauge), dating from 1865: interesting as the first railway engine to be turned out by Nydqvist and Holm of Trollhättan, who became, with the Motala works, the largest locomotive-builders in Sweden. (The first Motala engine is also here: *Carlsund*, a standard-gauge 0–6–0T built three years earlier.) The little railway system on the island of Gotland was laid out on the gauge of 2 feet 11 inches; it did not pass into the hands of the Swedish State Railways until 1948. Here is one of its early locomotives: *Gotland*, an 0–6–0T built by

---

[1] The move to Gävle is now in hand; the new museum should be open there in June 1970.

Nydqvist and Holm in 1878 and awarded a silver medal at the Paris Exhibition of that year. It remained in service until 1953.

Like Holland and other countries in northern Europe, Sweden looked largely to British manufacturers in early days, and pre-eminently to Beyer Peacock of Manchester. This firm built the oldest of the standard-gauge locomotives that are to be seen here: *Prins August*, a 2–4–0 of 1856 (Beyer Peacock No. 33). This engine remained in service for exactly fifty years. After another fifty, she was able to take part in the Swedish railways' centenary celebrations. She is still occasionally put into steam, and capable of running at 40 m.p.h. and more. In appearance she much resembles the engines Joseph Beattie began to put into service on the London and South Western Railway at just the same time, but in a simpler version, without the jet-condenser and other prominent boiler-mountings associated with his feed-water systems.

Two of the other engines built by Beyer Peacock also call for mention: a 2–2–2 with inside cylinders, *Göta* of 1866, the first express passenger locomotive to be used in Sweden; and *Jernsida* (class G), a six-coupled goods engine of the standard English type. In the 1890s, when no longer new, *Jernsida* and some of its fellows found an unexpected use. Many attempts had been made to exploit the rich iron deposits of Gällivare, in northern Sweden. British companies were much interested in them, and, with British capital, a Swedish and Norwegian Railway was built in 1884–88 to bring the iron down to the Baltic at Lulea. It was in constant financial difficulties,[1] and the task was successfully tackled only after a reorganization of the iron company and the purchase of the railway by the Swedish government in 1891. Class G engines were then dispatched to this far northern line, and they hauled the heavy trains—quite often working three in harness—over this difficult route, which crosses the Arctic Circle. Special locomotives were later designed for the work, one of which is to be seen in the Museum: the 2–8–0 class Ma, built by Nydqvist and Holm (1904). They in their turn were displaced when the line was electrified in 1915–22.

The last English engine here that demands mention is a little

---

[1] One consequence of which was that Messrs Sharp Stewart found it necessary to dispose of some powerful 0–8–0 engines, which this company had ordered but could not pay for. Accordingly it sold two of them in 1889 to the Barry Railway, which thus became the pioneer of that type in Britain.

0–4–0T, *Elfkarleö,* which spent all its long life (1873–1945) in industrial service in the little town from which it takes its name. It is one of the earliest surviving products of Hughes and Co. of Loughborough (later the Brush Electrical Co.), a firm noted for its tramway work, first with steam and then with electricity.

Of the more modern steam locomotives constructed in Sweden, two are particularly interesting, Both show strong American influence. No. 864, a 4–6–0 of 1906, is basically an American freight engine (look at its wheels, coupling rods, and cylinders), though built at Trollhättan. It is equipped to burn peat. As in the United States and several other European countries (cf. p. 248), the 4–4–2 Atlantic type had a brief vogue in Sweden for express passenger work in the early years of the twentieth century. Surprisingly, the engine of this type preserved here (No. 1001, built by the Motala Company) has inside cylinders. It has been sectioned, for purposes of demonstration.

A single electric locomotive is preserved. It is of class Z, built in 1910, one of the earliest to be owned by the State Railways. From 1914 until it was withdrawn from service in 1938 it worked on the iron-ore railways of the far north. There are also four steam rail-cars, all dating from around the year 1890 (in Britain, by contrast, not a single example is now extant), and a solitary diesel car, of 1932.

The Swedish assemblage of original passenger and freight rolling-stock is the most extensive in Europe: pretty certainly, within the confines of its period, the most extensive anywhere in the world. For it all belongs to the second half of the nineteenth century. There is nothing of the twentieth here whatever, except a frag-ment—comprising one compartment and the lavatory—of the earliest third-class sleeping car of the State Railways, which was in service from 1910 to 1938.

The most ancient pieces are a passenger vehicle and an iron-ore wagon from the Kroppa Railway in Värmland, built to the 2 foot 3 inch gauge; they date from 1850. Then comes a most interesting group of four vehicles from the Frykstad Railway, used before the introduction of locomotives: an open passenger carriage, which was hauled by horses, and—a truly remarkable rarity—a pair of timber-wagons that were placed in the charge of oxen when they were going uphill and coasted downwards by the force of gravity. A pair of standard-gauge passenger coaches, built to be hauled by horses in the 1850s, come from the Ammeberg Railway.

As with the locomotives, a good many of the earlier passenger and freight vehicles were bought outside Sweden. Lauenstein of Hamburg built sixteen of the first coaches for the State Railways in 1856; the one preserved here, No. 103, was in service until 1908. The Skandia Company, of Randers in Denmark (which is active in the business still), supplied a passenger and mail coach to the North Bergslag Railway in 1876 and an eight-wheeled vehicle to the Frövi–Ludvika line in the following year. Three well-known British firms are also represented here: Joseph Wright and Son of Birmingham with two coaches of 1854 for the Köping–Hult Railway; their successors the Metropolitan Carriage and Wagon Company with one for the Gävle–Dala Railway (1868); and Ashbury's of Manchester, with a vehicle that demands fuller attention. This is a four-wheeled first-class carriage supplied to the Bergslagen Railway, probably in 1873. It incorporates an early device for affording access from one vehicle to the next: the Chubb and Fry gangway, comprising a platform on hinges that could be drawn up flush with the end wall of the coach, in which there was a door that gave on to the platform when it was down. Though it was an English firm that had patented it, in 1866, it was not used in this country, which did not begin to take to the corridor principle, in any form, for ordinary travellers until the nineties. In Sweden, however, the State Railways adopted the Chubb and Fry device in 1872, and for a time it became widely popular.[1]

There are two royal saloons here, forming part of a five-coach train built in 1874 for the young King Oscar II and his Queen Sophia by the Norddeutscher Fabrik für Eisenbahnbetrieb in Berlin. The Queen's saloon has been subsequently reconstructed, but the King's audience-coach remains in its original state, with a pair of centrally-placed doors for formal receptions. No such vehicle was ever seen in Britain, where the sovereign's journeys were rapid and short; but in Sweden and Norway (Oscar reigned over both countries until 1905) they were slow and might extend over two or three days. The intricate brass decoration of the side

[1] Cf. H. Ellis, *Railway Carriages in the British Isles* (1965), 95, 179–80. This vehicle is illustrated in Plate 13 of Mr Ellis's book. The concertina gangway made a solitary appearance in Britain in 1869, to link the two saloons built for the Queen by the London and North Western Railway, now preserved (reconstructed as one vehicle in 1895) at Clapham (see p. 57).

panels of the coach, throwing up the roundels that display the three crowns of Sweden, reflects the King's taste, which ran to the elaborate; the vehicle must have been hard and unyielding to travel in—much less comfortable than Ludwig II's saloon (p. 51) or Queen Victoria's (p. 57).

At the opposite pole of the social and political world—and surely no other museum has such a vehicle—is a four-wheeled carriage built in 1873 for the conveyance of prisoners on the Uddevalla–Vänersborg–Herrljunga Railway. Its walls are covered with inscriptions scribbled by its occupants during their enforced, and doubtless very slow, journeys.

Except some signalling equipment that is also to be seen here, the display is confined to rolling-stock. Two things may be said about it, in conclusion. It is the largest single collection of nineteenth-century locomotives and vehicles in Europe—British Rail have preserved more locomotives, but they are dispersed in several places. The emphasis is laid heavily on the nineteenth century. One cannot help noticing that most of this rolling-stock was taken out of traffic a long time ago—well before the second World War—and wondering if the Swedish Railways have called a halt to further preservation. If so it will be a great pity; for in Sweden, as elsewhere, the railways have been changing fast in recent times, and the memorials of this change will be looked for by succeeding generations just as eagerly as those of the Railway Age. Is the first steel coach, or one of the first, still in service, for example, and if so can it be earmarked for preservation on its retirement? Or again, considering the important contribution that Sweden has made to electric traction in Europe, surely the State Railways cannot be content to see that represented by a single locomotive?

But such questions bring us back to our starting point. It is plain that no more material can be accommodated at Tomteboda. Nothing more can be done until new premises are available. (Meanwhile, we must be grateful for the holding operation that has at least made it possible for visitors to see something of this fine collection.) One must hope that the removal can be effected soon. When it does take place, and when the new museum is completed, may an Englishman venture to wish that it may be open for rather more liberal hours than are customary in Stockholm, where the major museums can be visited by the public, on an average, for only some four hours in the day?[1] This is a shorter time than in any other comparable city of northern Europe—shorter, indeed, than in Naples or Madrid.

[1] This comparison excepts the great open-air museum, Skansen, which serves other purposes besides that of a museum. It is based on the opening hours given in the latest editions of the *Blue Guides*. One might add that, in this matter, things do not improve: the Technical Museum, for example, now closes at 3 p.m. on Saturdays, whereas in 1952 it was open an hour longer (*Blue Guide to Sweden*, 1952, 136).

53a Stockholm: Atlantic locomotive built by the Motala Works for the Swedish
State Railways in 1907

b Nuremberg: Bavarian Atlantic locomotive (1906) beside German State Railways streamlined 4–6–4 (1935)

54a Clapham: Midland compound No. 1000. This photograph, taken in the open air, gives some idea of the superb quality of the Museum's restoration of the locomotive

b Beaulieu: the Southern Railway's 'Bournemouth Belle', which ran from 1931 to 1967, is happily commemorated here, with 'Schools' class locomotive *Stowe* attached to three Pullman cars. A Great Western signal stands on the right

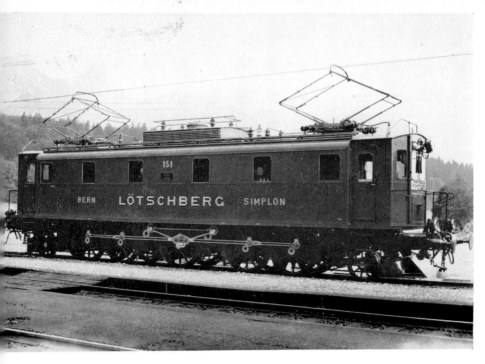

55a Lucerne: Lötschberg Railway electric locomotive (1913)

b Belfast: Co. Donegal Railways locomotive *Phoenix*, originally built as a steam engine and converted to diesel operation in 1933. It is seen here shunting at Strabane

56a Clapham: drawing-room in Queen Victoria's saloon, London and North Western Railway, 1869–95

b Nuremberg: saloon built for King Ludwig II of Bavaria

57a Clapham: electric kettle from Queen Victoria's saloon

Clapham: engraved glass from Queen Victoria's service

58a Stockholm: King Oscar II's saloon, built in Berlin in 1874

b Hamar: royal saloon for the Røros Railway (then metre-gauge) built in the USA in 1876

59   Science Museum: advertisement with cut of Robert Davidson's electric locomotive, tried out on the Edinburgh and Glasgow Railway in 1842. It also refers to a flying machine by Sir George Cayley

60a Science Museum: letter sent by balloon out of Paris during the siege of 1870

b Royal Scottish Museum: Percy Pilcher's glider *Hawk* (1896)

32

NORWEGIAN RAILWAY MUSEUM
HAMAR

Although the notion of a railway museum originated in Bavaria (cf. p. 245), the first museum of the kind to be opened to the public was in Norway. The initiative came from the Norwegian Stationmasters' Association; a committee was formed for the purpose in 1895, and the first group of exhibits was placed on show, in a room in the station at Hamar, during the following year. This arrangement continued until 1912, when the room was needed by the railway management for other purposes. Its contents had then to be put into store, and they remained there for fourteen years. In 1926 a fresh start was made, on a new site at Disen outside Hamar. Three wooden station buildings were presented to the Museum and re-erected there, to house the exhibits. By 1939 an old coach-shed had been added, containing engines and rolling-stock, and it soon began to become plain that there would not be room for continuing development. A new site was then acquired on the other side of Hamar, seven acres in extent, and the whole Museum has now been moved there. Since 1946 it has been directly under the control of the State Railways.

The site is a most charming one. Hamar lies eighty miles north of Oslo, on the Dovre railway to Trondheim. With 13,000 people, it is the biggest inland town in Norway: an ancient place, which can show the ruins of a small Romanesque cathedral, destroyed by the Swedes in 1567, beautifully situated on the eastern shore of Lake Mjøsa, a huge inland sea sixty miles long: delectable quarters for a quiet summer holiday, either in the town itself or in one of the country hotels in the hills behind it.

The ideal way to approach Hamar, supposing you are not in a

265

hurry, is to take the train to Eidsvoll (if you are coming from the south) or to Lillehammer (from the north) and then to embark on the steamer. This is partly for the same reason as urges one to take the steamer along Windermere—which Lake Mjøsa somewhat resembles, on a grander scale: in order to get a quiet and uninterrupted view of the lake and its whole shore. But there is another reason too, a compelling one to the student of transport. The service on the lake, which runs daily throughout the summer, is maintained by the paddle-steamer *Skibladner*, built in Sweden 112 years ago and, so far as I am aware, the oldest steamship now plying regularly in Europe. When she was new in 1856 she was the largest steamer in Norway. She was fitted with a new engine in 1888, and in 1921 she was converted to burn oil; she is still capable of 14 knots today. She has not been jazzed up in the degrading style that has been applied to so many old steamships: her funnel is still slender and tall. She moves calmly about her business on the lake with the unmistakable air of good breeding, the product of a secure and settled age.

The Museum is down by the shore of the lake, on the north side of Hamar; beyond the little bluff on which the cathedral stands, with the town's museum of antiquities adjoining it. This Norwegian Railway Museum is different from its fellows elsewhere in Europe. For, in a manner characteristic of Scandinavia, it has been laid out as, essentially, an exhibition in the open air. What could be more appropriate? No railway can be confined within train sheds. The right way to display it is surely, as far as possible, out of doors. To expose machines like these, unprotected, to the weather all the year round would clearly be unwise: so provision is made for bringing them indoors during the winter. But in the summer months a number of them are allowed to stand in the open, beside the timber station buildings that have the same timeless resistance to the elements as the Stave churches, their religious counterpart surviving from the Middle Ages. Best of all, a narrow-gauge railway is maintained in working order with a six-coupled tank engine (built at Chemnitz in 1895) and a small train, which runs up and down a 300-yard stretch of track when enough passengers offer themselves. Here is no model, no silent electrically-operated replica, but the real thing: a locomotive in steam. With every year that passes, the number of visitors who have never seen such a thing in their lives will increase; the wonder and fascination of it will continue to grow as long as the train goes on running. May it enjoy a long and prosperous life!

The main building of the Museum is a very simple one, two storeys high and fire-proof in its construction. It houses not only a series of exhibition rooms but a library (including archives), offices, and a caretaker's flat. Its display is confined to small objects and is designed to provide a general introduction to the history of railways in Norway, paying special attention to some elements in the story not illustrated elsewhere in the Museum. But this Museum aims not only at providing instruction about the past. When it came under the present management in 1946, it was laid down that one of its objectives should be to arouse interest in the development of railways and to promote appreciation of the importance of their work and the service they render to the community now. This could lead merely to a tedious exercise in sales promotion. But sensitively handled, as it is here, it can help to give a sense of actuality to what might otherwise be the presentation of no more than a quaint forgotten past. This policy is no doubt responsible for the main exhibit that confronts you in the entrance hall at the outset: a montage called 'The Railway Town'. It is designed to show the importance of the railway undertaking in the economy of the country as a whole. This it demonstrates by a theoretical assemblage in one plan of all the buildings of the railways and of the people employed in their service, to produce a town of 90,000 people, which would be bigger than any other town in Norway except Oslo and Bergen. That point established firmly at the outset, the exhibition turns back into history.

The first railway in the country ran from Christiania (as Oslo was then called) to Eidsvoll, near the southern tip of Lake Mjøsa. This was laid out under the direction of Robert Stephenson, with G. P. Bidder as his resident engineer. Brassey and Peto were the contractors, and associated with them was J. L. Ricardo, who became Chairman. (He was also Chairman of the North Staffordshire Railway in England.) Drawings of some of the main engineering works on the line are shown here, signed by Stephenson— notably one of a timber viaduct—together with a plan and section of the permanent way, which was laid both on longitudinal and on cross sleepers, all of timber. Here stands the decorated wheelbarrow and silver spade used by the Viceroy of the King of Sweden when the first sod of the railway was cut in 1851; above it an engraving from the *Illustrated London News* shows the opening of the line in 1854. Robert Stephenson's firm supplied the first locomotive—the manufacturer's plate that it bore is shown in the Museum, with the engine's number-plate and a series of pictures of it. So many Englishmen worked on this line in the early days that its first rule-book was printed in their language as well as in Norwegian.

Much attention is given to the special problems of constructing and operating the railways in this difficult country. They were extended only very gradually. It was not until 1909, for example, that Oslo and Bergen were linked by railway. (And what a railway, too! Its engineering and its scenery combine to provide an unforgettable experience in travelling.) A large model of the Bergen line, and of the branch down to Flåm, shows something of the problems involved. Not even in the Alps is snow a more formidable enemy. On this line, as on others, the train sometimes runs through an almost continuous series of snow-galleries, cut in the rock-face. An interesting section of these rooms is given up to snow-clearing equipment.

As you go upstairs you come to a large wall-map of Norway, extending the height of the building. This can be illuminated so as to show the growth of the railway system at ten-year intervals and the extension of electrification. You also encounter here a memorable railway clock; its case is a prodigious piece of wood-carving.

On the first floor there is a comprehensive display of telegraph, telephone, and block-signalling equipment, some of which can be demonstrated in use; of rule-books—here it might be suggested that some of the rules themselves should be shown, instead of a series of rather uninformative title-pages; of tickets and ticket-printing machines. Among the tickets one notices an ivory pass on the Trunk Railway for J. L. Ricardo, the Company's English Chairman; and several for fourth-class travel, a well-established Norwegian institution. A series of uniforms is displayed, some of considerable elaboration: the General Director is virtually in court dress. The last room brings us to publicity, with an interesting set of posters, the original drawings and paintings shown beside the printed versions. All are worth study, and one or two are really distinguished—for example Ben Blessum's poster of 1926 for the English market.

When you have come down and moved into the open air, the

full charm of the place begins to unfold. On the left is the lake, screened by trees; in front, a railway line with wooden buildings beside it; on the right, a little garden and a large hall, of wood and glass, which houses the rolling-stock and serves, on the far side, as a station for the narrow-gauge train. Everything is dignified and simple, entirely characteristic of the country itself; but though simple, the buildings are redeemed by the warmth of their timber from any suggestion of bleakness.

The first of these original station buildings is one of the oldest in Norway. It is from Kløften, a little north of Lillestrøm on the Christiania–Eidsvoll railway, and it continued in use, unaltered, from the opening of the line in 1854 until 1926, when it was dismantled and brought to Hamar for preservation. A bodily removal of this kind is, of course, a great deal easier with a timber building than it would be with a brick or stone one, of the sort we are accustomed to in Britain. The two waiting-rooms and the booking-office have been furnished as far as possible in the style of 1854. The rest of the building is used for a fascinating exhibition of photographs—a sample from the much bigger photograph-archive in the Museum itself—showing the construction and equipment of the Norwegian railways and the life led by the men employed on them. A whole room is filled with pictures of locomotives—one notices for how long the Norwegian railways bought them in Britain. Among the portraits of railwaymen, too, are several of the English servants of the Norwegian Trunk Railway: S. B. Shaw, its first manager; James Mollatt Smith, *Contorchef* from the opening until his death in 1875; H. Parker, Mechanical Engineer from 1861 to 1865.

On the platform of Kløften station is an interesting notice. It was the practice to attach to the rear vehicle on the afternoon train from Christiania boards showing triangles and squares, to give an indication of the weather that was being forecast by the experts in the capital for the next day; a poster explains these symbols to the public. Alongside the platform a length of the original track has been laid. It is interesting to see Stephenson and Bidder employing the bridge rails invented by Brunel and used in England almost exclusively on the broad-gauge Great Western Railway. A few yards away, where the track takes on a more modern form, you find rails bearing the stamps of the Dowlais and Rhymney companies, dated 1876–78.

The other two stations, erected along the line here, are very much newer: Ilseng, the next (from the Røros Railway, originally narrow-gauge, which ran from Hamar by Elverum to the north), dates from 1893; Bestum, the third, from 1890. Ilseng station contains a display of local material relating to the Hamar district. The stationmaster's living quarters on the upper floor of Bestum have been excellently refurnished in the style of the 1890s. In between the two stations is a platelayer's hut of 1889, with trolleys and other equipment inside; and by Bestum stands a double-armed signal on a steel lattice post 50 feet high.

The large hall opposite contains the full-sized rolling-stock. For antiquity, one machine claims pre-eminent attention: No. 17 of the Trunk Railway, *Caroline*, a 2–4–0 built by the firm of Robert Stephenson in 1861. The engine is attached to a pair of four-wheeled coaches and a royal saloon, upholstered in silk and with a prettily-painted floral ceiling. She continued in normal service until 1919, when she was sold for industrial use. In 1953 the State Railways took her back in exchange for another locomotive and in the following year she hauled visitors to the exhibition commemorating the centenary of the opening of the first Norwegian line.

Another early locomotive of unusual interest is the little metre-gauge 2–4–0 tank engine *Alf*, built by Beyer Peacock in 1870. With its tall enclosed smoke-stack and enormous single head-lamp, its front end has a distinctly American appearance. Among the standard-gauge locomotives of the early twentieth century are a 4–4–0 of 1901, the first to be turned out by the Oslo firm of Thune, and a 2–6–0 built at Hamar in 1914.

There are several passenger and service vehicles of note. An early fourth-class carriage from the Trunk Railway is without roof or seating; the only piece of furniture it contains is a cross-bar running its whole length, to which passengers could cling when the train was riding unsteadily. A great rarity in Europe is a royal saloon constructed for the metre gauge: it is an ingeniously roomy vehicle, plainer than most of its kind, supplied to the Røros Railway by Jackson and Sharp of Wilmington, Delaware, in 1876. In a country like this, special provision was needed in cases of accident: for the distances were great, the trains ran slowly, and it might be a long time before injured people could be got to hospital. Here is a four-wheeled first-aid coach (*Sanitetsvogen*) designed to be attached, when necessary, to a breakdown train.

There is an inspection vehicle of 1914, which is simply a motor-car mounted on railway wheels; and a diesel-driven railbus, with a timber roof, built for the Setesdal Railway (now disused) in 1930.

The closing phase of the age of steam is represented by a 2–8–4 freight engine, a product of Krupp's works at Essen: of enormous size (its running-board stands 7 feet 6 inches above the ground), it makes as violent a contrast as possible with even the most recent of the other locomotives. It is a splendid museum piece, but also a disturbing one: for this is an immensely elaborate and costly machine, whose career has reached a premature and untimely end.

The idea of a railway museum was launched here, as we have seen, seventy years ago. It was a particularly enlightened notion in Norway, where the railway itself was then little more than forty years old and the system was still in the process of being extended. (None of the present main lines to the north and west of Oslo had yet been completed.) Men do not commonly think of creating museums out of novelties. That these men did think in this way is perhaps to be seen as a tribute to the importance of the railway itself as a force in the development and unification of a country so extended, so sparsely peopled, and so mountainous as theirs. They saw the work in progress, and that may itself have moved them to turn their minds back to the past, to look to the rock whence they had been hewn.

However they thought, the museum they modestly set on foot grew and prospered, to become the remarkable thing it is today, commanding the instant respect of anyone who sees it. The whole project has been realized and controlled throughout by a sane economy in planning and execution. There is no waste here, no unprofitable repetition, no frills; yet at the same time nothing is flimsy, there are no gimmicks—and there is room for substantial further development, for only half the site has yet been used. It is a solid achievement, and built to last.

There is something to think about here. The Norwegian State Railways are poorer than those of Sweden and Denmark. One has only to look at the trains themselves: half the coaches in Norway are still of timber. I travelled recently on an express in which the second-class seating was five-a-side and without upholstery; and the Oslo–Bergen morning train then customarily included a first-class coach built in 1910. I know no main terminal station in Europe that breathes so completely as Oslo (East) the atmosphere of the years before the first World War. Yet the Norwegian State Railways have succeeded in producing a railway museum far ahead of that achieved by either of their wealthier neighbours. They have been enabled to do so through a combination of circumstances, local, personal, in a word historical. Grander plans may yet be realized in Sweden and Denmark. They will do well indeed if, in the result, they can match the intelligence, the combined liveliness and peace, the indescribable charm of the Museum at Hamar.

CONCLUSION

The museums discussed in this book are by no means the only places in which historical relics of transport are preserved. There are other transport museums in Britain that might well have been included: the Yieldingtree Railway Museum, for example, near Weston-super-Mare, with its original tank engine from the Cardiff Railway; the Army Transportation Museum at Longmoor in Hampshire; the Museum of the Royal National Lifeboat Institution on the beach at Eastbourne; the Nautical Museum at Castletown, Isle of Man, which displays the armed yacht *Peggy* of 1789 entire, in her own boathouse. Some of the larger municipal museums, like that at Coventry, have substantial transport collections, and two of them—those at Bristol and Leicester—are fast adding to their holdings, with a view to the establishment of museums of industry and technology, in which transport will play a large part. Bristol already has an interesting road transport gallery, including an unusual assortment of horse-drawn vehicles —fire-engines, four-in-hand coaches, a caravan, an ambulance owned by a colliery company and stationed at the pit-head when an accident occurred. Leicester has a similar collection, at present awaiting adequate premises for display; it has acquired eight locomotives (seven steam and one electric) dated between 1866 and 1924, four of which are now on show.

Many other museums, not specially concerned with transport, have individual objects or groups of objects of this kind that are worth seeing. There are fine horse-drawn vehicles, for example, at Halifax, Huddersfield, Nottingham, and Truro; the singularly elegant coach built by Barker for Lord Abinger in 1830 is in the Municipal Museum and Art Gallery at Brighton. You will find models of seaplanes at Rochester and of ships in the museums of many seaports—Barrow-in-Furness, Birkenhead, Brixham, Dundee, Plymouth, South Shields, Whitby. You will even come upon machines standing outside museums altogether, in public places: a London tram at Chessington Zoo; the Stephenson locomotive *Invicta* in a park at Canterbury, a Bagnall engine in front of the station at Stafford, *Locomotion* and *Derwent* mounted on the station itself at Darlington.

The twelve Continental museums discussed here are no more than a small sample of what is to be seen in Europe. They exclude the most ancient exhibitions of royal coaches; three very extensive French collections, the Museum of the Air at Meudon, the Tramway Museum in Paris, and the Carriage Museum at Compiègne— I have deliberately omitted the last of these because the ordinary visitor has no chance to study the carriages, being moved on at a smart pace by a continually-discoursing guide; the Dutch Tramway Museum at Weert; the Fiat Company's museum at Turin, and innumerable collections of motor-cars that have been assembled, often as tourist attractions, in recent years; the Maritime Museums of Stockholm and Gothenburg and Elsinore, and indeed of almost every other European country. Nothing has been said here of the museums of Eastern Europe—the railway museums of Russia, Yugoslavia, and Hungary, for example; or of the huge collections in America, such as those at the Smithsonian Institution in Washington, at St Louis and Montreal.

The number of museums described in this book could, thus, have been doubled or trebled. But the thirty-four that have been included[1] are a representative collection, and between them they exemplify every form of transport, from prehistoric times to the 1960s. There they are; and at the close of a survey like this it is natural to ask oneself two or three questions about them. What is their purpose? What, in broad terms, have they to tell us, to justify the labour and money spent on them? And what is their position with regard to the future?

Museums exist to preserve and to display. Though the number of collectors is immeasurably greater now than it has ever been in the past (witness the excitement that arises from the issue of each of our over-numerous series of pictorial stamps), very few of them have the facilities for storing the bigger kinds of object discussed in this book. If those are to be kept for posterity, nearly all of them will have to be accommodated, sooner or later, in museums. Transport museums face special difficulties here. Their problems are well summarized in a paragraph of the Standing Commission's 1963 *Survey of Provincial Museums and Galleries*, relating to scientific and industrial museums as a whole:

[1] Two each in Chapters 2 and 14.

Conclusion

'The main problem for these museums is space for exceptionally bulky exhibits, and qualified technical staff—not money for purchases. The objects, which, unless they are collected in time, may disappear on the scrap-heap, are not likely to be costly. Moreover, such museums are of especial interest to local industry, and have a claim on the generosity of local firms for funds and also, perhaps, for technical assistance. But their need for buildings is urgent. . . . The material of these museums cannot be collected until it can be housed, and although firms will no doubt co-operate by delaying the scrapping of objects in which museums are interested, they will not be able to delay indefinitely.'[1]

This is what explains the diversity of premises, some very unsuitable, in which these museums are housed and the over-crowding that is to be seen in a number of them, which makes it difficult to inspect the exhibits closely and to compare them adequately. When one is inclined to be critical of such insufficient provision, however, one should remember that it has sometimes been a choice between half a loaf and no bread, and that getting the important objects in, under some kind of protection, has often seemed the most pressing task.

This problem has been especially acute for transport museums, for two reasons. Most of them have come into existence at a time when the machinery and equipment with which they are so much concerned are becoming out-of-date at an ever-increasing speed. There were 19,000 steam locomotives in service on British Railways in 1955; the last disappeared from regular service in 1968. Their scrap value is substantial, and the running-sheds built to house them are fast being demolished. Most of those that are to survive must find their way somehow, as quickly as possible, into museums.[2]

The machines that are worth preserving need to be saved from scrapping. They also need protection against vandals and the thieves who are sometimes whitewashed under the name of souvenir-hunters. No precautions will altogether defeat these nasty pests. They will steal the name and number-plates off locomotives while railway officials are kindly doing them the courtesy to show

---

[1] *Survey of Provincial Museums and Galleries* (H.M.S.O., 1963), para. 76.

[2] I say 'most' because I am not forgetting the service that is being rendered in the preservation of railway rolling-stock by, e.g., the Bluebell Line.

them round the shed, or even after the engines have been brought on to the premises of a museum—as we have seen at Beaulieu. The best chance of preserving these machines intact seems to be to get them indoors, under lock and key.

The museum must often think it desirable to pursue its first task, of preservation, to the detriment of the second, of display; and who is to say that order of priority is wrong? These museums are almost all under-staffed—some of them shockingly. They are short of money for current expenses. The temptation for some of them must, at times, be very strong indeed to stand still, to squeeze in a few more things if they can be rescued and accommodated somehow, to tinker about with the display and, for the rest, to let it all quietly tick over, secure in the knowledge that a useful collection has been brought in and hopeful that one day the money may perhaps be found to enable its treasures to be adequately shown to visitors.

I do not think any one of the thirty-four museums I have visited and described in this book has succumbed to that temptation. In the face of what must often have been great difficulty and discouragement they have persisted in trying to improve the display they present to the public as well as enlarging their collections. Many of them are very young—more than half of those in Britain have been established since 1950; but in each of them, whether it is old or new, one can see that things are on the move, somewhere if not all along the line.

This is very much as it should be, for by common consent the standard of presentation in museums as a whole has been rising steadily since the end of the last war. There are many reasons for this: increased leisure, a greater visual awareness (stimulated, to some extent at least, by television), changing methods of education, which have often led to direct association between the museums and the schools. New types of lighting and lettering have become available, new materials for dressing a display. The old-style museum, crowded up with dingy cases, heavily framed in dark wood, has now become a rarity—almost a museum-piece in itself. Traces of it linger in some parts of two or three of those described here; but all of them have been affected by these changed modes of thinking, and most are dominated by them.

Moreover, in recent years transport, as such, has come to assume increasing importance in the everyday lives of people in Britain, and they have become conscious of that—with the multiplication of cars and the building of motorways, the enormous growth of foreign travel, the political and social controversies in which the railways have been involved since they were nationalized. From these and many other points of view transport has come to interest the ordinary Englishman more. The striking changes that have come over it in this generation have made an impression on many people who in earlier years merely took it for granted.

This has given these museums their opportunity. To take one example, it can be seen in a very clear way in relation to trams: lumbering, plebeian, utilitarian vehicles—and yet, what a fascination they exercise, when they are seen in museums, over people of all generations! The reasons are not difficult to find. In this country, they are almost extinct; yet they are well remembered by many young adults and familiar to most older people. For many millions they formed an integral part of the working day. Though the buses that replaced them enjoyed clear advantages, the change-over, when it arrived, came as an unconscious shock, and the sight of these old friends stirs something more than just a vague memory of the past. At the same time, these huge vehicles are so strange, so obviously unlike the buses we have become familiar with today, that children, who never saw a tram at work, are astonished, almost awe-struck, by them.

It is not quite the same on the Continent, where the tram continues to be a feature of life in all the great capitals except Paris; but the recent disappearance of the steam tram in Milan, and its commemoration in the Leonardo da Vinci Museum there, provoke very similar comments.

Are nostalgia and curiosity, then, the main emotions that these museums appeal to? They are certainly important ones, and neither of them is to be scorned. For nostalgia may be an ingredient of poetry, and as for curiosity—well, if museums do not exist to satisfy curiosity, what are they there for? But there is more to it than that. They serve, or they should serve, more strictly intellectual purposes too.

I said just now that we today, in Britain at least, have become aware of transport, its problems and the part it plays in our lives, more acutely than any of our forebears. We are beginning to see at the same time how great a factor it has been in the life of the past, to take a fresh interest in its history. The records of that history are copious, but imperfect. In particular, they often fail to make clear the relationship between technological progress and economic and social change. Here is one of the great contributions that the transport museum can make to our understanding, whether of the very recent past or of times more remote. And this is a contribution that, in large measure, has yet to be made.

The museum tends to concentrate on the object itself, on its arrangement and display and on the proper description of it as a piece of equipment or machinery. What it does too seldom is to demonstrate its significance—economic as well as technological—its relation to what had gone before or what was going on at the time when it was made. Or, to put the point in another way, we are not told nearly often enough why this particular object was chosen to be included in the museum at all. Was it an example of the normal, the characteristic? Not enough attention has been paid, it seems to me, to exhibits of that kind. In the British Rail museums, where over thirty locomotives are displayed, only one example of the standard six-coupled goods engine is to be seen, not a single open goods wagon nor one brake van. Yet these were the chief instruments by which the railways of this country earned their bread and butter for the best part of a hundred years. Or was this object a freak, like the 7-foot penny-farthing bicycle at Beaulieu or the locomotive *Dr von Klemm* at Nuremberg? Or if it was an important pioneer, just what was the secret of its success and what social and economic changes did it lead to? For these machines did not come into existence by accident: nearly all of them were designed—well or badly—to meet specific needs, to outstrip a rival, to carry more quickly or at a cheaper rate. And the machines do not themselves *make sense* unless they are explained in this way.

Let us take one specific example. At Clapham we are shown a B-type London bus. The accompanying description tells us that it was an outstandingly successful design, and that 2,900 of the type were put into service. Mr Charles Lee's *Early Motor Bus* (one of the admirable handbooks issued by the Museum) gives further particulars of it and points out that its introduction in October 1910 coincided exactly with the changeover from horse to motor traction. The proved merit of the B bus, which consisted above all in its reliability, was decisive. The General Company now had a really satisfactory machine in its hands; only a year later, on October 25, 1911, it withdrew the last horse-bus from its service. It staked a great deal on the success of this single vehicle; and won.[1]

Now all this could be much more excitingly demonstrated at Clapham if that B bus were made the centre-piece of a carefully-planned display, drawing attention to those features that made it superior to its predecessors, emphasizing the critical importance of the part this vehicle took in shaping the modern life of London.

To my mind it is quite useless to put things on display unless they are accompanied by a description that will at least give the visitor some idea of what he is looking at. If they are not described, he can only wander round aimlessly, his eye caught perhaps by something brightly painted here or something that looks funny there, asking himself, if he is a person of intelligence, 'Why are they in the museum at all? What makes it worth while to preserve them?' Those are questions that ought to be asked—and sometimes, to be frank, the only answers that can be given are rather unsatisfactory; for not everything in all these museums justifies its place. It seems to be self-evident that there is no point whatever in displaying a series of early bicycles or horse-drawn carriages unless they are explained and distinguished from one another. They mean nothing—but nothing—to the visitor today until he is given a little guidance. With that, their history can be made to come alive, and fascinate him.

I am sometimes told by museum men that it is a waste of time to prepare elaborate descriptions, since so few visitors will read them; that the things are there to be looked at, to be appreciated visually, and that if information is wanted about them that should be sought from an attendant or from books. But what if the attendant is otherwise engaged, or if his explanation is inadequate? And what books?

The answer to that last question may well be supplied in part by the museum itself. It may even be practicable to keep a copy of some relevant book alongside the object it refers to. The museum may be able to produce good guide-books and catalogues of its own. Its labels can then be kept as brief as possible, since the visitor who wishes fuller information can reasonably be expected to seek it in a readily-accessible and inexpensive handbook. How far have the museums studied here adopted this practice?

[1] Cf. *London General* (London Transport, 1956), 44.

Twenty-eight of these thirty-four offer general guide-books, ranging from the neat little ninepennyworth of the National Maritime Museum to the sumptuous volumes, with notably fine coloured plates, from Munich and Nuremberg. General catalogues, in the true sense of the word, listing the exhibits with explanatory comment, are to be found at Maidstone, at Brighton and Beaulieu, at Old Warden, Newcastle, and Utrecht. Sectional catalogues of very high quality—some of them standard works in their own right—are produced by the Science Museum.[1] The same practice is also followed at Greenwich (for ship-models and paintings), Glasgow, the Arts et Métiers, and Milan.

Two other series stand out from the rest by the excellence of their format as well as the merit of their texts: those issued by the Swiss Museum at Lucerne and by British Railways. The account given by Herr Max Troesch of the motor-cars at Lucerne, in the fifth of that Museum's booklets, seems to me to provide almost exactly the sort of historical description that is needed by exhibits such as these, and Dr W. F. Dollfus's two booklets on Swiss aviation are admirable. The British series (designed with feeling and imagination by Charles Hasler and printed by the Shenval Press) are unquestionably the most distinguished of all in their production. They provide an excellent historical background to the vehicles exhibited at Clapham, written by such authorities as Mr Hamilton Ellis, Mr Charles E. Lee, and Mr L. T. C. Rolt. And to my taste Mr Bryan Morgan's *Transport Preserved*, which surveys the Museum at Clapham, is the best introduction that any of our thirty-four can show.

With the sole exception of a few of the Science Museum hand-books, which date back to the 1930s, all this considerable body of literature has been published in the past twenty years. Here, on the shelf that accommodates it, is the final proof of the enterprise and intelligence that have gone into the making of these museums. The visitor should be thankful for what he is offered—and buy it, for his money will generally be well spent; he should also be insistent in asking for more. These museums afford us endless ways of enlarging the dimensions of our knowledge and refining its quality. They must be used in close conjunction with libraries and record offices. Indeed, the plan of combining two of these, or all three, together into a single unit, as at Hamar and Lucerne and the

[1] I have discussed them above, p. 48.

61a Shuttleworth Collection: Deperdussin monoplane (1910)

b Science Museum: Avro triplane, 1909

62a Science Museum: Col. S. F. Cody standing by his biplane at Lark Hill in 1912

b Science Museum: another historic photograph. Alcock and Brown take off from Newfoundland on their transatlantic flight, June 14, 1919. The aeroplane is in the Museum

63a Shuttleworth Collection: aeroplane starter devised by B. C. Hucks

b Munich: the Aeronautical Gallery

64 Science Museum: the Aeronautical Gallery

German museums, at South Kensington and Greenwich, has much to recommend it. For they complement one another. As a distinguished French museum director has remarked: 'The knowledge books give is only potential: the aim of museums is to make it real.'[1]

And that is what, at their best, these museums do, as it can be done nowhere else. You can read MacDermot's magisterial *History of the Great Western Railway*, you can go behind the book to the Company's archives, to newspapers and pamphlets and timetables; you can look at the railway itself as it stands today, a hundred years and more after most of it was built. But nothing will give you the same sense of actuality, of being in the presence of the thing itself, as you get from the first moment of your encounter with it in the Museum at Swindon. For a railway, after all, is not an abstraction. It is an economic device that expresses itself in eminently tangible terms; and the instruments created for its purposes are part of the stuff of the history of the railway itself and the service it provided. You cannot really understand Brunel's timber viaducts—the strengths and weaknesses of their design, accounting for their erection and their supersession—from descriptions, plans and sections, photographs alone; you need to examine the model of the one at Ponsanooth shown at Swindon as well. And to study all these things in conjunction with Brunel's instruments and drawings which appear in the same gallery, brings you as near as perhaps you can get to the mind of the man himself.[2] Or again, we read much of the development of passenger travel across the Atlantic in the age of steam. It is easy to measure it in terms of statistics—much harder to see and feel the life led by the passengers and crews, especially since, as Mr Archibald points out,[3] photographs of the interiors of passenger steamships are unaccountably rare. Exhibitions like those devoted to this topic at Munich are an important aid to our understanding.

The main purpose of museums is unquestionably educational:

[1] 'Le but du musée est de rendre actuelle la connaissance virtuelle donnée par le livre': L. Benoist, *Musées et Muséologie* (1960), 102.

[2] It must of course be understood that the Museum exhibits cannot tell the whole story on their own. No one can hope to understand these bridges without reading, for example, the article on them by H. S. B. Whitley in the *Railway Engineer*, lii (1931), 384–92.

[3] E. H. H. Archibald, *Travellers by Sea* (H.M.S.O. for the National Maritime Museum, 1962), plate 9.

to instruct, and to store up materials for research. This is what must always justify the expenditure of public money on them. But if they exist to teach, they exist also to give pleasure, pure delight, and these museums can certainly offer that abundantly: in small objects, like the elegant bridge-plates of the London and Birmingham Railway at Clapham or the gay furnishings of the narrow boats at Stoke Bruerne, like the marvellous models at Nuremberg and the Science Museum; in paintings, many times at Greenwich and again at Utrecht and Copenhagen; in the vehicles and machines themselves—man has made few things more beautiful for his own use than the best of the carriages at Maidstone, Glasgow, and Brussels, than No. 1 at York and No. 737 at Clapham, than *Golden Arrow* at Beaulieu, than *Cutty Sark*. And many people must return in their minds over and over again, as I do, to the grandeur of the great hall at Swindon, to the unending varieties of Lucerne, to the simplicity and calm of that far northern lakeside at Hamar.

The majority of these museums are new. A hostile observer of them might say that they are the product of a fashion, that there is a vogue for them at present that will soon pass away, leaving them stranded, high and dry, in a backwater. He might point, for example, at the figures of attendance at one of the newest of all, that at Swindon, which showed a large total in the first year, followed by a steady decline in the second and third. Yet the decline was arrested in the fourth year (1965–66), and the upward trend was resumed very markedly in the fifth.[1] The inference to be drawn from these figures is plain. A large number of visitors came at first, simply because this was a new show. The museum builds up its true and lasting public gradually, but—if it is as good as this one —surely enough, to become an established and highly valued institution.

Private museums are bound to be particularly vulnerable to changes of taste; and those that are run by volunteers, like the museums at Towyn and Portmadoc and the tramway museums at Crich and Schepdaal, are at the mercy of changes of enthusiasm. All that can be said here is that at present they are keeping their ends up remarkably well. As for the museums at Beaulieu and Lucerne, which are private ventures on a large scale, it is clear

[1] Great Western Railway Museum, Swindon: Annual Reports of the Curator, 1962–67.

that both of them, from the visitor's point of view, are a continuing success.

The long-term future of museums such as these may perhaps not be entirely assured—a very severe economic recession, which drastically reduced holiday-making, might be fatal to any of them. But their collections are now so considerable that, if anything so unhappy should ever occur, one might reasonably hope that government, either central or local, would intervene. What is more immediately disturbing is the uncertain future of two of those in public ownership: the museums at Clapham and York.[1] They are among the most important in Europe; and this book may fitly conclude with a brief discussion of their fate.

The origins of these two museums, as we have seen, are different. That at Clapham was created by the British Transport Commission, in accordance with the recommendations of the Report of 1951.[2] The York Museum was set up some forty years ago under the auspices of the London and North Eastern Railway, and inherited by the Commission as part of that Company's property. The establishment of the Commission's own Museum, in permanent premises in London, proved to be a slow business, completed only in 1963, when the present premises at Clapham were fully opened. Nearly 100,000 people visited the Museum in the first year: yet even before that year was out it was common knowledge that its future was in jeopardy. As for the Museum at York, it has recently been deprived of the premises in which its small exhibits were shown. We have no indication that they are to be replaced by others: only persistent rumours that even the one building left to the Museum is in danger of demolition.

The new British Railways Board, created by the Transport Act of 1962, was less friendly towards these museums than its predecessor the British Transport Commission; and in so far as the reasons for this attitude were economic, they could be understood and respected. But the want of sympathy went somewhat further than that, as an official of the Board revealed when he said to a journalist, 'We have a certain moral obligation to maintain these museums, but it also is *our duty not to waste money on things*

---

[1] The Great Western Railway Museum is in a different position, since its maintenance is provided for by an agreement between the British Transport Commission and the Corporation of Swindon.

[2] Cf. p. 50.

283

like this which are not in the public interest,[1] going on to add that they 'should be the job of sociological and educational people, that is, the Ministry of Education'.[2]

The Board had already tried to persuade the Government to transfer the financial responsibility for its museums to the Treasury, but without success.[3] Long discussions with the Ministry of Transport ensued, which led then to no clear-cut result.[4] Two things could be said positively. First, the Government specifically laid on the British Railways Board the duty of preserving the historical relics for which the Commission, its predecessor, had assumed responsibility.[5] Second, the Museums still continued to be open, on the old basis; for the moment they weathered the storm of 1964.

But this was only an interlude in the story. No permanent solution has been found. Though the Board was obliged to preserve relics, it was also given very wide powers to dispose of them by gift, loan, or sale. It is now quite certain that the enlightened policy, initiated by the Commission, of preserving all the locomotives and vehicles on a limited and carefully-prepared list, will never be carried to completion. Moreover, the Board was not now specifically enjoined to continue to display any or all of its historical relics to the public.[6] Nobody could feel that, on this basis, the future of the Museums was secure; especially when it was realized that, from a financial point of view, it would be most profitable to the Board to sell the premises they occupied—the value of those at Clapham was estimated at half a million pounds.

Various possibilities lay open: the maintenance of the existing arrangements; the transfer of the Museums to the care of the Department of Education and Science, side by side with the Science Museum; their administration under a separate trust. In 1968 the Government decided in favour of the second of these options; but it appeared in a new form. The Museum at Clapham was now to be closed, and its contents to be dispersed. The main

---

[1] My italics. [2] *The Times*, May 30, 1964.

[3] *Daily Telegraph*, March 9, 1964.

[4] Cf. *Guardian*, August 11, 1964; *The Times*, August 18 and 24, 1964.

[5] British Transport Historical Relics Scheme, 1963, which came into force on July 1, 1965: *Hansard*, H. of C., July 2, 1965, cols. 141–4.

[6] 'The Railways Board may make such arrangements as they think fit for the exhibition either privately or publicly of such of the relics as it may from time to time be convenient and practicable for them to exhibit' (Scheme, para. 3a: *ibid.*, col. 143).

collection was to be moved to York, to join that in the Railway Museum already there, the whole being rehoused in new quarters. It was intended, however, that those exhibits relating specifically to transport in London should be retained in London. And it was made clear that those relics for which no place could be found would be disposed of—either to provincial museums that might wish to acquire them, or by sale.

If any proposals like these were to be implemented, it would be necessary to give the Railways Board power to part with the relics in its charge, which enjoyed some degree of protection under the Transport Act of 1962. It became clear that the Government intended to confer that power by means of provisions inserted into the large-scale Transport Bill it was then preparing. The terms of the proposal, when they were announced, were amply drawn. They related to records as well as relics; and they gave the Board the widest possible freedom to dispose of them, subject only to the consent of the Minister of Transport.

These proposals were vehemently opposed, in Parliament[1] and outside it. There was no lack of alternative suggestions. If the Clapham site was to be vacated, what about the Crystal Palace[2] or St. Pancras station?[3] Miss Jennie Lee (Minister of State, Department of Education and Science) received a deputation from the London Boroughs Association on August 14th, protesting against the proposal to remove the Museum from London, but she 'did not hold out much hope that the Government would change its mind'.[4] *The Times* carried a leader stating that the Bill failed to safeguard the Board's relics and that they could not be adequately housed at York.[5] But the Government went on its way, undeterred, and the original proposals were incorporated, with no important modifications, in Section 144 of the Transport Act, 1968.

It is outside the scope of this book to describe the controversy or to pass any judgment on its outcome. Potentially dangerous as these proposals are, everything must depend on the way in which the Act is made to work. Two things, however, may be said here in conclusion.

---

[1] See, especially, the Parliamentary debates of January 31, 1968 (Commons), July 20th and October 8th (Lords).

[2] Stephen Stewart, July 22nd. [3] Lord Montagu, July 23rd.

[4] *The Times*, August 15th. [5] *Ibid.*, October 19th.

First, this continuing indecision has been deeply discouraging to the Curator of Historical Relics and his staff. They have shown abundant energy and many touches of real imagination in assembling and presenting to the public the collections in their charge. But good museums can never stand still, and the uncertainties that have hung over these have denied their staff the opportunity to plan for their improvement and orderly growth.

Second, their railway collections are not merely of national, they are of international importance. For the railway as we know it was pre-eminently a British achievement; and here, in these Museums, that achievement is made manifest, to the British people themselves and to visitors from all over the world. However the matter of their administration is decided in the long run, the collections in the Museums of the Railways Board must be worthily provided for. Great Britain has good reason to look on them with affection and a special pride.

VISITOR'S GUIDE

It would not be helpful to include here a list of times of admission to the museums, or of admission fees, since these are liable to change. For those in Britain see *Museums and Galleries in Great Britain and Ireland*, issued annually by Index Publishers, 27 Finsbury Square, London E.C.2. Particulars of admission to Continental museums can usually be obtained from the tourist office of each country in London. The location of each museum is given below, together with an indication of the means of reaching it by public transport. Bus services (of varying frequency and convenience) are available from the railway stations mentioned. In a few instance, where access is difficult, the nearest main road has been indicated. Direction is given *from* the point of access *to* the museum.

Chap.	Museum	Location	Route
1	Science Museum	S. Kensington, London S.W.7	Underground: S. Kensington stn.
2	Museum of British Transport	Clapham High St., London S.W.4	See p. 51.
3	National Maritime Museum	Greenwich, London, S.E 10.	See p. 74.
4	Tyrrwhitt-Drake Museum of Carriages	Mill St., Maidstone, Kent	Maidstone E. or W. stn.
5	Brighton Motor Museum	Madeira Drive, Brighton	Brighton stn.
6	Montagu Motor Museum	Beaulieu, Hants.	Brockenhurst stn. or bus from Hythe (opposite Southampton).
7	Great Western Railway Museum	Faringdon Rd., Swindon	Swindon stn.
8	Shuttleworth Collection	Old Warden, Beds.	Biggleswade stn. (3m. W.). Road: A1.
9	Waterways Museum	Stoke Bruerne, Northants.	Northampton stn. (8m. S.). Road: M1 (4m.).
10	Tramway Museum	Crich, Derbyshire	Matlock stn. (7m. S.W.). Road: M1 (6m. W.).
11	Museum of Science and Industry, Birmingham	Newhall St., Birmingham 3	Birmingham New St. stn.

Transport Museums

Chap.	Museum	Location	Route
12	Narrow-Gauge Railway Museum	Towyn, Merioneth	Towyn stn.
12	Festiniog Railway Museum	Portmadoc, Caernarvonshire	Portmadoc stn.
13	Penrhyn Castle Museum	Penrhyn Castle, near Bangor, Caernarvonshire	Bangor stn. Road: at junction of A5 and A55.
14	Maritime Museum, Hull	Pickering Park, Hull	Hull stn.
14	Transport Museum, Hull	High St., Hull	Hull stn.
15	Railway Museum, York	Queen St., York	York stn.
16	Museum of Science and Engineering, Newcastle upon Tyne	Exhibition Park, Gt. North Rd., Newcastle	Newcastle Central stn.
17	Royal Scottish Museum	Chambers St., Edinburgh 1	Edinburgh stn.
18	Transport Museum, Edinburgh	Leith Walk, Edinburgh	See p. 166.
19	Museum of Transport, Glasgow	Albert Drive, Glasgow S1	Pollokshields E. stn.
20	Transport Museum, Belfast	Witham St., Newtownards Rd.	Belfast stns.
21	Musée des Arts et Métiers	Rue St Martin, Paris IIIe.	Underground: Arts et Métiers stn.
22	Belgian Railway Museum	Brussels Nord stn.	Brussels Nord stn.
23	Carriage Museum, Brussels	Musée d'Art et d'Histoire, Brussels	See p. 202.
24	Tramway Museum, Schepdaal	Schepdaal, 7m. W. of Brussels	See p. 205.
25	Netherlands Railway Museum	Maliebaan stn., Joan van Oldenbarne-veldtlaan, Utrecht	Utrecht stn.
26	Swiss Museum of Transport	Verkehrshaus, Lucerne	Lucerne stn.
27	Leonardo da Vinci Museum	Via S. Vittore, Milan	Milan Central stn.
28	Deutsches Museum	Museums Insel, Munich	Munich Hbf.
29	Transport Museum, Nuremberg	Lessingstrasse, Nuremberg	Nuremberg Hbf.
30	Railway Museum, Copenhagen	Sølvgade, Copenhagen	Copenhagen Cent. stn.
31	Swedish State Railways Museum	See pp. 8, 259	See pp. 8, 259.
32	Norwegian Railway Museum	Hamar, 80m. N. of Oslo	Hamar stn.

INDEX

Index

Index

Index

Index

North Brabant Rly., *52*
North British Locomotive Co., 169, 176, 177, 215
North British Rly., 164
North Eastern Rly., 59, 62, 149, 151, 153, 154–6
North London Rly., 39, 58, *50*
North Staffordshire Rly., 71, 267, *51*
North Union Rly., 69
Northampton, 85
Northcliffe, Lord, 45
Northern Counties Committee, 181
Norwegian
   Rly. Museum: *see* Hamar
   State Rlys., 265, 270, 271–2
   Trunk Rly., 269
Nottingham, 273
Nuremberg, Transport Museum, 23, 24, 245–53, 277, 280, 281, 282, 288
Nydqvist and Holm, loco. builders, 259, 260

Oakham Canal, 118
Oporto, 124, 217, *33*
Oscar II, King of Sweden, 262–3, *58*
Oslo, 265, 267, 268, 270, 271–2
Ostend, 78, 205, 207, 212

Padarn Rly., 142, *43*
Paisley, 124, 174
Paris, 44, 45, 76, 238, 260, 277, *60*
   Musée des Arts et Métiers, 23, 30, 33, 79, 189–95, 232, 241, 280, 288
   Tramway Museum, 274
Park, J. C., 181
Parsons, Charles, 159–60
Pavia, 238
Peckett, loco. builders, 134
Pegler, Alan, 137
Penn-Gaskell, The Misses, 47
Penrhyn Castle Museum, 141–3, 288, *43, 49*
Penrhyn Rly., 138, 141–2, *37*
Pepys, Samuel, 81
Perambulators, 87
Perth, 58
Pettit, Paul, 78
Pevensey, 76
Pilcher, Percy, 45, 163, *60*
Pius IX, Pope, 57
Plymouth, 62, 273
Poole, 76

Port Carlisle, 185
Portmadoc, Festiniog Rly. Museum, 136–40, 383, 388, *37*
Portsmouth, 71, 99
Portugal, 21
Postal services, postal museums, 47, 225, 247, 258
Praed, W., 120
Preston, 69, 80
Pullman cars, 17, 59, 99, *54*

Quadricycles, 112, 147

Racing cars, 97
   Types:
      BRM, 97
      Golden Arrow, 97, 282, *29*
      Railton Special, 132, *29*
      Romulus, 97
Railways,
   representation of, in museums, 19–21
   rolling-stock (freight), 59, 138, 154, 161, 179, 201, 249, 261, *37, 42*
   rolling-stock (passenger), 39, 56–9, 69, 99, 138, 142, 154, 180–1, 184, 192, 200–1, 215, 221, 249, 251–2, 256, 261–3, 270, *42, 43, 50*
   royal saloons, 56–8, 69, 251, 256, 261–2, 270, *56–8*
   signalling, 39–40, 99, 204, 205, 253–4, 161, 230, 250, 256, 268, *48*
   stations, 39, 269, 270, *32, 39, 45*
   track, 39, 142, 151–2, 199, 243, 256, 267, 269, *43*
   see also Locomotives
Ramsbottom, J., 53, 69
Randers, 262
Regent's Canal, 117
Reims, 47
Rhymney Iron Co., 269
Rhymney Rly., 104
Ricardo, J. L., 267, 268
Richards, J., 78
Rickshaw, 87
Roads, construction of, 36–7, 237–8
Robinson, J. G., 56, 205
Robinson, Sir Joseph, 95
Rochester, 273
Rolt, L. T. C., 150, 280
Rome, *57*
Rootes, W., 90
Røros Rly., 270
Rotterdam, 211, 213, 214, 216

297

Index